THE REGENERATION OF
LOCAL ECONOMIES

The Regeneration of Local Economies

HUGH MORISON

CLARENDON PRESS . OXFORD
1987

Oxford University Press, Walton Street, Oxford OX2 6DP
Oxford New York Toronto
Delhi Bombay Calcutta Madras Karachi
Petaling Jaya Singapore Hong Kong Tokyo
Nairobi Dar es Salaam Cape Town
Melbourne Auckland
and associated companies in
Beirut Berlin Ibadan Nicosia

Oxford is a trade mark of Oxford University Press

Published in the United States
by Oxford University Press, New York

British Library Cataloguing in Publication Data
Morison, Hugh
The regeneration of local economies.
1. Regional planning—Great Britain
2. Great Britain—Economic policy—
1945– I. Title
330.941'0858 HC256.6
ISBN 0–19–828551–5

Library of Congress Cataloging in Publication Data
Morison, Hugh
The regeneration of local economies.
Bibliography: p.
Includes index.
1. Scotland—Economic policy.
2. Scotland—Economic conditions—1973–
3. Industry and state—Scotland.
4. Enterprise zones—Scotland. I. Title.
HC257.S4M67 1987   338.9411   86–281123
ISBN 0–19–828551–5

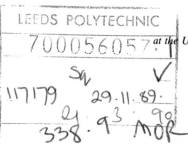
Printed in Great Britain
at the University Printing House, Oxford
by David Stanford
Printer to the University

Acknowledgements

I should like to thank the Warden, Fellows, and students of Nuffield College, Oxford, for providing me with the facilities to write this book and for making my stay among them so enjoyable. Thanks are also due to the Scottish Office for granting me a year's sabbatical leave; Dr Gavin McCrone, Secretary of the Industry Department for Scotland, who first aroused my interest in the problems of local economic regeneration; the many people in central and local government, the Scottish Development Agency, and other organisations concerned with local renewal, who gave up valuable time to discuss their activities and the issues which they raised, and on whose ideas I have freely drawn; the librarians of both Nuffield College and the Scottish Office for their help with source material; Her Majesty's Stationery Office for their permission to quote from government copyright material; the typing staff of St Andrew's House who typed the manuscript; and my secretary, Miss Betty Fender, who kept track of it during its gestation. Above all, I should like to thank my wife and children for their encouragement and support while I was engaged on this project.

Needless to say, all errors are my own, and the views expressed are mine and not those of the Scottish Office.

Edinburgh   HUGH MORISON
November 1985

Contents

Introduction

This study is about the creation of employment. It is written from the viewpoint of a serving civil servant who has been involved in the development and delivery of such policies, and hence is concerned more with their theoretical foundations and the practical problems associated with their implementation than with the political pressures which led to their adoption, which have been fully treated elsewhere.[1] It considers some of the ways in which the central government and local authorities in Great Britain have sought to stimulate economic activity in urban areas of high unemployment over recent years, and particularly during Mrs Thatcher's first administration of May 1979 to June 1983. Some more recent developments are covered, however. I have considered in particular the extent to which initiatives in the field of local economic regeneration tackle constraints on economic development identified in recent research, and overcome the considerable problems of implementation which arise when multiple organisations become involved in activities with diffuse or unclear goals. I have examined initiatives at the local level, not the national level or the level of the economic planning region, but have deliberately avoided defining 'local' in a way which would exclude initiatives of interest to the urban policy maker: the most extensive initiative considered here—the Merseyside Task Force—indeed takes in a conurbation. While the keynote of most of the initiatives which I have examined is local delivery, I have also given some consideration to regional policy, which is an important component of many of the initiatives.

Employment creation at the local level is a subject of increasing interest, both in Britain and abroad, as structural and technological change affects the industries on which localities have relied and as social change affects their populations. Thus in 1982 the Organisation for Economic Co-operation and Development established a programme 'to promote the exchange of experience and information on local initiatives to create employment';[2] in the 1982–3 session of Parliament the House of Commons Environment Committee began a major study of the problems of management of urban renewal (which was, however, abandoned after the 1983 election); and in 1983 the Archbishop of Canterbury established an Archbishop's Commission to examine the problems of Urban Priority Areas which led to the report 'Faith in the City'.[3] Academics have also turned their attention to these issues, notably Peter Hall and the Inner Cities Working Party team, Lawless on urban deprivation and the inner cities, Butler and Massey on enterprise zones, and Wannop and Keating on some of the Scottish initiatives.[4] Forthcoming studies are considering the mechanisms and impact of policies to regenerate local economies in particular conurbations, for example Lever and Moore's study of policies for economic regeneration in Clydeside.[5] But no excuse is needed for a further study, both because few researchers have sought to draw the various strands of policy together, and because events are moving so fast. While any book of this kind is an attempt to hit a rapidly moving target, the study of particular initiatives does enable us to draw general conclusions about how such initiatives should best be structured.

The regeneration of local economies involves a wide variety of disciplines and policies. Economists, planners, geographers, statisticians, and political scientists all have a contribution to make, as do regional policy, inner city policy, and training policy. Sociologists, social administrators, and educationalists also play an important part in regeneration, although within the compass of this study it has not been possible to do justice to their contribution. Reflecting this diversity there is a plethora of organisations with responsibility for the health of declining areas, including the Departments of Industry, Employment, and the Environment, the Scottish and Welsh Office, the two tiers of local government, centrally and locally sponsored development agencies and corporations, and various private sector bodies. There is, moreover, a bewildering variety of tools—regional grants, financial assistance from the local authorities and the development agencies, advice and support from various agencies of central and local government, factory space at concessionary rentals, assistance with environmental rehabilitation, help with training, and so forth. It is hardly surprising that the subject is complex and raises complex political, social, economic, and organisational issues.

A few words about the structure of the study. It opens with a consideration of the causes of local economic problems, the organisational framework within which such problems must be tackled and the arguments for tackling them at all. We shall find that analysis of the causes of the problems can give useful insights into how to solve them, and that examination of the organisational framework casts light on some of the formidable difficulties of implementation. The identification of appropriate policies and the design of appropriate organisations to implement them does not, however, imply that they should be used. For the free market economist, local decline simply reflects the inevitable changes which must take place in a healthy economy; any attempts to reverse decline by interfering with the free play of market forces, far from helping, may well make matters worse. We shall see, however, that the social and political arguments for action remain compelling, and that while recent experience casts doubt on some of the traditional economic arguments for spatially discriminatory economic policies, there remains a case for action to improve the supply side of local economies in the interest not only of the local but also of the national economy.

Having set out the theoretical justification for action, we shall consider some of the practical tools of local economic regeneration, and in particular the extent to which they tackle the basic causes of decline and overcome the fundamental problem of implementation, how to concert the activities of the variety of institutions which are involved. Finally, we shall examine in depth four major and recent attempts to overcome this problem: the encouragement of private sector involvement in regeneration, enterprise zones, the Merseyside Task Force, and area initiatives in Scotland.

Throughout the study there is a particular emphasis on Scotland. There are three reasons for this. Firstly, Scotland, unfortunately, is well endowed with the problems which local employment initiatives seek to tackle, and has developed some particularly imaginative approaches to their solution. Secondly, my own practical experience of local economic regeneration has been gained in Scotland (albeit from the somewhat detached position of the central government administrator). Finally, most recent books on the subject treat Scotland in a somewhat cursory manner (a notable exception is Maclellan and Parr's volume *Regional Policy*[6]); readers who have found references in the literature to the interesting things which are happening at Glengarnock or in the East End of Glasgow may wish to know something more about them.

But this is not an academic treatise designed simply to redress an unfortunate imbalance in academic research (and I am conscious that I am myself open to the charge of having ignored Wales). It deals with a subject of pressing social and political importance, and it is addressed not only at academics and students, but also at policy-makers and practitioners in central and local government and other public organisations, and at the increasing number of people in the private sector who are becoming concerned with their own role in economic regeneration. Through drawing to the attention of this wider audience the insights of recent economic research and policy analysis it hopes to make a practical contribution to their own most vital task.

Notes

1. See, for example, Grant, W., *The Political Economy of Industrial Policy*, Butterworths, London 1982.
2. OECD, *Decision of the Council Concerning a Co-operative Action Programme on Local Initiatives for Employment Creation*, C(82)99 Final, Paris, 26 July 1982.
3. Archbishop of Canterbury's Commission on Urban Priority Areas, *Faith in the City*, Lambeth 1985.
4. See bibliography.
5. Lever, W. F. and Moore, C., *City in Transition: Policies and Agencies for Economic Regeneration in Clydeside*, Oxford University Press, Oxford 1986.
6. Maclellan, Duncan and Parr, John B., *Regional Policy, Past Experience and New Directions*, Glasgow Social and Economic Research Studies 6, Martin Robertson, Oxford 1979.

1

The Problem

It is axiomatic that, if policies are to succeed, they should be both consistent and directed at the causes of the problem which they are intended to solve. Initiatives designed to tackle local and regional economic problems, however, have been bedevilled by unclear or outdated diagnosis of their causes; institutional complexity and conflicting objectives make implementation difficult; and both theory and recent developments in the British economy have called into question the desirability of such policies at all. In this chapter, we shall review the nature and causes of local and regional economic problems, the institutional and policy constraints on action, and the rationale for government policies to tackle such problems, in order to set the scene for an assessment of the bundle of policies and initiatives which constitute present attempts at the regeneration of local economies.

1. The Nature and Causes of Local Economic Decline

The Economic Background

Local economies may get into difficulty for a number of reasons. Some places, like Clydebank, might have experienced decline over a long period as a result of structural changes in the economy. Others, like Glengarnock or the Ayrshire mining villages, might experience the loss of a major employer through a reduction in demand for his product or depletion of a natural resource. Still others, like the East End of Glasgow, might be suffering from the collapse of their economic base but have their problems exacerbated by the effects of previous policies (inner city redevelopment, dispersal of jobs and people to the New Towns and elsewhere). All might be affected by the centralisation of decision-making; and all will be profoundly affected by the management of the national economy.

Local economies get into difficulty, however, in a variety of circumstances. One local economy experiencing difficulty may be located in an area of relative prosperity: examples would be the Medway towns or Leith. Another, such as Clydebank, may be situated in a region which is itself suffering acute problems. It is by no means self-evident that the prosperity of the surrounding region will be sufficient to enable the former kind of area to solve its own problems, or that the same remedies will be appropriate to every set of circumstances. Yet policy in the past has too often been founded on such assumptions.

Local economic difficulties, moreover, manifest themselves in a variety of ways. Unemployment is the most visible symptom. A local economy is said to be in difficulty if its unemployment rate is persistently above the national average, or if it is somewhat above the regional level which is itself above the national average, or if it has suffered major employment loss leading to a substantial increase in unemployment. But difficulties may be reflected also in underemployment: people in areas of difficulty may be discouraged from seeking work because of the poor chance of finding it. They may be reflected in lower than average income per head (although national wage bargaining in the UK tends to reduce such differentials among the employed and the relative levels of income per head are largely explicable in terms of the greater number of dependants per worker in the problem areas) or in lower than average growth in output or productivity. They may result in higher than average net migration. And they may be seen in the whole gamut of inner city problems: environmental dereliction, social disorder, selective migration, poverty, and squalor.

Concentration on the symptom, however, may well inhibit the cure. To tackle one symptom—and especially the symptom which the published figures make most visible—can have unfortunate, though predictable, results. To take steps to increase wages in distressed areas, for example through minimum wage legislation and centralised pay bargaining, may well decrease employment there. To seek to reduce migration, a major concern of the Scottish Office in the late 1960s, may do nothing for unemployment. To improve productivity through subsidising capital expenditure—a favoured regional policy instrument—might actually tend to increase unemployment in the short run through encouraging a shift to more capital-intensive means of production. And to attract jobs to the inner city may do nothing for those who actually live there. But, given the divergent nature of the symptoms, and the difficulty of distinguishing local economic problems from regional problems (of which they form a set) and from inner city problems (which they include), can we say with any certainty what the objectives of policy should be?

A review of the history of UK regional policy over the past fifty years does indeed suggest that policy-makers have found this a difficult question. At times, policy has been directed at alleviating the problems of 'black spots', at others at stimulating self-sustaining growth through government assistance in 'growth points'. Sometimes action has been focused on small areas: the Special Areas of the 1930s or the Development Districts of the 1960s. Sometimes it has been diffused over virtually half of the country: before the reforms of 1979, the assisted areas covered some 40 per cent of the working population. At times it has encouraged migration: the first specific regional policy measure was, indeed, the establishment of the Industrial Transfer Board in 1928 to assist workers, and particularly miners, to move to places where work was to be had. At others, it has sought to reduce it, as in Scotland in the late 1960s.

Policy has generally subsidised capital investment—highly relevant to the restructuring of a region's economy but less appropriate if the immediate object is to reduce unemployment. Sometimes, however, it has subsidised labour. When most effective it has added to the carrot of investment the stick of controls aiming to reduce overheating in more prosperous regions. It has largely concentrated on manufacturing industry, while the main employment growth has been in services. It has often sat uneasily alongside related policies. Until the mid-1970s, for example, a major objective of policy appears to have been the dispersal of people and jobs away from the inner city. While such dispersal was clearly necessary to reduce congestion—itself a major cause of economic decline—it did little to solve the social problems which inner city policy was then seeking to tackle, and it contributed to the legacy of decay with which many of the initiatives considered in this study are grappling. Also, it has often been implemented against a background of scepticism. Much of the complexity and confusion has, indeed, arisen through attempts to treat the symptoms rather than the causes of regional and local economic problems.[1]

Recent work on sub-regions, particularly that by Fothergill and Gudgin[2] and Gudgin, Moore, and Rhodes,[3] has, however, cast further light on the differing performances of regional economies. Differences in the rate of growth are seen as the major determinant of varying performance. Despite its declining share of employment, manufacturing is confirmed as the 'primary engine' of growth. Differences in industrial structure and the effects of regional policies are shown to be less important than hitherto in determining differential growth rates; and the main causes of the differences are identified as the extent to which the region is urbanised and the typical size of firm—rural regions with a large number of small firms are favoured over predominantly urban regions dominated by large firms. Also important, and related to firm size, are the extent to which control of the region's firms is centralised elsewhere and the capacity for innovation within the region. Because of the importance of these findings for the development of policies directed at local and regional economic difficulties it is worth considering them in a little more detail.

'The Leading Role of Manufacturing'

Regional policy has traditionally concentrated on manufacturing industry. Some assistance was available for service industry under the Local Employment Acts, and such aid was strengthened under the OSIS Scheme in 1973, but in 1983 *The Economist* commented that 'only 5% of regional aid today goes to labour-intensive services'.[4] The implication that there should be greater help for service industry is plausible, and the raw figures do indeed support such an approach. Between 1952 and 1979 service sector employment in the UK increased by 18.7 per cent while manufacturing employment declined by 3.1 per cent. But, as Fothergill and Gudgin show, the main cause of this shift of employment is the relative growth of labour productivity. In the period, output grew by about the same amount in services and manufacturing, but labour productivity in services grew by only 29 per cent by contrast with 115 per cent in manufacturing. Because, moreover, of the increase in part-time employment in services, the employment growth in this sector has been less than the raw figures suggest.[5]

Employment in services appears, therefore, to be closely related to employment in manufacturing—and this is what one would expect. Service sector activities are largely dependent on the income and demand created by other sectors of the economy: there is, over the long term and very approximately, a one-for-one relationship between basic sector jobs (primary, manufacturing, and non-dependent services) and dependent service jobs—although, over time, fewer basic sector jobs are supporting more jobs in dependent services.[6] Some 15 to 20 per cent of service sector activity might be regarded as non-dependent or basic, in that it provides services for people or firms outside the region or the country: examples are some banking and financial services, R. & D. activities, head offices, ports, and universities. It is clear that the attraction of such basic services might form a component of policy to assist the regions, although, as experience with civil service dispersal suggests, much of this activity is not particularly footloose. Hence, while Fothergill and Gudgin might be overstating the case when they argue that 'the potential for a successful regional policy in the service sector must be very restricted indeed', and the dependent sector can indeed contribute to the efficiency of the basic sector and hence to regional competitiveness and growth, it is apparent that one cannot place too great a reliance on the service sector as an 'engine' of regional economic growth.

The same considerations do not apply, however, when it comes to the regeneration of local economies. Dependent services may provide highly suitable employment for inner city residents, many of whom are relatively immobile. Many of the distressed labour market areas are close to city centres and suitable on locational grounds for such activities. While the encouragement of dependent service activities in such locations will not lead to an increase in economic activity within the region, it may be of great benefit to the locality, particularly when it lies within a generally prosperous region. Here, as Pressman and Wildavsky observe in their pioneering study of attempts at urban regeneration in Oakland, California,

the problem is not one of bringing a regional economy up to the strength required to employ an under-employed population, but one of rigging a stable and well developed metropolitan economy so as to reduce the disparity between the location and characteristics of jobs available and the location and skills of the distressed population.[7]

Even within the distressed region, the balance of advantage may be in encouraging dependent services within the inner areas. Hence it may be appropriate to take steps to assist such services as part of a closely focused spatial policy while it remains inappropriate as part of a more general regional policy; and many of the initiatives which we shall consider do just that.

Industrial Structure

The industrial inheritance of particular regions has in the past been a crucial determinant of differential growth rates and hence of the regional problem, and it remains an important component of localised employment problems. Changes in the demand for particular products affect regions differently according to their industrial structure: the increased demand for the output of heavy industry between the end of the war and the late 1950s, for example, did far more to alleviate the difficulties of the problem regions than did regional policy, and the subsequent fall in that demand made a considerable contribution to the re-emergence of an acute regional problem. Current difficulties in the West Midlands, where over the period 1979 to 1983 unemployment rates overtook Scotland's, may be attributed to a considerable degree to shortfall in demand for that region's products in engineering, metal-working, and motor manufacturing, although this may reflect supply-side as well as demand-side problems. But in most regions the effect of industrial mix as such has declined since the mid-1960s, both because since then there have been fewer growth industries to boost the performance of regions favoured by their presence, and because the declining industries, becoming smaller, have had less of an effect. Regional policy has also tended to improve industrial structure. Fothergill and Gudgin go so far as to suggest that 'industrial structure is now little more than a minor cause of disparities between local and national employment trends'.[8]

Nevertheless, the presence of potential growth industries in a region's economy may place it in a better position to take advantage of economic upturn when it occurs: Scotland's relative strengths in micro-electronics and the non-dependent tertiary sector are a clear advantage.[9] Also, the dependence of a local community on a declining industry may give rise to acute local economic problems, even though the consequent loss of employment and output are offset by developments within the same region. Electronics developments in Fife do not help redundant steelworkers in Glengarnock. Thus industrial structure remains important both as a cause of local economic problems and as a means of predicting where they are likely to arise.

The Urban–Rural Shift

The major component of differential growth rates identified by
Fothergill and Gudgin is the so-called urban–rural shift. Regions
containing large conurbations have shed jobs faster, or gained them
more slowly, than those without. Particular gainers have been small
country towns and rural areas. Between 1971 and 1976, for example,
the Highlands of Scotland and rural Northumberland recorded the
fastest growth in industrial employment, and during this period 19
out of 20 counties or regions recording growth could be described
as 'rural' or 'less urbanised'. Again, the six counties recording the
highest job loss were the six largest industrial conurbations.[10]
Fothergill and Gudgin suggest that

in the main, the decline of cities has occurred because a wide range of
existing manufacturing establishments have grown more slowly in cities
than in small towns... probably due to a higher proportion of city-based
firms finding themselves in locations where they are unable to expand
because their factories are hemmed-in by existing urban development.[11]

And, with the increasing floor-space required by manufacturing
industry and the high rent, rates, and land values, and congestion
and planning problems associated with urban areas, there is
increasing pressure on expanding firms to move out.[12] Thus the
shift can be associated with a number of factors, some of which
are amenable to policy (such as planning constraints and rates) and
some of which are not, or only in the longer term (such as
congestion and limited space for expansion).

One must, however, exercise some caution both in interpreting
the data and in drawing conclusions. An undeveloped rural region
may show a high growth rate with a gain of very few jobs, thus
giving an exaggerated impression of the attractivenesss of such
locations for industrial activity. Regions may grow for reasons
unassociated with rurality. The very considerable advances made
in the Highlands in the early 1970s are directly attributable to the
growth of oil-related activities in Easter Ross and have nothing
whatsoever to do with the region's highly rural character; indeed,
other parts of the Highlands continue to suffer from acute
underemployment. The Borders region and Dumfries and Galloway
did not share in the experience of some rural areas closer to the
main centres of population, and in particular East Anglia. It seems
clear that peripherality—remoteness from major markets—does

confer disadvantage. Transport costs may not be crucial; additional cost here may be outweighed by lower costs for other factors of production. Also, for companies serving local markets remoteness may offer a form of protection. But firms in peripheral areas are likely to be hampered by distance from ancillary services and centres of innovation, poor access to market information, shortages of skilled labour, and the quality of transport; such factors are likely to inhibit the relocation of firms or the birth of new firms in these areas.

Recent work commissioned from the Centre for Urban and Regional Development Studies at Newcastle University by the Scottish Economic Planning Department has sought to develop an 'economic potential' index taking account of these factors. Not surprisingly, the highest (i.e. most favourable) scores were for Greater London, followed by the areas surrounding the main conurbations of Birmingham, Manchester, Liverpool, and Newcastle. The so-called 'coffin belt' between NW and SE England attained relatively high scores, although only some 30 per cent of that attained by Greater London. Central Scotland attained 20 per cent, while the more peripheral rural areas—rural SW England, the Lakes, West Wales, the North Pennines, and the Scottish Borders— attained between 10 and 20 per cent, and the Grampian region (outside Aberdeen), the Highlands and Islands, and West Cornwall less than 10 per cent.[13] Policy needs to take account of factors such as these as well as the urban-rural shift identified by Fothergill and Gudgin.

Size of Firm

A third factor considered by Fothergill and Gudgin is the mix of firm size. Their evidence suggests that the growth rates of manufacturing companies are higher in areas with a relatively high proportion of small firms, and that, while newer firms, which tend to be smaller, have a relatively high failure rate, employment growth overall is higher in new firms.

One can speculate why manufacturing companies grow faster in areas favoured with a high proportion of small firms; and this has important implications for policy. The smaller firm might provide the mix of generalist experience required by a potential entrepreneur who is considering setting up on his own. Areas such as the North-West, having a high proportion of large branch plants, provide a less fertile soil for such developments. Again, entrepreneurs are likely to establish themselves in the industry with which they are familiar; and some industries—particularly those which attain large economies of scale—require more capital to start up. There may be differences in access to capital in different regions, influencing the historical structure of the region and making it easier to establish new small firms in some places than in others. Finally, large firms may be less likely to subcontract than small firms, or may subcontract only to established firms with a proven track record. Thus there may be less opportunity for a new small firm to establish itself in a town dominated by a few large plants than in one with a greater proportion of smaller plants and companies. All of this suggests the need for policies to ease the path of entrepreneurship, for example through training, encouraging co-operation between large and small firms, filling the 'management gap' by providing advice and support for the new firm, and facilitating access to finance; many of the initiatives which we shall consider pursue such aims.[14]

Centralisation

Size of firm, then, is a determinant of the success of regional economies. But the degree to which firms are controlled from outside the region is also of importance. A region with a relatively large number of small firms is, indeed, likely to enjoy more local control than one relying on a smaller number of larger firms, not simply because of the greater number of decision-makers there, but also because of the succession of take-overs, mergers, and nationalisations which have affected large firms over the last thirty years. Commenting in 1970 on the loss of control of large manufacturing firms in Scotland, the Scottish Council (Development and Industry) noted that 'This process is accelerating. It inevitably detracts from the independent initiative of Scottish concerns. Equally important, it drains from the community the kind of people upon whom the vitality and energy of its public affairs, in all their forms, largely depend.'[15] Scotland, like other regions of the UK, was becoming a 'branch factory' economy, isolated from the most important decisions, lacking the research and development facilities which are essential to product diversification and long-term growth, and exposed to the first winds of economic depression.

A series of spectacular closures and cutbacks in the 1970s and early 1980s, including Singers at Clydebank, Massey Ferguson at Kilmarnock, British Aluminium at Invergordon, Chrysler and Peugeot at Linwood, and more recently Timex at Dundee, emphasised the problems of the branch economy.[16] The issues were considered exhaustively by the Monopolies and Mergers Commission in its examination of proposals for the take-over of the Royal Bank of Scotland and Anderson Strathclyde Ltd.,[17] and the disadvantages were highlighted in evidence led by Scottish organisations. In summary, they argued that economies dominated by branch plants and subsidiaries were more vulnerable to recession than those which were not. In a telling phrase, the Fraser of Allander Institute described the branch firm as a 'neutered cat'. Innovation and enterprise were inhibited by the lack of the more senior posts and, with them, the people whose creative flair was vital to economic development. The 'information-rich environment' which stimulates innovation was damaged by the process of centralisation, so that changes would take place elsewhere or not at all. (Work by the Science Policy Resource Unit[18] has, indeed, shown that in 1968 about 49 per cent of all research establishments were in the South-East, which at that time had 24 per cent of manufacturing employment. Adjusting for industrial structure, the South-East produced 33.6 per cent of 'significant inventions' over a specified period with some 25 per cent of manufacturing employment, while Scotland produced 6.9 per cent with 9 per cent of manufacturing employment.) Centralisation also damaged the range of professional and support services on which head offices rely, and, more generally, social life, voluntary activities, and the whole range of public affairs in the regions were weakened by the departure of the potential leaders of public life. In the case of the Royal Bank, the transfer of control of financial institutions could lead to lower levels of involvement and a weaker economy and prove to be a decisive barrier to attempts to pursue a more self-reliant regional economic development strategy.[19]

In the event, the Monopolies and Mergers Commission ruled by a majority against both mergers. In its report on the Royal Bank it notes that it was 'impressed by the argument' that a merger 'may be seen as part of a process of economic centralisation which has been damaging to Scotland and to some other regions of the UK'. It accepted that 'in certain cases the comparative economic difficulties of the regions... have been accentuated by the acquisition of locally managed and controlled businesses by companies from outside'. The commission recognised that there were dangers of closures of branches in times of recession, and that, even if the firm flourishes, it becomes responsible for fewer and less important functions: 'Overall direction of the enterprise is typically moved to the head office of the acquiring company, and with it, major decisions in such areas as corporate finance and market strategy, financial policy, labour relations and the employment of senior personnel.'[20] This, for the Commission, could have a number of serious implications. It could reduce the responsiveness of the business to local needs because 'an element of judgement enters into almost all business decisions, which are not made on the basis of cold reason alone'. It could affect the vigour of the local economy, which is 'seriously affected by the general level of professional and business skills available there. Good managers learn from their peers in other local businesses, through social contacts, business clubs and commercial dealings with suppliers and customers.' It could lead to a loss of morale and business confidence, which were crucial elements in creating and sustaining entrepreneurship and business leadership. Whatever assurances were given, major decisions on marketing, investment, and company strategy would naturally be the concern of the centre. Hence the Commission concluded that 'there is value in preserving such independent centres of business initiative and opinion as survive in the UK'.[21]

Clearly not all mergers are against the public interest: a take-over may be necessary to improve management or secure the future of a firm, and inefficient firms cannot be protected from the effects of their inefficiency even if that means the loss of another centre of decision-making. Neither are branch plants necessarily a bad thing: they can enjoy advantages relative to local firms, such as access to group resources, better access to markets via the group, and access to information and specialist management skills. Branches may be newer and more efficient than indigenous firms. Problems are likely to arise, however, when branches predominate, and the impact of centralisation on local and regional economies does suggest a number of lines of policy. First it suggests that there should be major effort to stimulate the growth of new firms (although the process might be more difficult simply because of the extent of centralisation), and, where appropriate, to encourage 'management buy-outs'. Secondly, it suggests that steps might be taken to remind large firms of their responsibilities to the regions in which their branch factories are located, something which, as we shall see, Mr Heseltine has done in relation to Merseyside and Business in the Community is attempting for the whole country. Finally, it suggests that something might be done to strengthen the regional responsiveness of the financial institutions.

The Inner City

Since the early 1970s increasing emphasis has been given to the economic aspects of inner city decline. Lawless suggests that 'To the major investigative projects exploring the realities of urban decline in the early and mid-1970s it seemed increasingly obvious that the primary causes for the "urban crisis" were the reduction in employment together with the shrinkage of individual and community wealth.'[22] The White Paper *Policy for the Inner Cities* (1977) commented that 'the decline in the economic fortunes of the inner areas often lies at the heart of the problem',[23] and the work of Forthergill and Gudgin on the urban–rural shift does suggest that regional and urban economic problems are closely related.

But this is not the whole story. Within metropolitan labour markets there are often significant variations in unemployment levels. Job loss in the inner areas is not a sufficient explanation; because of travel flows such losses will, over time, be diffused throughout the labour market. Further factors are at work.

Traditional explanations of variations in unemployment rates within travel to work areas have pointed to differences in the personal characteristics of the residents of particular areas (the 'competitive explanation'), job loss or gain in particular areas (the 'equilibrium explanation'), locational advantage or disadvantage, for example in transport and access to jobs within the labour market (the 'locational explanation'), and the stigmatisation of certain areas or poor access to informal job information networks (the 'area explantion'). Work by A. McGregor on differential unemployment rates within the Glasgow conurbation[24] has confirmed the intuitive judgement that the dominant strand is the competitive position of residents of different areas. Inner city residents tend to be the poor, the unskilled and semi-skilled, ethnic minorities, and others at relative disadvantage in the labour market.

The housing market, in particular, tends to concentrate those who are particularly vulnerable to unemployment within the inner urban areas. Such people are also less mobile than those living elsewhere. Of the other possible explanations, apart from in the peripheral housing estates (such as Easterhouse), locational, area, and equilibrium factors appeared to have little effect on unemployment experience: there was no evidence of an 'inner city' problem in locational terms. Thus McGregor comments that 'building factories and creating extra employment in (say) Maryhill is unlikely to give any differential benefit to Maryhill workers in the sense of improving their unemployment situation relative to workers from Govan or Drumchapel'—except in so far as the creation of unskilled jobs is likely to lead to greater net employment gain for the deprived areas having a relatively high proportion of unskilled residents.[25]

Thus, even when new jobs are created in the inner areas—a major aim of present policy—the main beneficiaries are likely to be commuters from elsewhere in the travel to work area. Net inward commuting on Clydeside has indeed increased more than threefold in the years 1951 to 1976, so that while there has been a greater loss of population than of jobs from inner Glasgow, there remains a net shortage of jobs for residents of the inner area. The same holds true of the other conurbations.[26]

The creation of new jobs in inner city areas will not, then, provide the whole answer to concentrations of unemployment there. A powerful manpower element must be added to provide inner city residents with the opportunity to train for jobs which are, or might be, attracted. (Of course, such an element is desirable in any attempts to tackle local economic problems—redundant steelworkers, as we have noted, are not well endowed with the skills required of micro-electronics technicians.) In addition, housing policies might be designed to reduce the concentrations of the severely disadvantaged and to create a greater social mix. Such policies, like environmental refurbishment, have the additional benefit of making the areas a more attractive location for entrepreneurs. As we shall see, tentative steps are being taken on both fronts: private houses for sale are being built both in the East End of Glasgow and in inner Liverpool, and the Manpower Services Commission, through the New Training Initiative, is taking steps to raise the skills of the least skilled in the workforce.

Conclusion

Recent studies have, then, provided a number of useful insights into local economic problems. There appears to be a close relationship between such problems and the regional problem; consistent policies require to be developed to deal with both sets of problems (although some measures, such as assistance for dependent services, are more appropriate to local than to regional regeneration). Constraints imposed by inner city locations appear to be an important component both of local and of regional problems; while some such constraints are immovable, steps might usefully be taken to deal with others, such as shortages of attractive sites and premises. There appear to be barriers to entrepreneurship in some areas; policy might be developed to overcome them. The centralisation of decision-making in the economy has implications both for the health of local and regional economies and for private sector involvement in local economic regeneration; in particular, steps might be taken to encourage greater private sector involvement in such matters. Finally, a strong manpower dimension seems desirable. As we shall see, however, the institutional framework within which such policies must be developed and implemented is complex in the extreme.

2. Policy Conflict and the Institutional Background

The fast-developing science of policy analysis suggests that measures to solve particular problems are likely to be successful in proportion to the extent of agreement on their objectives, the clarity with which they are defined, the directness with which they address the problem, the smallness of the number of organisations involved in their design and delivery, and the closeness of the relationship between design and delivery of the measures.[27] On these criteria, an ideal mechanism for securing the regeneration of a local economy would possess a number of characteristics unlikely to be found in the real world.

In the first place, there would be general agreement on what it was that should be achieved. But, as we have seen, there has over the past fifty years been far less than full agreement on the objectives of policy. Indeed, even the consensus that 'something should be done' appears at present to be breaking down in the face of increasing unemployment throughout the country. The Labour party's 'Alternative Regional Strategy' urges us not to forget that 'the South East and South West between them suffer absolute levels of unemployment that are almost 30 per cent above those of Scotland, Wales and the Northern Region combined',[28] while monetarist economic theory stresses the need to allow the free play of market forces in a way which, at first sight, appears to leave little room for regional or local economic policies. (We shall consider these arguments further below.)

Secondly, there would be agreement on how the objectives of policy were to be achieved, and as direct a relationship as possible between the problem which it was agreed should be tackled and the measures which were addressed at it. If it were agreed that unemployment was the real problem, then labour subsidies would be preferred. If, by contrast, it were concluded that the problem lay in barriers to the operation of market forces, so that, for example, labour markets did not clear because wages were set too high by national wage bargaining, then steps would be taken to make the market work better, not to compensate for its inefficiencies through subsidies.[29] The causes of regional and local economic problems are complex, however, so that the policy-maker, however ingenious, is unlikely to find a single 'efficient' solution under which his measures operate directly on the one underlying cause of the problem. Policy-makers, hardly surprisingly, are far from clear what they are trying to maximise—employment, factory space, inward investment, regional income, output, or productivity— although recent research, as we have seen, has cast some light on the matter.

Thirdly, there would be a single organisation possessed of adequate powers and resources and charged with the solution of the problem. It would have no other responsibilities to give rise to competing priorities; and its individual members of staff, at all levels, would be involved both in the design of programmes and their execution and monitoring—apart, perhaps, from a privelged breed of 'policy analysts' who would not have responsibility for implementation. In fact, as Table 1 shows, a large number of organisations are members of the 'regional policy network' and involved to a greater or lesser degree in the delivery of programmes to alleviate local and regional economic problems.

Table 1. *The Regional Policy Network*

Organisation	Functions	Priority Accorded To Regional Regeneration	Level of Resources Available For Regeneration	Potential Policy Conflict
HM Government	Overall management of national economy	Medium	High	
HM Treasury	Macro-economic management Control of public expenditure Improving supply side of economy	Low/medium	High	Macro-economic management and public expenditure controls vs. expenditure on supply-side improvements
Dept. of Industry	'A profitable, competitive and adaptive productive sector' 'Reduction of UK regional disparities in resource utilisation through industrial adaptation'[a]	High	High	Sectoral vs. spatial schemes
Dept. of the environment	Local government, urban renewal, and infrastructure	High	High	Control of local government expenditure and reallocation of Rate Support Grant vs. expenditure on urban renewal
Dept. of Employment	Manpower policy, training and services for the unemployed	Low	High	Concept of 'single GB labour market' vs. training to meet local needs
Manpower Services Commission	Training and services for the unemployed	Medium	High	As for Department of Employment
Local authorities	Infrastructure, local authority services, health of local economy	Varying	Low/Medium	Conflicting priorities at time of expenditure cutbacks
LA Industrial Development Units	Factory building and letting promotion and industrial development	High	Low	
SDA/WDA	Economic development	High	High	Sectoral vs. spatial support
Scottish Office, Welsh Office	Central government services (including functions of DI, DOE, and DE)	High	High	Conflicting priorities

[a] Department of Industry 'Strategic Aims', 1983

The majority of the organisations concerned have other responsibilities, giving rise to problems of competing priorities. Some have to struggle with inconsistent objectives leading to policy conflict—Keating *et al.* have instanced the area of conflict which has emerged

'between the Department of the Environment's policy of withdrawing resources from cities by withdrawing Rate Support Grant aid, and its special measures to put extra resources into cities, including the Urban Programme, Inner City Partnerships and Enterprise Zones.'[30]

Quite apart from intra-organisational conflicts, there is ample opportunity for conflict between organisations: central government departments with national responsibilities do not necessarily see eye to eye with local authorities on the promotion of inward investment; regional development agencies may feel that other bodies could do more to assist the achievement of their objectives, for example in the training field. Not all of the organisations involved give local economic regeneration a high priority; and, as Pressman and Wildavsky have shown, there is likely to be considerable delay in the implementation of programmes where organisations with a high level of resources to address at the problem have different aims and accord it a low priority.[31] Not only is there a split between design and implementation within many of the organisations (in the Scottish Development Agency, for example, area initiatives are designed in the Programmes and Planning Directorate and implemented by the Area Development Directorate), there is often such a division between organisations (for example, between the Department of the Environment and SDD who have 'policy responsibility' for the urban programme, and the local authorities on whom the main burden of delivering it falls). At first sight there appears to be an organisational nightmare, although one which is somewhat less acute in Scotland and Wales because of the wide functions of the Scottish and Welsh Offices and the existence of their Development Agencies.[32] Success depends on agreement between 'a diverse group of participants with diverse organisational objectives'.[33]

This apparent confusion, and the ideal type of organisation which casts it into relief, have had a profound influence on observers of the regional and urban policy scene. Booth, Pitt, and Money, for example, criticise the Scottish Development Agency's attempts to

co-ordinate action to regenerate the East End of Glasgow as diverting attention from the need for 'powerful united organisations
to cope with urban problems'.[34] Co-ordination of the organisations
concerned in the Urban Programme is described by John Edwards,
who worked in the Home Office on its evaluation, as an 'administrative opiate'. It is, he suggests, believed that 'So long as there
are co-ordination machinery and inter-departmental forums for discussion, all else will come right. All too often, the corporate approach
and co-ordination machinery serve no other purpose than to cloak
an absence of effective problem-directed strategy.'[35] For Pressman
and Wildavsky, co-ordination covers up the very problems—conflict
versus co-operation, coercion versus consent—that its invocation is
supposed to resolve.[36] Thus for many, academics as well as politicians—although, to give them their due, not Pressman and Wildavsky—the creation of a new organisation is the only way through
the maze.

The large number of organisations involved in local economic
regeneration and their conflicting and competing priorities do indeed
create acute difficulties, and co-ordinative machinery is sometimes
ineffective. But co-ordination is not the opiate, nor reorganisation
the panacea, that some observers suggest.

Two basic criticisms are levelled against co-ordination. First, it is
presented as an end in itself, as the solution to a problem, whereas
problems quite patently do not disappear when the co-ordinative
machinery is established. Secondly, it is seen as a means of covering
up rather than resolving difficulties. The co-ordinator is cast in the
position of having to secure the agreement of other organisations to
his will; often (it is alleged) he does not know whether to bargain
with them or coerce them; and if he is a public servant he will be
as much concerned to spread the blame for failure as to achieve
success.[37]

There is much in the first criticism. In politics and public administration, as in other walks of life, there is a strong temptation
to mistake the will for the deed. Once agreement has been reached
on the regeneration of an area and the machinery to carry it through,
'all that remains is the carrying out of the plans'.[38] But general
agreement among organisations on objectives can rapidly get lost
in disagreement about how to achieve those objectives; and the
establishment of co-ordinative machinery will not, of itself, cause all
else to come right.

Nevertheless, if a variety of organisations have a relevant input to local economic regeneration, then some mechanism is needed to concert their actions, to secure the resolution of inter-organisational conflicts, and to encourage the participants to rethink their priorities. Co-ordinative machinery provides such a mechanism. At times its use involves bargaining, at times persuasion, and at times even co-ercion, but it is naïve to suppose that these activities are inappropriate, or that the co-ordinator does not know in which activity he is engaged at any particular point. Sometimes, moreover, co-ordination will not work: if differences of approach between organisations of equal weight or resources are such that they will not co-operate on a particular issue, no amount of co-ordination can make them do so. But the facts that co-ordination is sometimes presented as an end in itself, and that it sometimes does not work, are not reasons for rejecting it out of hand. Co-ordinative machinery can be a necessary and effective component of measures to tackle local economic problems.

If, however, co-ordination presents such difficulties (exaggerated though they may be), might it not be better to sidestep them by creating a new organisation having within itself all the necessary powers and resources to do the job, and avoiding the bureaucracy of established organisations? There can indeed be a use for new organisations. Scotland has benefited considerably from the establishment of the Scottish Development Agency. But the idea that institutional reform can provide an easy solution to the administrative complexity of local economic regeneration is open to four very serious objections.

First, as Keating *et al.* have observed,[39] a wide range of central and local government activity is relevant, including housing, social work, and the provision of infrastructure as well as industrial support and general economic and monetary policy. Some services are delivered at the national level, some regionally, and some locally. The officials concerned are in the main accountable to elected representatives. Quite apart from the implications for local and national democracy of the establishment of 'powerful united organisations to cope with urban problems', it would be impossible to construct an organisation with responsibility for all the appropriate programmes, even if one were to leave out activities which lie towards the fringe of the policy field. Reorganisation simply shifts the boundaries of inter-organisational conflict.

Secondly, reorganisation does not necessarily remove policy conflict even if the new organisation is relatively comprehensive: it merely shifts it from between to within organisations. The Department of the Environment, as we have noted, is faced with the problem of cutting local government expenditure and shifting resources from the cities to the shires at the same time as it is seeking to divert additional resources to the inner cities. Within the Scottish Development Agency there is a potential conflict between area-based approaches to economic recovery, which seek to unlock the potential of particular places, and sectoral approaches, which seek to encourage the growth of particular sectors of the economy wherever they might be located. As Pressman and Wildavasky note, agencies that seem to be single organisations can turn out to be several sub-organisations with different wills.[40] The establishment of a unitary organisation may facilitate the solution of problems of conflicting priorities and objectives, but it cannot remove them.

Thirdly, as Hogwood notes, the complex pattern of the 'regional policy network' is likely to be altered by the transfer of functions,[41] and this is unlikely to help the smooth operation of the network in the short term. Clients of existing organisations may be confused about where responsibilities lie, and officials may simply forget to consult the new organisation on matters which concern it.

Finally, any new organisation takes time to settle to its task, and in doing so will inevitably develop bureaucratic modes of its own. Initially its senior management will consume a good deal of energy in developing its structure, decision-points, and communications networks, and ensuring consistency of approach (its 'bureaucracy'), resolving differences between the different organisations which it has absorbed, and—to put it crudely—jockeying for position. It was, as we shall see, some years before the Scottish Development Agency began to pursue its task in a corporate way. If the establishment of co-ordinative machinery will not provide an instant solution to spatial problems in the economy, nor will the creation of new organisations. While co-ordination might be criticised as an administrative opiate, reorganisation as such must be regarded as an academic chimera.

There are, then, no ready solutions to the organisational and policy problems raised by local economic regeneration. Policy conflict is a fact of political life, and when the success of programmes depends on the co-operation of a number of organisations with differing aims and objectives and answerable to different constituencies, hiccups are inevitable. Even where there is agreement over the general objective, there may be considerable difficulty in carrying out the tasks necessary to its achievement because of incompatibility with other programmes or organisational preference for them, dependence on the actions of others with a lesser commitment to the general objective, lack of resources, differences of view on leadership of the project or the proper role of the different organisations involved, and technical and legal difficulties.[42] The Minister arriving at the scene of the riots and announcing a £120m. co-ordinated package of regeneration to be master-minded by a new organisation has only just begun the task.

In our consideration of particular initiatives we shall examine a number of ways of resolving the difficulties to which present organisational arrangements give rise, from reorganisation (the creation of the Urban Development Corporations and the Development Agencies) through co-ordination (the Glasgow Eastern Area Renewal project and the SDA Task Forces and Integrated Projects) to unilateral or bilateral action designed to draw the other parties along in its wake (the Merseyside Task Force). Many involve the appointment by the bureaucracy of progress-chasers 'to circumvent its own restrictions'.[43] None provides the ideal solution—indeed, given the complexity of the problems and the structures there can be no ideal solution—but they do offer some insights into both the problems of implementation and the most effective ways of dealing with local economic decline.

Despite its sometimes tenous relationship with the real world, policy analysis may tell us much of relevance to the design and management of such initiatives. Effective policy-making involves a number of stages: agenda setting, or a decision to consider whether something should be done; formulation, or a definition of the problem to be tackled; design, or the planning of a programme to tackle the problem and its assignment to an organisation; the setting of objectives and targets; the development of arrangements for implementation and control; means of evaluation and review; and termination, or arrangements to end the programme.[44] Only too often initiatives to tackle local economic problems have been started with inadequate arrangements for implementation and review, scanty methods of evaluation and control, and no arrangements for termination. This is not to say that they are of no effect: in the real world political and other pressures often require action to be taken too rapidly to permit a detailed analysis of all the stages of policy, and much can be achieved by 'muddling through'. But programmes whose design has taken account of these elements are, on the face of it, likely to be more effective than those which have not. Also, we now have a clearer perception of the nature and causes of local economic problems than was enjoyed by the policy-makers in the past, a perception which should be of considerable help in defining the problems to be tackled, designing programmes, and setting objectives and targets. But the prior question of whether something should be done raises complex economic, social, and political questions of its own.

3. The Rationale for Spatial Economic Policies

A recent book by two lecturers in Business Studies declares confidently that

We have established a strong case for government intervention to help solve the regional problem, arguing, in particular, that such intervention is necessary due to the apparent lack of an equilibrating mechanism in the free market, or at least one that works in something less than the very long term. In addition, it can be argued that regional policy may reduce the social costs of location decisions, increase the rate of economic growth and facilitate demand management policies.[45]

In fact, not only the case for government intervention but also the very existence of a 'regional problem' as such are under scrutiny, although, paradoxically, in a way which strengthens the argument for policies to deal with local economic problems. The regional problem is in the course of being redefined as a complex of problems associated with inherited urban and industrial structures, congestion, and manpower resources, affecting not only the traditional assisted areas but also some cities in more prosperous parts of the country, while the traditional arguments for regional policy are under challenge from both theory and circumstances.

Traditional arguments for regional policy have suggested, as Green and Clough observe, that regional disparities are not self-equilibrating. Because of loss of earnings and output a less favoured region will fall into a cycle of decline from which it finds it impossible to raise itself unaided. Unlike a nation state, it cannot adjust its 'exchange rate' with other regions to make its goods more competitive. Thus intervention by the state is needed to break the cycle of what Professor Myrdal termed 'cumulative causation'.[46] Such intervention can be justified as enabling the best use to be made of the nation's resources. It permits a higher level of output for a given level of inflation than would otherwise be the case. It reduces pressure of demand for labour in the more favoured regions, and it utilises available infrastructure in the less favoured regions while reducing the need to provide such social capital elsewhere. It can lead to increased efficiency in firms which have been encouraged to relocate in the less favoured regions because they avoid the congestion costs which they would have to meet elsewhere. It also has benefits for the community as a whole in excess of the benefits accruing to the individual firm: the public benefit of expenditure to bring an additional person into employment in an area of high unemployment will considerably exceed the private benefit to his employer; and, as Professor Thomas Wilson has observed, expenditure on regional policy measures, unlike other government transfer payments addressed at the problem of unemployment, is designed to make the less prosperous regions more efficient, and hence, over time, will reduce the need for other transfers.[47]

The theoretical challenge to this case suggests that the failure of declining regional economies to move into equilibrium may be attributed not to 'cumulative causation' (which need not go on for ever, as the economy of North-East Scotland shows) but to institutional constraints on the attainment of equilibrium. Social security and unemployment benefits may pin minimum wages at a level at which the regional labour market will not clear; national wage bargaining aggravates the process. If this is the case, one does not need a regional policy, which may even aggravate the problem by attracting high-wage firms which will increase the cost of labour. One needs measures to make the market operate more efficiently through removing, or at least reducing, the constraints, so that the equilibrating mechanism may come into play.[48]

To this theoretical challenge has been added experience during the current recession, which has cast doubt on the validity of many of the arguments for regional policy at a time of high unemployment nationally. It might, for example, be suggested that even if the constraints are removed it may take a considerable time for the regional economy to move into equilibrium, so that there remains a case for assisting the regional economy in the meantime. But, apart from the fact that such action might very well inhibit the attainment of equilibrium, the case is considerably weaker at a time when even the most favoured regions are suffering levels of unemployment considerably in excess of the 4.5 per cent necessary to trigger action under the Local Employment Act 1960, than it was at a time of full employment. It is to the national benefit to bring into use underused resources, wherever they might be; and expenditure to encourage development in the less favoured regions might indeed make it more difficult to create the conditions in which the national economy will prosper through putting pressure on the necessary controls on the money supply and government borrowing.

What, then, of the argument that regional policy leads to a more efficient use of social capital? The fact is that much of the social capital of the less favoured regions is in urgent need of replacement, and environmental recovery and the provision or replacement of infrastructure has formed an essential component of policy to encourage development in the regions since the early 1960s.[49] Despite the considerable investment in social capital in these areas over the last thirty years, the encouragement of industrial development in the less favoured regions rather than the relatively more prosperous areas of the country is unlikely to reduce significantly the need for new infrastructure; indeed, since people moving to the growth areas (wherever they may be) generally have to wait for the provision of new services, while such provision is essential to the attraction of new industry to the less favoured areas, the argument might well run the other way.

Congestion clearly imposes costs on firms in the more favoured areas. But it is no less of a problem in parts of the less favoured areas, for exemple Clydeside and Merseyside, and, as we have seen, it appears to be a major component of regional decline. The remedy is not to shift development from one region of the country to another, but to seek to tackle the problems caused by congestion wherever they occur.

Thus both theory and experience during the current recession have cast doubt on the traditional arguments for regional policy. Indeed, the prevailing view, echoing that of the Minister of Labour in 1933, appears to be that 'no direct intervention in the employment market, through the provision of public works, etc., can do anything to the employment figures comparable with the effects of ordinary trade improvement which flows from the soundness of the Government's general policy'.[50]

There do, however, remain theoretical arguments for a spatially discriminatory economic policy. It is arguable, firstly, that the non-inflation-accelerating rate of unemployment (NIARU) may be lower if unemployment is distributed more evenly throughout the country rather than being concentrated in particular places or areas. By improving the workings of the labour market, policy may moreover help to reduce the natural level by removing constraints on labour market adjustment. (There is, it must be said, as yet no robust econometric evidence for this view.) There is also, as we have seen, evidence that the less favoured regions are less innovative and less likely to spawn new enterprises than more favoured areas. Spatially discriminated measures to encourage entrepreneurship, innovation, and the adoption of new technology in the less favoured areas would have national economic advantages, for it is the case that measures to improve the supply side of regional economies will both encourage growth and place the national economy in a better position to cope with the upturn when it occurs.

Thus there remains an economic case for spatially biased policies, although not necessarily policies designed primarily to subsidise capital investment attracted from abroad and from the more prosperous parts of the country to the traditional Development Areas. As Hallett observes, the complex of problems with which policy must deal today is 'very different from the "regional problem" which, implicitly or explicitly, has underlain policy for the past 45 years'.[51] But there now appears to be a convergence of views as to the causes of regional and local decline, which is of considerable relevance to the design of appropriate policies.

Nevertheless, it has to be admitted that the case for *locally* biased policies, on economic grounds alone, is far from conclusive. Gudgin, Moore, and Rhodes, indeed, go so far as to concede that 'There is no strong case on economic grounds for removing the urban concentrations of the unemployed. But there is a case on social grounds.'[52] The arguments on social and political grounds are, happily, less ambiguous. Widely differing unemployment rates in different parts of the country are socially undesirable, and, as Sir Ian Gilmour has stressed, 'the social consequences of industrial change and decay cannot be neglected'.[53] Multiple deprivation in the inner cities and peripheral housing estates can lead to social disorder, as the experience of the summer of 1981 showed only too clearly; for that reason Lord Scarman's report into the Brixton disorders urged a more consistent and concentrated attack on inner city deprivation.[54] Such deprivation can impose economic costs on the community, so that its alleviation is an economic as well as a social priority. But even if its alleviation imposed costs in excess of the immediate economic benefits, the state is concerned with more than the pursuit of economic efficiency for its own sake. Its primary concern is with the welfare of all its citizens. Given constraints on mobility (not everyone who wants to can leave the inner city) and people's preferences about where they wish to live and work (not everyone wants to move to the Home Counties, and those who are already there would not welcome them if they did), there is a case for state intervention to stimulate economic activity in the less favoured areas. Indeed, as Professor Nove has pointed out, the reflection of people's wishes as to where to live and work is not necessarily 'inefficient' in economic terms.[55]

Disparities may, moreover, be so wide as to be politically unacceptable. Politicians of all parties press Ministers for measures to assist their constituencies or regions, either in response to high unemployment, or to deal with the impact of particular redundancies or closures. As Wyn Grant has argued, they see spatially orientated policies as both desirable and capable of influencing voters—this despite the results of polls suggesting that regional policy is of low political salience and the second least favoured form of public expenditure after social security. (In a MORI poll published in the *Sunday Times* on 30 March 1980, only 9 per cent of respondents favoured increases in regional policy expenditure, 37 per cent favoured cuts, and over half the respondents offered no views at all.[56]) Both the main political parties have argued, when in opposition, against modifications or reductions in regional aid programmes. It was not regarded as odd for Conservative MPs from parts of Scotland due to be downgraded in the reforms of 1979 to lobby the Government for a reprieve for their areas, and MPs, faced with a large closure in their constituency, will almost inevitably join forces with the local authority, the local trade unions, and community organisations to campaign for a rescue (using regional aids if they are available) or for special measures to assist the area to recover from the impact of closure.

While, then, regional policies in the abstract may be of low political salience, closures and high levels of local unemployment are not, as a glance at any local newspaper in a declining area will readily demonstrate. Hence measures to regenerate local economies are likely to attract considerable political support.

Widely differing unemployment rates in different parts of the country are, in addition, seen as inequitable. Dr P. Damesick argues that 'A spatial economic policy is needed to prevent the impact of the recession falling disproportionately on certain regions or districts and to try to ensure that the benefits of national economic recovery are shared with some degree of equity between different areas of the country.'[57] Of course, it might be regarded as inequitable to expect the more prosperous regions to bail out the less prosperous, particularly if regional policies simply transfer economic activity from some parts of the country to others, possibly at the expense of national economic recovery. But measures to improve the supply side of local and regional economies cannot be held to be at the expense of other parts of the country, except in so far as they involve inter-regional transfers of public expenditure. (Government expenditure is in fact higher than the tax take not only in the traditional problem regions, but also in the South-East and East Anglia, where the inward migration of firms has led to a considerable need for infrastructure investment.) Spatial economic measures should not, moreover, be judged only in the short term. They attempt to deal with long-term distortions in the economy, and in the longer term national economic recovery will depend on the performance of the less as well as the more prosperous regions of the country.

What, then, remains of the rationale for spatially discriminating economic policies? The traditional economic arguments have been weakened by changed circumstances and by the rise of the market economy school. Traditional social and political arguments have been weakened by the spread of unemployment to the previously prosperous areas. Nevertheless, there remain interlinked economic, political, and social arguments for spatially differentiated policies, which, together, add up to a convincing case. Economically, a more even spread of unemployment and improvements in the supply side of the less prosperous areas may both encourage growth and place the economy in a better posture to benefit from it. Socially, policies may alleviate the problems of the deprived areas, which contributed, for instance, to the Brixton and Merseyside riots. And politically there remains considerable pressure for measures to alleviate the problems of the hardest-hit areas. By seeking to meet this pressure through measures to deal with the social consequences of industrial change and decay, central and local government can, indeed, help to create the conditions for growth.

Notes

1. For a concise history of regional policy see J. D. McCallum, 'The Development of British Regional Policy' in Maclellan and Parr, op. cit., pp. 3–41; also McCrone, R. G. L., *Regional Policy in Britain*, Allen and Unwin, London 1969.

2. Fothergill, Stephen and Gudgin, Graham, *Unequal Growth: Urban and Regional Employment Change in the UK*, Heinemann, London 1982.

3. Gudgin, Graham, Moore, Barry, and Rhodes, John, 'Employment Problems in the Cities and Regions of the UK: Prospects for the 1980s', *Cambridge Economic Policy Review*, vol. 8, no. 2, December 1982.

4. *The Economist*, 19–25 February 1983, p. 21.

5. Fothergill and Gudgin, op. cit., p. 27. Their argument may be bolstered by selective data: between 1960 and 1980 output in manufacturing grew by 28 per cent compared with 57 per cent in services. But the general argument holds true.

6. Ibid., p. 39.

7. Pressman, Jeffrey L. and Wildavsky, Aaron B., *Implementation*, University of California Press, London 1973, p. 153.

8. Op. cit., p. 67.

9. See for example the speech by the Secretary of State for Scotland on 'Scotland's Economic Renaissance' at the Scottish Council's International Forum, Aviemore, November 1981; and Lythe, Charlotte and Majmudar, Madhavi, *The Renaissance of the Scottish Economy?*, George Allen and Unwin, London 1982. Qualifications must, however, be made. Within the tertiary sector consumer services are relatively over-represented and business services relatively under-represented. Between 1971 and 1981 private sector services, unlike public sector ones, grew more slowly in Scotland than in Great Britain.

10. Information supplied by Scottish Economic Planning Department.

11. Op. cit., pp. 111–2.

12. See Gudgin, Moore, and Rhodes, op. cit., p. 32.

13. Owen, D. W. and Coombs, M. G., *An Index of Peripherality for Local Areas in the United Kingdom*, SEPD, Edinburgh 1983.

14. See Storey, D. J., *Entrepreneurship and the New Firm*, Croom Helm, London 1982, and especially chapter 10, for an interesting discussion of these issues.

15. Scottish Council (Development and Industry), *The Influence of Centralisation on the Future*, Aviemore 1970, pp. 2–3. See also Firn, J., 'External Control and Regional Policy' in *The Red Paper on Scotland*, EUSPB, Edinburgh 1975.

16. See Hood, Neil and Young, Stephen, *Multinationals in Retreat: the Scottish Experience*, Edinburgh University Press, 1982.

17. Monopolies and Mergers Commission, *The Hong Kong and Shanghai*

Banking Corporation, Standard Charter Bank Ltd. and the Royal Bank of Scotland Ltd., HMSO, London 1982, and *Charter Consolidated PLC and Anderson Strathclyde PLC,* HMSO, London 1982.

18. Information provided by Scottish Economic Planning Department. See also Rothwell, Roy, 'The Role of Technology in Industrial Change: Implication for Regional Policy', *Regional Studies,* vol. 16, no. 5, October 1982, p. 366.
19. Monopolies and Mergers Commission, op. cit., para. 10.17.
20. Ibid., para. 12.8.
21. Ibid., chapter 12, *passim.*
22. Lawless, P., *Britain's Inner Cities: Problems and Policies,* Harper and Row, London 1981, p. 7.
23. *Policy for the Inner Cities,* Cmnd. 6845, HMSO, London 1977, p. 2, para. 7.
24. McGregor, A., 'Labour Market Disadvantage' (mimeo), 1980 (summarised in McGregor, A., *Urban Unemployment: A Study of Differential Unemployment Rates in Glasgow,* Central Research Unit, Scottish Office, Edinburgh 1980).
25. Ibid., para. 9.15-17.
26. Gudgin, Moore, and Rhodes, op. cit., p. 41.
27. See in particular Pressman, Jeffrey L. and Wildavsky, Aaron B., op. cit., and Hogwood B. and Peters B. G., *Policy Dynamics,* Wheatsheaf Books, Brighton 1983. Hood gives an interesting analysis of 'perfect administration' in Hood, C. C., *The Limits of Administration,* John Wiley, London 1976.
28. The Labour party, *Alternative Regional Strategy, a Framework for Action,* Parliamentary Spokesman's Working Group, London 1982.
29. See, for example, West, E. G., 'Pure versus Operational Economics in Regional Policy' in *Regional Policy for Ever?,* Institute of Economic Affairs, London 1973.
30. Keating, M., Midwinter, A., and Taylor, P., *Enterprise Zones and Area Projects,* University of Strathclyde, Glasgow 1983, p. 2. In a leader on 23 April 1984 *The Times* commented that 'the resultant tension is not creative. It is tearing sensible policy-making apart'.
31. Op. cit., p. 117.
32. See below, chapter 2.5 and chapter 6.1.
33. Pressman and Wildavsky, op. cit., p. 30.
34. Booth, S. A. S., Pitt, D. C., and Money, W. J., 'Organisational Redundancy? A Critical Appraisal of the GEAR Project', *Public Administration,* vol. 60, no. 1, spring 1982, pp. 56-72.
35. Edwards, John, in Higgins, Joan *et al., Government and Urban Poverty,* Basil Blackwell, Oxford 1983, p. 64.
36. Pressman and Wildavsky, op. cit., p. 134.
37. Ibid., p. 134.
38. Ibid., p. 34.

39. Op. cit., p. 1.
40. Op. cit., p. 92. A similar point is made in Hood, Christopher and Dunsire, Andrew, *Bureaumetrics*, Gower, Farnborough 1981, p. 38.
41. Hogwood, B., 'The Regional Dimension of Industrial Policy' in *The Territorial Dimension in UK Politics*, ed. Madgwick, P. and Rose, R., Macmillan, London 1982, p. 62.
42. See Pressman and Wildavsky, op. cit., pp. 99–102.
43. Ibid., p. 78.
44. See for instance Hogwood, B. and Peters, B. G., *Policy Dynamics*, Wheatsheaf Books, Brighton 1983, p. 8 and Hogwood, B. and Gunn, L. A., *Policy Analysis for the Real World*, Oxford University Press, Oxford 1984, p. 4 for description of the policy cycle.
45. Green, W. and Clough, D., *Regional Problems and Policies*, Holt, Rinehart and Winston, London 1982, p. 39.
46. Myrdal, G., *Economic Theory and Underdeveloped Regions*, Methuen, London 1956, cited in Green *et al.*, op. cit., p. 28.
47. Wilson, T., 'Regional Policy and the National Interest' in Maclellan and Parr, op. cit., p. 107.
48. See, for example, Friedman, M. and Friedman, R., *Free to Choose*, Martin Secker and Warburg, London 1980, chapter 8, for an exposition of such views, and Gilmour, I., *Britain Can Work*, Martin Robertson, Oxford 1983, pp. 147–50, for a critique.
49. See, for example, Scottish Council (Development and Industry), *Inquiry into the Scottish Economy 1960–61* (Toothill Report), Edinburgh 1961, and the Regional Plans produced in the mid-1960s.
50. CAB 24/247: CP 189(33) memorandum by Minister of Labour, 21 July 1933, cited by Bush H. J. in 'Local, Intellectual and Policy Responses to Localised Unemployment in the Inter-War Period: the Genesis of Regional Policy', Oxford 1980 (unpublished D. Phil. thesis in library of Nuffield College, Oxford).
51. Hallett, Graham, *Second Thoughts on Regional Policy*, Centre for Policy Studies, London 1981, p. 28.
52. Gudgin, Moore, and Rhodes, op. cit., p. 2.
53. Gilmour, I., op. cit., p. 170.
54. Great Britain, *The Brixton Disorders April 1981: Report of an Enquiry by the Rt. Hon. Lord Scarman OBE*, Cmnd. 8427, HMSO, London, p. 131, para. 8.44.
55. Nove, Alex, *Planning—What, How and Why*, Scottish Academic Press, Edinburgh 1975, p. 7.
56. Grant, Wyn, *The Political Economy of Industrial Policy*, Butterworths, London 1982, p. 57.
57. Damesick, P., 'Issues and Options in UK Regional Policy: the Need for a New Assessment', *Regional Studies*, vol. 16, no. 5, October 1982.

2

Seven Pillars of Wisdom:
Some Tools of Economic Regeneration

In chapter 1 we argued that there remains a case for initiatives to regenerate local and regional economies and suggested what the components of such initiatives might be. We noted, however, the complexity of the institutional and policy framework within which they must be developed and implemented. Hardly surprisingly, this complexity has led to the creation and maintenance, by both central and local government, of a complex edifice of interrelated and interlocking measures and organisations. Some have been abandoned or allowed to atrophy; others have been continued, perhaps beyond their usefulness, as a result of inertia or pressure from the 'regional policy community'.[1] The result is a 'complex patchwork of areas and powers',[2] involving for example specific measures administered by organisations with wider responsibilities (regional policy measures, local authority initiatives, manpower measures, and the traditional urban programme), arrangements designed to co-ordinate the activities of different organisations (the new urban programme), and specific organisations established to regenerate areas (the Scottish and Welsh Development Agencies, Local Authority Development Boards, and the Urban Development Corporations). In this chapter we shall briefly consider the extent to which such initiatives (summarised in Table 2) overcome constraints on economic development and problems of implementation, before turning in later chapters to detailed consideration of the role of the private sector, enterprise zones, and the use of the tools for economic regeneration on Merseyside and in Scotland.

1. Regional Policy

Regional policy is not specifically directed at the regeneration of *local* economies; and, since it is administered at arm's length in an essentially reactive manner, it offers no solution to the difficulties of implementation which we considered above. It can, indeed, add to such difficulties, and at times in the past it may have contributed to some of the problems which measures to secure the regeneration of local economies are designed to tackle. But it forms a pervasive background to the activities of those concerned with local economic regeneration, and is an essential component of many of the packages which they design. It is, therefore, appropriate to begin our consideration of measures to regenerate local economies with a brief examination of the regional policy background.

Traditionally, regional policy has sought to tackle the dual problems identified by the Barlow Commission of congestion in the south and east and underused resources in the north and west by diverting economic activity from the one place to the other.[3] Recent research, as we have seen, has shown that the causes of the regional problem are more complex than Barlow's analysis would suggest; regional policy measures have, moreover, been altered frequently and were the subject of major changes in 1979 and, following a further fundamental review, in November 1984. The mechanisms of regional policy have generally involved a mix of automatic investment-related grants and selective employment-related grants—the former until 1984 exclusively and the latter primarily directed at manufacturing industry—and, until 1981, controls on development in the non-assisted areas. Eligibility and rates of grant for projects within the assisted areas have varied according to whether the location has been within an intermediate, development, or special development area, and the overall coverage of the assisted areas has varied from over 40 per cent of the working population in the mid-1970s to some 28 per cent between 1979 and 1984 and 35 per cent from 1985 (when the map was simplified to produce a two-tier system of development areas and intermediate areas).

Traditional regional policy has been the subject of much criticism over recent years.[4] Regional policy measures, it is suggested, run across the grain of market forces and distort the decision-making processes of firms, causing them to locate in less than optimal places. (Both anecdotal evidence and research results do, however, suggest that it is physical and locational factors rather than government grants which are the main determinant of location decisions.)[5] The subsidisation of capital is not the most appropriate way to deal with the problem of excess labour, since it encourages manufacturers to become more capital-intensive. The provision of RDGs, by far the largest component of traditional regional policy measures, is essentially reactive, while pro-active measures are needed; where policy is actively promoted, however, as through the Invest in Britain Bureau or Locate in Scotland, the result has often been the introduction of large branch factories, doing nothing to stem the flow of decision-makers to the centre, vulnerable to recession, and damaging the indigenous economy through pushing up the wage level. The attraction of activity to the periphery of the conurbations, as on Merseyside, has contributed to inner city decline, while its diversion from the non-assisted areas has contributed to their own relative decline, as in the West Midlands. While the main area of employment growth is the service sector, almost all support goes towards assisting manufacturing industry. Regional Development Grant is criticised because it is automatic— large sums of money have gone towards assisting oil developments in Scotland which would have been located there anyway—and because it was not hitherto dependent on the creation of jobs, while the discretionary nature of Selective Financial Assistance is said to create uncertainties for firms who find it difficult to plan ahead. Planning is rendered yet more difficult by the frequent changes in the measures. Finally, critics question how effective the measures are and whether expenditure is cost-effective.[6]

Nevertheless, there does remain a case for traditional regional policy measures to support industrial development in the less advantaged regions and localities. Many of the criticisms outlined above are self-contradictory: measures cannot, for example, be both more and less discretionary at the same time. Moreover, policy is about more than the creation of employment; assessments which ignore its contribution to industrial restructuring, activity rates, output, capital formation, and lower levels of migration are less than complete. The attraction of firms from elsewhere or abroad contributes to technological diversity and the improvement of management in the regions; and the availability of factory space, for example through advance factories, has been shown to be a critical determinant of the distribution of new manufacturing industry through the regions.[7] Support for capital-intensive manufacturing industry gives rise to employment benefits through the generation of downstream service sector jobs. Regional incentives can be a useful part of the promotional package of areas in need

Table 2. *Tools of Economic Regeneration*

Tools and Powers	Objectives	Activities	Actors	Comments
Regional Policy Industrial Development Act 1982 Co-operative Development Agency and Industrial Development Act 1984	to stimulate economic growth and restructuring in disadvantaged regions	provision of grants and loans— RDG: for plant and machinery in SDAs and AAs (automatic, although with grant per job ceiling except in the case of small firms); certain service activities now eligible SFA: additional support; also covers mobile services (subject to employment creation and 'additionality test')	DI, SO, WO	Essentially reactive; bias towards manufacturing and capital-intensive industry reduces its aptness to tackle local economic problems, although valuable for restructuring regional economies.
Local Authority Initiatives Local Government Act 1972 Local Government (Scotland) Act 1973 Various Local Acts	to stimulate economic development in local authority areas	(i) provision of sites and premises (ii) grants and loans (iii) promotion of the authority's area	Regional and District Councils in Scotland; Metropolitan County and City Councils in England and Wales	Provision of smaller factories and workshop units a useful component of local regeneration. Land assembly important though hampered by lack of resources. Promotion arguably counter-productive. Metropolitan Counties abolished from April 1986.
Urban Programme Local Government (Social Needs) Act 1968 Inner Urban Areas Act 1977	to reverse inner city social and economic decline	75% grants for projects of benefit to multiply deprived areas; programme and partnership arrangements to co-ordinate policy	Local government in designated areas, subject to central approval	'Traditional programme' is diffuse but flexible. Not an effective means to co-ordinate action.

Urban Development Corporations Local Government, Planning & Land Act 1982	to secure regeneration of their area	land acquisition and development; factory building; provision of finance for industry and commerce	Urban Development Corporations appointed by Secretary of State	Confined to the docklands of London and Merseyside. A useful means of bringing land into use; but doesn't solve problems of co-ordination.
Development Agencies Scottish Development Agency Act 1975 Welsh Development Agency Act 1975	to further the development of the economies of Scotland and Wales and improve their environment	land acquisition and development; environmental improvement; factory building; provision of finance for industry; promotion	Development Agencies appointed by Secretary of State	Well fitted in range of functions and relations with local authorities to tackle local economic problems in integrated way.
Local Authority Development Agencies Local Government Act 1972 Local Government (Miscellaneous Provision) Act 1982	to stimulate economic development in their areas	provision of finance for industry and commerce; promotion; sometimes factory provision	Development Boards appointed by local authority	Can undertake many relevant functions; but possibility of conflict with central government policies. Will move to ownership of Boroughs after abolition of Greater London Council and Metropolitan County Councils.
Training Initiatives Employment and Training Act 1973	to meet the training needs of residents of deprived areas; and of companies developing in such areas	provision of training services	MSC, education authorities, firms	MSC national priorities are not well matched to meeting needs of disadvantaged inner city residents.

of regeneration: the Corby Enterprise Zone, for example, has made much of the fact that it is the closest Development Area to London.

Recent experience does, however, suggest that a heavy reliance on the attraction of branch plants is not particularly appropriate at present; instead, more might be done to encourage joint ventures between UK and foreign firms, which avoid many of the problems of the branch factory. There is also a case for encouraging non-dependent services and indigenous enterprise, and for relating RDG to job creation. The changes announced in November 1984 following the White Paper *Regional Industrial Development* of December 1983, and the Co-operative Development Agency and Industrial Development Act 1984 did indeed contain proposals on these lines.[8] In particular, certain service sector activities, including business services, data processing, and software development, and technical design and analysis, have been made eligible for RDG, and a grant per job ceiling has been introduced for all but small firms undertaking modernisations and other projects of less than £500,000. Above all, it seems desirable to forge closer relationships between those who administer the instruments of regional policy and those who are concerned with the regeneration of local economies, particularly in relation to the safeguarding of employment in existing enterprises. The creation of new jobs in small firms, important though it is, can only be a long-term answer to local economic problems, and action to safeguard employment in potentially viable firms, and to identify difficulties in advance of their arising so that appropriate steps can be taken, is a vital arm of policy.

2. Local Authority Initiatives

Local authorities are at first sight well placed to design and implement measures of direct relevance to the regeneration of their area's economy, and with their breadth of functions they might seem well able to overcome difficulties of implementation. They have been involved in economic development for a long time through their responsibilities for planning and infrastructure. Over the past two decades they have increasingly adopted positive measures to stimulate economic development through the provision of sites and premises for industry, through offering advisory services and finance, and through promoting their area as a location for industrial investment. Such activities are often highly relevant to local economic regeneration. But they raise in acute form problems not only of competition between areas and proliferation of measures, but also of the relationship between central and local government and between the various organisations concerned with economic redevelopment.

The reasons for the increasing involvement of local authorities are complex. Declining prosperity and rising unemployment have clearly been a major stimulus, although the power to provide sites and premises dates from 1957, when unemployment was very low. Developments in planning form a second important element; in particular the requirement to produce Structure Plans which took into account economic and demographic factors gave local planners 'a statutory responsibility to consider the economic development of their area'.[9] Local government reform in the mid-1970s created authorities with the staffing resources, expertise, and political weight to undertake a major role in economic development; for an authority like Strathclyde, with half the population of Scotland and some of Scotland's most intractable economic problems, the assumption of such a role must have seemed inevitable. The close involvement of local authorities in the delivery of the Special Programmes for the unemployed may have encouraged them to consider whether they could use their powers to produce a more permanent solution to high unemployment. But perhaps the most important stimulus has been described by Norman Holmes, director of the West Midlands Enterprise Trust, as the feeling among local authorities that 'we are best able to define what's needed and to tailor the available measures to our needs'.[10] While, however, they may be best fitted to define what is needed for their own area, they are by their very nature unable to consider the best way to meet the needs of the community at large.

Local authorities throughout Great Britain have used their powers to provide land and buildings to offer premises in particular to small and medium-sized firms. It is, as Johnson and Cochrane point out, 'widely accepted that the private market is not always able to provide premises for the smaller firm'[11]—although more might be done to encourage private sector activity here. Financial assistance in the form of loans, grants, or equity participation is offered under a hotchpotch of private act powers (many of which are due to expire in 1986), and under general powers to incur expenditure of benefit to their area under section 83 of the Local Government (Scotland) Act 1973 and section 137 of the Local Government Act 1972. These general powers limit total expenditure to the product of a 2p rate (which would, however, permit expenditure of up to £6m. per year by the Greater Manchester Council and £38m. by the GLC). They were not generally used before 1982, even by those authorities who saw them as capable of providing surrogates for the Development Agencies enjoyed by the Scots and the Welsh, because of financial constraints and doubts about the *vires* of using them to assist industry. Thus Johnson and Cochrane note that, amongst the authorities which they studied, direct grants to industry were rare; loans were made to private developers although developers rarely found it difficult to raise private funds; and while one authority proposed to use its superannuation fund to purchase equity in firms in its area, the conditions were so strict that the facility was not used.[12] As we shall see, however, authorities have become more active in these fields of late, and even by 1979 South Yorkshire County Council's County Regional Investment Scheme, which makes use of the Council's superannuation fund to provide finance on a commercial basis to small unquoted companies, had provided equity funding of £2m. for such companies in tranches of from £100,000 to £250,000.

Local authorities have various powers to promote their areas as locations for industrial investment, and such activities, as Johnson and Cochrane point out, are an attractive form of activity for authorities facing political pressures because of high unemployment: 'they require little additional manpower and finance to initiate, yet they create the impression that action is being taken'.[13] The provision of advice to firms in the area and potential incomers, covering both the authority's own services and those available from other institutions, is also regarded by authorities as an effective use of their resources.

Many of these activities are aimed directly at constraints on local economic development. Factory space has been a considerable inhibition on the development of small firms; local authorities can help to fill the gap. Falkirk District Council has, for example, provided small factories and workshop units which, it claims have provided several hundred jobs, many for redundant workers.[14] Finance is helpful to fill the 'equity gap' for small and medium-sized firms (although the gap appears to be very much smaller than was thought on the establishment of the Wilson Committee on Financial Institutions), as is advice to fill the 'management gap' which might constrain their development. Yet central government has been particularly concerned at two elements of local authority involvement in industrial development—promotion, and the provision of finance.

The use of industrial promotion powers created little difficulty until the 1980s: expenditure was generally low, and bodies such as the North East Scotland Development Authority (NESDA) more or less successfully co-ordinated the activities of the authorities in their areas without distorting national priorities. But increasing unemployment has caused authorities to become more active, while the reduction in the amount of footloose industry looking for a home has increased central government's concern at the effects of unstructured promotional efforts, which could be counter-productive and contrasted unfavourably with the 'one door' for promotion and financial support offered by the Irish Industrial Development Authority. It was concerns such as these which underlay the efforts of the Locate in Scotland bureau (the promotional arm of the Scottish Office and the Scottish Development Agency) to co-ordinate the promotional activities of the Scottish New Towns and local authorities and the removal of powers from the District Authorities in Scotland to promote their districts overseas. South of the border, the Department of Industry explained its decision not to grant aid to the North West Development Association as generously as to the North of England Development Council on the grounds that the local authorities and new towns in the North-West had not demonstrated 'the requisite degree of commitment to a full and effective co-ordination of programmes'.[15]

If uncoordinated industrial promotion by local authorities can be counter-productive, the provision of finance carries with it the risk of competitive bidding-up of incentives and the gratuitous shifting of activity from one area to another. Cornwall County Council, for instance, was reported as agreeing to pay an international mining company £100,000 to create 200 jobs at Cambourne even though it believed that, as a result, the company would close its plant in Buckingham.[16] (It has to be conceded that central government activity can have similar results.) Local authorities may not be in the best position to appraise investment propositions, and some of the schemes in which they involve themselves—for instance job subsidy schemes to encourage recruitment of the long-term unemployed—may carry considerable deadweight. The central government viewpoint was expressed by the Parliamentary Under-Secretary of State at the Department of Industry during the Second Reading of the Greater London Council Bill, which sought to extend the GLC's private powers to assist industry:

> There is no doubt that local authorities can create a better environment for the development of industry through sensitive planning policies and procedures. However the Government are concerned at the prospect of what I might call a proliferation of powers for local authorities to give financial assistance to industry, whether by means of loan guarantees... or by giving grants and loans on favourable terms.[17]

Authorities nevertheless remained keen to secure new powers to assist industry; the Government's response was to establish a group under the chairmanship of Sir Wilfred Burns (Deputy Secretary and Chief Planner at the Department of the Environment) to review the local authority role. The group concluded that authorities had a proper role in relation to the fostering of local employment—any other conclusion would indeed have been politically impossible—but stressed that their activities must be complementary to, and not competitive with, the activities of central government and the private sector. Such complementarity could be achieved either through restricting authorities to specific forms of assistance, or through giving them a closely circumscribed general power.

The Government followed the latter course. It made it clear in a Consultative Paper[18] that it saw the main function of local authorities as stimulating the development of smaller firms 'which underpin the local economy and which are relatively less mobile between different areas', and in encouraging enterprise generally through the proper exercise of their statutory powers and through avoiding excessive rates burdens and bureaucracy. Apart from in the designated inner city areas, therefore, the powers under sections 83 and 137 of the Local Government Acts would be replaced by a 'widely drawn power' to assist industry and commerce in any way considered appropriate by the local authority, but subject to two limitations: support should be limited to independent firms employing twenty-five or fewer people, and total support by any one authority should be limited to the product of a $\frac{1}{2}$p rate. The use of the power to create 'special economic development agencies through which to channel assistance' was not favoured because of the danger that they might develop into separate bureaucracies and absorb some of the available resources; rather the government wished 'to encourage local authorities to use their new powers to assist industry and commerce directly'.

In short, the Consultative Paper, despite its genuflections in the direction of local autonomy, constituted a significant attack on the ability of local authorities outwith the inner urban areas to assist industry. Private Act powers were to be removed, the available finance was to be cut by three-quarters, the new power was restricted to the smallest firms, and local authorities were to be discouraged from establishing their own development agencies. Hardly surprisingly, the proposals gave rise to vigorous opposition from the local government lobby, and in the event, and despite the Government's concerns, the local authority view prevailed. In response to pressure in the House of Lords, particularly from Lord Northfield (the former chairman of the Development Commission), the Government modified its approach in such a way that the powers under sections 83 and 137, far from being restricted, were enhanced to the extent that any remaining doubts as to their legality were removed. The sums available to all but the largest authorities nevertheless remain small, and it seems likely that the bulk of local authority support will continue to be concentrated on the small and relatively immobile firm—activity which, in addition to the authorities' planning and infrastructure powers, can make a useful contribution to local economic revival. As we shall see, however, a few of the larger authorities have used the powers to establish regional development agencies of their own.

3. The Urban Programme

The Urban Programme provides a means of channelling additional resources to support urban regeneration in some of the most disadvantaged areas in such a way as to avoid many of the problems of competition, co-ordination, and competing priorities which concerned the Burns Group and which bedevil attempts at economic regeneration. The programme consists of two elements. The 'traditional urban programme' introduced in 1968 provides 75 per cent grants towards the capital and current costs of projects of benefit to multiply deprived urban areas (or areas at risk of becoming multiply deprived). The 'new urban programme', dating from 1977, added a structure of Partnership and Programme Authorities to co-ordinate the work of central and local government over the whole range of urban renewal activities in the hardest-hit areas.

Initially, the traditional programme concentrated on social projects directed at the alleviation of multiple deprivation in order to break the 'cycle of deprivation' which was thought to be at the roots of the inner city problem. In this respect it was in tune with the two other spatially discriminatory measures introduced to alleviate inner city problems at about the same time, Educational Priority Areas and the Community Development Programme. Most of the Urban Programme's expenditure in its first four years was, indeed, on day nurseries, nursery education, and child care.[19]

The turning-point came in 1977 with the White Paper *Policy for the Inner Cities*,[20] which Hall *et al.* describe as 'the biggest single policy shift since inner urban policies were introduced'.[21] The White Paper had been considerably influenced by the Inner Area Studies set up by the previous government, and it identified economic problems as being at the heart of the problem. It therefore proposed that the emphasis of the Urban Programme should be shifted in the direction of support for projects of benefit to the local economy in order to 'strengthen the economies of the inner areas and the prospects of their residents'.[22] Local authorities should therefore seek to stimulate private sector investment in industry, commerce, and housing, and should continue efforts to improve the fabric of the inner areas and to make their environment more attractive. But the alleviation of immediate social problems continued to be of importance in order to provide what the Secretary of State for the Environment subsequently described as 'the first comprehensive policy for the inner cities that this country has ever had'; a policy designed to halt the 'downward spiral' of physical, social, and economic decline, to 'strengthen the economic and social structures of the inner cities at the same time as we improve their physical environment', and to 'create confidence in the future of the inner cities as places to live, work and invest'.[23] The mechanism was to be the pattern of Partnership and Programme Authorities designed to secure co-ordinated action tailored to local needs, together with continuation of the traditional Urban Programme with a greater emphasis on action to assist economic development. For the

Partnership and Programmes Authorities, annual rolling programmes of expenditure covering both Urban Programme money
and main programmes would be approved by the Partnership and
Programme Committees (on which were to be represented the
relevant central and local administration bodies); in the Partnership
Authorities in particular an elaborate structure of committees and
subcommittees was established to oversee the programme.

The shift towards measures of benefit to the local economy was
given new emphasis under the Conservative Government of 1979–
83, which was concerned that 'wherever possible, funds... should
be used for schemes which will assist in wealth creation rather than
consumption; and which will engage the private sector, directly
or indirectly'.[24] Reviews of the Programme, which was initially
considered at risk because of its uneasy relationship with the
economic philosophy of the new government, confirmed both its
future and the shift to an economic orientation. The shift was less
marked in Scotland, where the Scottish Development Agency does
much which would be supported by Urban Programme funds in
the south; and in Scotland much of the work supported by the
Programme continued to be in the traditional fields of social work
and community education. But the Programme does support a
certain amount of economic and environmental development in
Scotland, for example the provision of very small workshops and
nest factories (which the SDA was initially reluctant to provide)
and, in consultation with the SDA, environmental rehabilitation to
remove constraints on economic development. It is also doing
useful work in supporting community businesses and the Scottish
Co-operative Development Committee.[25]

How well does the Urban Programme match up to the high
hopes expressed by Peter Shore, and how apt is it to the reversal
of inner city decline? Despite the hope that it would constitute a
comprehensive policy, it is difficult to trace any consistent strategy
among the variety of projects which the Programme supports—
everything, as John Edwards points out, from vasectomy facilities
to the care of the terminally ill by way of VD contact tracing.[26]
The control exercised by central government may reduce conflict
between the activities of agencies concerned to stimulate economic
development, but this control is essentially reactive, and since the
Programme relies on a mass of individual proposals submitted by
the local authorities it is hard to produce a comprehensive approach.

Nor have the partnership and Programme arrangements solved problems of conflict within and between the central and local government agencies concerned with inner city regeneration. Central government is criticised by the Partnership and Programme Authorities for having failed to develop a corporate approach to inner city problems, while individual departments within the Authorities tend to see the Programme as a means of restoring projects which would otherwise be cut. Thus the apparatus of committees and sub-committees has failed to secure any significant 'bending' of main programmes in the direction of inner city policies, or to produce a concerted programme of initiatives addressed at the causes of the problem.[27] In the words of John Edwards, the Urban Programme has 'signally failed to make a connection between the problems that it poses and the solutions that it provides'.[28]

Some of the more obvious anomalies of the traditional programme have been tackled by modifications introduced in 1984–5. Revised criteria for grants issued by the Scottish Development Department in November 1984[29] emphasise that the Secretary of State will increasingly be looking to authorities to submit applications for projects 'which are part of a co-ordinated local strategy for tackling deprivation'. In England, the Urban Programme Management Initiative is designed to achieve 'clearer objectives for the Urban Programme (UP) at national and local level' and 'clearer linking of programmes and projects to the local objectives'.[30] Both sets of directives, in line with the managerial stance which has characterised Mrs Thatcher's second administration, require a clear statement of objectives and wherever possible quantified targets against which performance can be assessed; the English guidelines also reiterate that

The role of the Urban Programme is to encourage local authorities to develop a coordinated approach and an action programme to tackle the problems of their areas; to work with the private and voluntary sectors; to involve other agencies including central government Departments; to develop new and more cost-effective solutions to problems; and to promote and encourage economic activity, enterprise and private investment.[31]

There remains a presumption in favour of economic projects in the English Inner Area Programmes, and the possibility of support for housing projects. The Urban Programme does provide a flexible, if somewhat *ad hoc*, means of tackling the full range of inner city problems; its very diversity can be a strength. Many of the initiatives which it supports are directly relevant to regeneration, particularly environmental recovery and assistance to small firms and co-operative enterprises, and if, as we have suggested, inner city residents are at a disadvantage in the labour market, the continuation of support for social measures, and particularly community education, seems highly desirable. The Urban Programme has given local and central government much useful experience in the development of policies aimed at specific social and economic problems,[32] and it has highlighted some of the problems of implementation. While the Urban Programme has not developed into a comprehensive policy for the inner city, and is unlikely to do so, even with the most recent changes, it can and does provide a useful component of integrated approaches to inner city regeneration.

4. The Urban Development Corporations

The partnership arrangements under the Urban Programme sought through improved co-ordination to resolve the conflicting priorities, institutional rivalries, policy conflicts, and bureaucratic inertia which can inhibit attempts at local economic regeneration. The Urban Development Corporation, by contrast, offers an organisational solution. The Corporations established under the Local Government, Planning and Land Act 1980 to regenerate the London and Mersey Docks have assumed many of the powers of the local authorities in their areas. Their proponents argue that they can accordingly avoid both the bureaucracy and the slowness of decision-making associated with local democratic control. Unlike the local authorities, they have a single objective: 'to secure the regeneration of their area' through bringing land and buildings into use, through encouraging industrial and commercial development, through improving the environment, and through ensuring the provision of housing and other social facilities.[33]

The Corporations, which are appointed by the Secretary of State for the Environment, consist of a chairman, a vice-chairman, and between five and eleven other members, some of whom must have experience of local government. They are akin to New Towns in their powers and relationship to the local authorities. Unlike the New Towns, however, they are consciously slim-line organisations.

Both Corporations have small staffs and rely on outside consultants and contractors for the preparation of detailed plans and for . the work of physical development. The Merseyside Development Corporation (MDC), for example, established in March 1981 to regenerate 865 acres of dockland on either side of the Mersey, had in December 1982 a staff of 44 and had commissioned some 90 pieces of work from the private sector, many from local firms.[34] They do, however, have quite considerable financial resources at their disposal by way of grant and loan facilities (grants are available to bring land up to developable state: the Corporations are expected to make a commercial return on development thereafter, which is accordingly funded by loan). The MDC spent £24.5m. of a budgeted £26m. in 1982-3; the London Docklands Development Corporation (LDDC), established in July 1981 to regenerate 5,000 acres in Newham, Southwark, and Tower Hamlets, spent £40m. in the same period and considered that it would require to spend about the same amount every year for the following ten years.[35]

These resources are addressed primarily at physical renewal and 'pump priming' to encourage private sector investment in the docklands areas. The MDC has developed a three-point strategy, in consultation with the local authorities, local community bodies, and other interests, involving physical, social, and economic development; to mid-1983 the vast bulk of expenditure was on physical development and environmental renewal, including the preparation of the site of the 1984 Garden Festival. Work was, however, in hand on factory buildings, the development of industrial sites, and the provision of roads and other infrastructure.

The LDDC has elaborated a five-point approach to regeneration addressed at many of the constraints which lie at the heart of inner city decline. It aims to create the economic infrastructure and physical environment which will attract private sector investment; to use its powers as a planning authority (UDCs have development control functions but not the power to produce statutory plans); to ensure and encourage high standards in quality and design of buildings; to promote the area, especially to developers and financial institutions; to stimulate development in the Isle of Dogs through its powers as an Enterprise Zone Authority; and to use some of its resources to assist community groups and small firms to undertake innovative schemes in the economic, social, and environmental fields.[36] The Corporation is making a particular effort to diversify housing tenure in the docklands and is promoting industrial development, both generally in the Isle of Dogs and on specific projects elsewhere.

It is early days yet to assess the effectiveness of the Urban Development Corporations as a means of ensuring that regeneration becomes 'a self generating process without the need for further major injections of public resources'.[37] The LDDC noted that intially there had been a slower than expected response from the private sector; Dr Noel Boaden, a member of the MDC, has suggested that redevelopment on reclaimed sites will not be nearly as easy as reclamation.[38] But the London Docklands Development Corporation, in particular, has made significant progress. The Corporation's report for 1984–5 shows a high degree of activity over the full range of regeneration. Infrastructure investment of £141m. had produced a total private sector commitment of over £800m.; 200 new companies creating some 5,700 jobs had moved in; over 1.8m. square feet of new industrial floor-space had been completed or was under construction; major programmes of private house building were in progress, with 9,500 houses completed, under construction, or planned for 1985–6; and work was proceeeding apace on transport improvements and environmental recovery. For the Western Docklands at least the Corporation considered that it had passed the 'critical development threshold' beyond which regeneration is self-sustaining.[39] But, notwithstanding the considerable amount of private investment which has been attracted by public sector pump-priming, this achievement has required a large investment of public funds. And to what extent do the Urban Development Corporations avoid the difficulties associated with other means of local economic regeneration?

The short answer is very little. They do permit central government to channel and regulate the use of substantial resources for urban renewal in a way which avoids the vicissitudes of the Rate Support Grant and block capital consents (under which funds may not be earmarked for specific purposes), and they do provide 'single-minded bodies' which are not troubled, internally, with problems of competing priorities. But they do not remove the need for co--ordination. As the MDC comments, both economic regeneration and social rehabilitation require effective co-ordination with the initiatives particularly of other public sector agencies operating on Merseyside... If we are to successfully integrate the redevelopment of the docklands area with the Inner City... more effective means of co-ordination must be found... Without adequate co-ordination we may compete for private sector investment and in the attraction of industrial and commercial occupiers and in initiatives for the encouragement of small businesses.[40]

Nor has the creation of Urban Development Corporations removed problems of competing organisational objectives and priorities. The chairman of the MDC put the matter succinctly when he noted, in relation to a problem about the acquisition of land from the Mersey Docks and Harbour Board, that 'He (the chairman of the Board) is pursuing his objectives as a Dock Company; I clearly have to pursue redevelopment objectives.'[41] The division of planning responsibilities, with the local authorities remaining responsible for development planning, while the Corporations have assumed responsibility for development control, is another potential source of difficulty.

The creation of the Urban Development Corporations does, moreover, raise in acute form the problem of the relationship between local and central government. Members are accountable not to the local community, but to the Secretary of State and, through him, to Parliament. While both existing Corporations have taken steps to minimise the difficulty, it is possible that the consequent tensions could inhibit effective action. The GLC notes waspishly in evidence to the Environment Committee that 'the Council does not have a formal working relationship with the Corporation', and argues that 'the docklands should be rehabilitated and developed through normal democratic processes rather than by the special machinery of the Corporation'.[42] While Liverpool City Council formally welcomed the establishment of the MDC, the Merseyside County Council initially had strong reservations, although good working relationships have subsequently been developed.[43]

Urban Development Corporations form one model for the management of local economic regeneration. Their combination of powers, which brings together industrial investment, factory building, and environmental functions in the one organisation, gives them the potential to tackle economic regeneration in an integrated way. The Corporations in London and Merseyside are beginning to tackle some of the fundamental constraints on growth, and their work on land assembly and rehabilitation, industrial building, and the diversification of housing tenure is particularly appropriate. But they leave unresolved many of the problems which they were designed to solve, and, imposed as they are from above to replace in effect some of the more important and politically sensitive of the local authority's functions, they are at risk of inhibiting the close working relationship with the local authorities which is essential for the effective management of regeneration. Such a drawback is avoided by the Scottish and Welsh Development Agencies, which are not tied to specific local areas and which generally enter an area at the request of, or in consultation with, the local authority. It is to these bodies that we shall now turn.

5. The Development Agencies

It is perhaps an over-simplification to say that if Scotland had not had oil, she would not have been given a Development Agency, and that if Scotland had not been given one, Wales would not have been given one either. The political pressures resulting from oil development did, however, play a considerable part in strengthening the case of what Frank Stephen described, in an article advancing the case for a wide-ranging development agency for Scotland, as 'a new approach to development'.[44]

In fact, as Stephen points out, there was nothing new about the suggestion. The Highlands and Islands Development Board, established in 1966, provided a ready model. In 1971 Bill Rogers MP presented a Private Member's Bill seeking to establish a Regional Development Corporation for the North. The Scottish Council of the Labour party proposed a Scottish Enterprise Board in 1973, and Santosh Mukherjee of Political and Economic Planning simultaneously proposed a wide-ranging Employment and Development Agency for Strathclyde, which would have powers of environmental regeneration as well as industrial support, and which would address itself in particular to industrial relations, identified (wrongly) by Mukherjee as the single most important cause of Scotland's economic problems.[45]

In the event, the Scottish Development Agency (established in December 1975) and its Welsh counterpart (established in January 1976) were given both environmental and industrial powers. This combination of powers, embracing as it does the rehabilitation of environmental dereliction, the provision of industrial premises, the giving of advice and consultancy services to companies (and particularly small firms), and the provision of finance for industry through loans, grants, and equity participation, fits the Agencies particularly well to tackle local economic problems. The problems of co-ordination were, in short, to be overcome by the creation of unitary organisations having extensive powers and resources. In the words of William Ross, Secretary of State for Scotland at the time, the Scottish Development Agency would be able

to undertake the whole process of redevelopment from clearing dereliction to providing factories and attracting the jobs to fill them. We have seen from past experience how building new roads, new houses and new towns has done much to attract industry and workpeople to Scotland. The Agency will be applying these lessons to our older industrial communities.[46]

It was in fact some years before the Scottish Development Agency brought its functions together in an effectively corporate way. Initially the Scottish Agency devoted the major part of its senior management effort to its industrial investment role, a role which Bruce Millan, the Minister of State, had described as 'the basic function of the Agency'.[47] The Agency's annual report for 1977 comments interestingly that the link between economic development and environmental improvement 'may not be so immediately apparent' as that between development, the safeguarding of employment, and industrial efficiency, although environmental improvement 'is properly associated with these, because so much of Scotland's environment bears the scars left by past industrial development'. Investment, therefore, could not be seen as 'a thing in isolation', but must be recognised as 'integral and interacting with the landscape and townscape in which it lies'.[48] Nevertheless, by 1979 the Agency was writing that 'the removal of the scars of earlier industrialisation is a necessary adjunct, and indeed preliminary, to the promotion of new investment. As well as providing land for new industry, the improvement of the environment has a marked tonic effect on local communities.'[49]

Through their combination of powers the Agencies are uniquely fitted to tackle problems of urban decay and industrial decline. Being separate from central government they can develop a closer and more intimate relationship with the local authorities than is perhaps possible even with the regional offices of central government departments; but unlike the Urban Development Corporations they are not potential rivals of the local authorities. They can, moreover, develop close working relationships with the financial institutions — essential not only for the effective discharge of their industrial investment functions, but also to stimulate a closer involvement of the private sector in local economic regeneration. Through their financial and advisory powers they can make a useful contribution to filling the 'management' and 'equity gaps' which inhibit the growth of small and medium-sized enterprises. Finally, they can provide a 'single door' for providing advice, assistance, and financial incentives to potential investors, a facility of considerable value to the attraction of such mobile investment as there is.

Despite these potential benefits, the Agencies are not without their critics. Grant argues that 'The Agencies have been a disappointment from a number of viewpoints. In business terms they have not been a great success.'[50] Following Dawson,[51] he suggests that the SDA has neglected Scotland's traditional industries and that its industrial policy has relied on attracting branch factories. It has, moreover, upset regional opinion by appearing to favour Strathclyde. It has inadequate resources to tackle the problems which it is expected to solve, and insufficient staff. Thus, in Dawson's words, 'it is fundamentally trapped into accepting Scotland's increasingly peripheral economic position'.

Whether or not Scotland's economy is 'increasingly peripheral' (a slightly far-fetched assertion in relation to one of the fastest-growing regional economies in the UK), much of this critique seems now to be beside the point. If the Agency is to concern itself with the development of the Scottish economy it must support growth sectors: this it is doing through its support for developments in electronics, health care, energy-related industries, and production engineering.[52] It has, however, paid attention to some of the more traditional sectors of the economy, such as timber production. The attraction of branch factories (which as we have seen can have benefits as well as disadvantages) is matched by efforts to stimulate indigenous enterprise and to encourage joint ventures between Scottish and foreign companies. If the Agency has been seen to favour Strathclyde, this is where half of the population and many of the problems which the Agency was established to tackle reside, and the Agency is involved in imaginative work elsewhere in the country. Finally, as we shall see, the Agency has begun to play a most effective role in local economic regeneration. Despite the much-publicised early industrial failures, the Agency has begun to take effective action to overcome constraints on development in the Scottish regions and districts.

6. English Local Authority Development Boards

The potential of the Scottish and Welsh Development Agencies to tackle spatial economic problems and encourage sectoral growth has, not surprisingly, led to demands for the establishment of similar bodies for the English regions. The National Enterprise Board, which, partly as a response to such pressures, established regional offices in the North and North-West, had neither the powers nor the manpower to replicate the detailed work of the Agencies on local development; its main preoccupations were elsewhere. Thus both the Labour party's 1979 manifesto and its Alternative Regional Strategy[53] called for the establishment of Regional Development Agencies in England. No such bodies have so far been created, and in the meantime four English metropolitan authorities—Greater London, West Yorkshire, West Midlands, and Lancashire—have sought to fill the gap by establishing Development Boards of their own.

The Local Authority Development Boards do not have quite the range of powers available to the Development Agencies. Typically they are funded from section 137 of the Local Government Act 1972 together with contributions from the local authority's pensions fund (made on a commercial basis) and perhaps from other institutions. Funds are deployed in providing loans, guarantees, and equity for small and medium-sized companies, in assisting with the development of new products or the provision of premises, in encouraging the application of new technology, and in aiding 'management buy-outs' of branch firms faced with closure. In addition, Boards may undertake promotional work and the provision of premises for industry.

Supporters of the Local Authority Development Boards argue that they have a number of advantages. They can avoid the normal bureaucratic processes of the local authority, facilitating speedy decisions. Unlike private sector financial institutions, which are in any event sparsely represented in the English regions, they can concentrate on long-term capital growth rather than short-term returns, and thus help to meet the unsatisfied demand for long-term loan capital.[54] Because of the element of non-commercial funding which they enjoy, they can look for a lower financial return than the private institutions, and they can accordingly take account of social costs and benefits in assessing their rate of return. Their close links with and knowledge of the local economy will moreover enable them to act as a bridge between financial institutions and local firms. For all these reasons they are well placed to make an effective contribution to the restructuring and development of the metropolitan economy.

The Boards do, however, differ substantially in their approach, reflecting perhaps the political philosophies of their founding authorities. Like the Scottish Development Agency, the West Midlands Enterprise Board is seeking to identify sectors of the economy on which to concentrate and is developing strong links with the private sector, and particularly the financial institutions for whom, in effect, it offers a brokerage service. Its main emphasis is on the provision of development capital for medium-sized firms, for whom it has identified a gap in the financial markets. It sees itself as 'a public sector development capital body' designed to 'lubricate the necessary changes in the industrial structure of the West Midlands'.[55] Hence, despite such features as the Planning and Investment Agreements which are required of companies seeking funds from the Board, and the assessment of investments on the basis of social as well as economic criteria, the Board is a relatively orthodox institution.

The West Yorkshire Enterprise Board shares this basic orthodoxy. Established in October 1982, its primary role is to fill a perceived gap in the provision of finance for small and medium firms, in particular to help them modernise and diversify, and to provide premises for high technology and service industries and for research and development facilities.[56]

The Greater London Enterprise Board, in principle at least, is far more radical. It quite overtly puts social needs before profits, and applications for support are assessed not on conventional market criteria, but according to the extent to which the project involves co-operative or municipal ownership, the number of women, blacks, and apprentices employed, the relations of the firm with the unions, and whether jobs will be created in sectors or areas of particularly high unemployment. The aims appear to be the development of social ownership, human technologies, industrial democracy, and trade union power.[57] In addition, the Board undertakes the more traditional local authority functions of factory building and industrial promotion.

Local authority Enterprise Boards provide a direct response to the absence, in England, of Development Agencies on the model of the SDA and WDA and of strong regional financial institutions; they are capable of providing a fine-grained approach to economic development arguably more appropriate to the local economy than the broad and reactive brush of regional policy (which in any case is inapplicable in London and was until November 1984 in the West Midlands). They are perhaps better placed than the local authorities from which they sprang to harness the experience and resources of the private sector. They are beginning to have some impact in their areas: in its first six months of operation the West Midlands Enterprise Board evaluated 100 enquiries and made five investments totalling £1m., thereby securing £3m. of private funds and creating or safeguarding 700 jobs.[58] How effective the more radical approach of the Greater London Enterprise Board will be remains to be seen, although in principle co-operative enterprises and community businesses seem appropriate components of initiatives to regenerate the local economy.[59] But, while Local Authority Development Agencies offer some of the benefits of the Scottish and Welsh Development Agencies, their powers are not sufficiently wide to offer a fully integrated approach to local regeneration. Like other English bodies concerned with regeneration, they must work in collaboration with others—a need which will be even greater following the abolition of their parent authorities.

7.   Training and the Manpower Services Commission

We argued in chapter 1 that an active manpower policy was an essential component of measures to regenerate the local economy. Apart from the relatively small in-plant training scheme operated under section 7 of the Industrial Development Act, the primary responsibility for such a policy rests with the Manpower Services Commission (MSC), although education authorities also have a part to play, in particular through their Further Education provision. Both arms of the Commission have relevant tasks: the

Employment Services Division in providing assistance and advice to job-seekers from the disadvantaged areas, and in counselling workers faced with redundancy, and the Training Services Division in providing training for the unemployed and in helping to meet skill shortages inhibiting growth (less of a problem during the current recession than hitherto).

The Commission administers some imaginative schemes of direct relevance to local economic regeneration. The Enterprise Allowance Scheme, which provides business advice and grants of £40 per week for a year in lieu of unemployment benefit to unemployed workers who are prepared to put £1,000 of their own resources into starting a business, is in a small way encouraging entrepreneurship. Between April and December 1982 a pilot scheme led to the creation of over 1,700 jobs in the pilot areas,[60] and the scheme was subsequently extended nationwide. By September 1985 it had provided support for 100,000 people, 65 per cent of whom had established themselves in the service sector; monitoring studies showed that 70 per cent of those supported were still in business three months after the end of their support.[61] (There is, however, likely to be a high rate of substitution.) Ever since the Job Creation Programme began, the Special Programmes for the adult unemployed have made a useful contribution to environmental regeneration. The Commission has, moreover, an area organisation whose existence, in principle at least, should assist the development of programmes appropriate to the needs of the local labour market and relevant to local economic regeneration.

Yet both staffing constraints and Commission philosophy have inhibited the development of such programmes. The Employment Services Division no longer has the specialist staff to run the Special Employment Needs Service, which was introduced in 1977 to provide intensive counselling for those, such as disadvantaged inner city residents, who found it difficult or impossible to secure employment, although 10 per cent of the time of employment office staff is dedicated to counselling those with such difficulties. Because of concerns about the rapid loss of skill by those who do not find appropriate work on completion of training, and the belief that industry should pay the costs of its own training, the Commission has set its face against 'training for stock', for example to provide the residents of a particular area with the skills likely to be sought by incoming firms or local entrepreneurs. It is not yet clear that the network of 55 Area Manpower Boards which the MSC has established to oversee its programmes on the ground will be 'sufficient to permit identification and response to local needs, let alone the proper co-ordination of training, education and unemployment programmes'.[62] Response to local labour market needs does indeed require very close attention to detail on the ground, yet the MSC found it impossible, for staffing reasons, to second an official to work with the Scottish Development Agency's Clydebank Task Force on the area's manpower needs,[63] while the West Midlands County Council observed in evidence to the Environment Committee that the MSC's policy imperatives 'do not reflect the special needs of deprived areas'.[64]

Over recent years the Commission has been heavily preoccupied with coping with increasing levels of unemployment, with its own internal reorganisation, and with the implementation of the Youth Training Scheme. Both the Enterprise Allowance Scheme and the Youth Training Scheme do point the way for it to play a more active part in local economic regeneration: support for Information Technology Centres, jointly funded by the Department of Industry and the Commission to provide computer training for the young unemployed, has for instance been biased in the direction of disadvantaged areas. In view of the importance of manpower policies for the regeneration of local economies it is to be hoped that the Commission will build on such experience, in particular through providing training for entrepreneurship, training for the new technologies (in concert with the education authorities), and assistance for those inner city residents who are disadvantaged in the labour market.

8. Conclusions

The measures which we have considered in this chapter are all, to a greater or lesser degree, addressed at the constraints on local and regional development which we identified in chapter 1, although some could be made more effective through a change of emphasis. The institutional arrangements have, for the most part, been designed specifically to overcome difficulties of implementation and co-ordination, although neither the co-ordinative approach of the new Urban Programme nor the organisational approach of the Urban Development Corporations have been entirely successful in removing problems of organisational rivalry and conflicting priorities. Such problems, indeed, appear to be part of the fabric where public bodies answerable to different constituencies are involved. The initiatives which we shall consider in the remainder of this study illustrate three separate ways of tackling them: the 'private sector approach', where difficulties inherent in the use of public sector bodies are side-stepped by encouraging the private sector to do the job; the 'charismatic approach', where inspired political leadership from the centre seeks to draw the other bodies whose co-operation is essential along in its wake; and the 'co-operative approach', where action depends on a negotiated settlement between equal partners. Each has its advantages as a means of drawing together measures to reverse decline and encourage self-sustaining growth; and each raises difficulties of its own.

Notes

1. The Environment Committee notes, for instance, that Merseyside has 'benefited from a plentitude of initiatives over the past 15 years but has also suffered from the subsequent abandonment or atrophy of each of them' (Environment Committee, *The Problems of Management of Urban Renewal (Appraisal of the Recent Initiatives in Merseyside)*, HMSO, London 1983, vol. 1, p. xi). Dr Wyn Grant considers the influence of the regional policy community in *The Political Economy of Industrial Policy*, Butterworths, London 1982, pp. 58-9.

2. Environment Committee, op. cit., p. xi.

3. Great Britain, *Royal Commission on the Distribution of the Industrial Population*, Cmnd. 6153, London 1940. A reading of this report, which was concerned primarily with the problem of excessive concentration of activity in the more prosperous areas and the concomitant dangers of aerial bombardment, suggests that economic historians have overemphasised its role in the development of regional policy, which owes more to the experience of the direction of industry during the war.

4. See, for instance, Damesick, P., 'Issues and Options in UK Regional Policy: the Need for a New Assessment', *Regional Studies*, vol. 16, no. 5, October 1982; Grant, W., op. cit., chapter 3.4; Hallett, G., *Second Thoughts on Regional Policy*, Centre for Policy Studies, London 1981.

5. See Hallett, op. cit., p. 8.

6. For assessments of the impact of regional policy, see for instance Marquand, J., *Measuring the Effects and Costs of Regional Incentives*, Government Economic Service Working Paper 32, London 1980;

Fothergill, S. and Gudgin, G., *Unequal Growth*, Heinemann, London
1982; Gudgin G., Moore B., and Rhodes, J., 'Employment Problems
in the Cities and Regions of the UK: Prospects for the 1980s',
Cambridge Economic Policy Review, vol. 8, no. 2, December 1982;
Ashcroft, B. and Taylor, J., 'The Effects of Regional Policy on the
Movement of Industry in Great Britain' in Maclellan, D. and Parr, J.
B., *Regional Policy, Past Experience and New Directions*, Martin
Robertson, Oxford 1979, chapter 2. While by the mid-1970s policy
had created some 200,000 jobs in the four main assisted areas, it
appears to have been far less effective subsequently; Fothergill and
Gudgin suggest, indeed (p. 147), that after 1973 it had ceased to have
any measurable effect.

7. See Slowe, P., *The Advance Factory in Regional Development*, Gower,
   Aldershot 1981.

8. Great Britain, *Regional Industrial Development*, Cmnd. 9111, HMSO,
   London 1983; OR, 28 November 1984, vol. 68, cols. 936–7.

9. Johnson, N. and Cochrane, A., *Economic Policy-Making by Local
   Authorities in Britain and Western Germany*, George Allen and Unwin,
   London 1981, pp. 15–16. It is a pity that while the interesting discussion
   here is couched in terms of Great Britain, the examples, case studies,
   institutional framework, and statutory references relate entirely to
   England.

10. Address to conference on 'Local Enterprise Agencies: their Role in
    Regional Development', Regional Studies Association, Manchester,
    November 1982.

11. Op. cit., p. 47.

12. Ibid., pp. 139–40.

13. Op. cit., p. 141.

14. Falkirk District Council Planning Department, *Application for the
    New Scottish Enterprise Zone*, Falkirk, September 1982, p. 1.

15. OR, 19 January 1983, vol. 35, WA cols. 144–5.

16. *Sunday Times*, 27 February 1983.

17. OR, 12 June 1979, vol. 968, col. 343.

18. *Local Authority Powers to Assist Industry and Commerce*, DOE, SEPD,
    and WO, March 1982.

19. See Hall, Peter (ed.), *The Inner City in Context*, final report of the
    SSRC Inner Cities Working Party, Heinemann, London 1981, for a
    useful analysis of the genesis of the Urban Programme. See also Home,
    R. K., *Inner City Regeneration*, E. & F. N. Spon, London 1982, and
    Higgins, J., *et al.*, *Government and Urban Poverty*, Basil Blackwell,
    Oxford 1983, chapter 3.

20. Great Britain, *Policy for the Inner Cities*, Cmnd. 6845, HMSO, London
    1977.

21. Hall, Peter (ed.), op. cit., p. 95. The policy shift was, of course, foreshadowed by the abandonment of Stonehouse New Town in 1976.
22. *Policy for the Inner Cities*, op. cit., para. 26.
23. Shore, Peter, speech to Royal Institute of Chartered Surveyors, Harrogate, 26 August 1978, cited in Higgins *et al*, op. cit., p. 133.
24. DOE Urban Programme Circular no. 20, 1979, cited in Higgins, Joan *et al.*, *Government and Urban Poverty*, Basil Blackwell, Oxford 1983, p. 83.
25. Interview with Scottish Development Department, November 1982.
26. Higgins, Joan *et al.*, op. cit., p. 69.
27. For criticisms of the partnership arrangements, see for example Boaden, N., evidence submitted to the Environment Committee study *Problems of Management of Urban Renewal* (*Appraisal of the Recent Criticisms on Merseyside*), minutes of evidence, 14 December 1982, pp. 162–4; and evidence submitted to the same enquiry by the City of Birmingham Council and the West Midlands County Council, 13 December 1982, especially pp. 67–72. (References hereafter to evidence to the enquiry will simply be called 'Evidence'.)
28. Higgins, Joan *et al.*, op. cit., p. 74.
29. Scottish Development Department, circular 35/1984.
30. Department of Environment, *Urban Programme Management Guidance Note No. 1*, May 1985.
31. Department of the Environment, Urban Programme, *Ministerial Guidelines for Partnership and Programme Authority Areas*, DOE, May 1985.
32. See Mawson, J. and Miller, D., 'Agencies in Regional and Local Development', paper presented to Regional Studies Association conference, 'Local Enterprise Agencies, their Role in Regional Development', Manchester, 12 November 1982, p. 18.
33. Local Government and Planning Act 1980.
34. Evidence, q. 481.
35. Evidence, qs. 472–4 and 1054.
36. Evidence, p. 457, memorandum submitted by the London Docklands Development Corporation, para. 6.
37. Evidence, p. 461, memorandum by LDDC, para. 11.
38. Ibid., para. 10.5; Evidence, p. 164, memorandum by Dr Noel Boaden.
39. London Dockland Development Corporation, *Annual Report and Accounts 1984–5*, LDCC London 1985.
40. Evidence, p. 178, memorandum submitted by Merseyside Development Corporation, para. 5.
41. Evidence, q. 519.
42. Evidence, pp. 389–90, memorandum submitted by GLC, paras. 35 and 41.

64   *Some Tools of Economic Regeneration*

43. Interviews with Liverpool City Council and Merseyside County Council, March 1983.
44. Stephen, Frank, 'The Scottish Development Agency' in *The Red Paper on Scotland*, EUSPB, Edinburgh 1975, p. 223.
45. The Scottish Council of the Labour party, *Scotland and the NEB*, 1973; Mukherjee, Santosh, *Strathclyde Employment and Development Agency: A Proposal for Discussion*, Scottish International Educational Trust, Edinburgh 1973.
46. OR, 25 June 1975, vol. 894, col. 467.
47. OR, 25 June 1975, vol. 894, col. 581.
48. SDA, *Annual Report 1977*, Glasgow 1978, p. 6.
49. SDA, *Annual Report 1979*, Glasgow 1979, p. 48.
50. Grant, Wyn, op. cit., p. 119.
51. Dawson, M. W., 'The Scottish Development Agency', *Public Enterprise* 19, autumn 1980, p. 13, cited by Grant, op. cit.
52. See SDA, 'Sectoral and Area Initiatives: the Experience of the Scottish Development Agency', paper delivered to the Regional Studies Association, Manchester, November 1982.
53. The Labour party, *Alternative Regional Strategy*, Parliamentary Spokesman's Group, London 1982, pp. 15-16.
54. See Carrington, J. C. and Edwards, George, *Financing Industrial Investment*, London 1975, and *Reversing Economic Decline*, London 1981, for a discussion of the impact of bank lending policies on economic growth in the UK.
55. N. Holmes, Director, WMEB, speaking at conference of the Regonal Studies Association 'Local Enterprise Agencies: their Role in Regional Development', Manchester, November 1982.
56. Mawson J. and Miller D., op. cit., p. 27.
57. See *Jobs for a Change*, GLC Popular Planning Unit, GLC, London 1983; and Marks, Stephen, 'Making London Work', *New Statesman*, 1 April 1983.
58. Holmes, N., op. cit.
59. See Pearce, J., *Can We Make Jobs?*, Local Government Research Unit, Paisley College of Technology, Glasgow 1978, for a discussion of local community-based approaches to industrial development.
60. OR, 21 December 1982, vol. 34, col. 807.
61. *Glasgow Herald*, 16 September 1985.
62. Fairley, J., 'Training Policy: The Local Perspective', *Regional Studies*, vol. 17, no. 2, April 1983, pp. 140-2.
63. Interview with deputy head of SDA's Special Programmes Division, October 1982.
64. Evidence, 13 December 1982, memorandum by West Midlands County Council, p. 68 para. 5.6.

3

Enlightened Self-interest:
the Role of the Private Sector

The difficulty of securing collaboration between the different public sector bodies involved in the regeneration of local economies can, on the face of it, be side-stepped by encouraging the private sector to do the job. For a government intent upon encouraging values of self-help and initiative and pledged to reduce the size of the public sector, to curb bureaucracy, and to reduce public expenditure, this constitutes a powerful incentive to seek greater private sector involvement. So it was that, while previous post-war governments had sought to regenerate declining areas by creating conditions amenable to private investment, the Conservative administration of 1979–83 encouraged the private sector to participate itself in the creation of such conditions.[1]

Commentators have been doubtful both about the possibility of securing greater private investment in declining areas, and about attempts to secure direct involvement of the private sector in regeneration. Robert K. Home, for instance, suggests that

The private sector has remained sceptical about the contribution it might make to inner city regeneration, since the inner city, with a weak economy, poor labour force and antiquated physical fabric, was unlikely to compete with other areas for profitable investment. The objective of securing the best return on investment was essentially incompatible with the social objectives of inner city policy.[2]

In fact, both encouragement from the Government and self-interest has led to an encouraging upsurge in private sector involvement in local economic regeneration, and the private sector is now making a substantial and effective contribution.

There are a number of reasons why it should benefit a firm to involve itself in local regeneration. First, and most important, large firms which have been compelled to contract or close their facilities in a particular area because of market loss or technological change have discovered that the process can be eased through helping to create alternative jobs in the area. Secondly, encouragement of the development of small firms can assist large firms in the area, for example in the sourcing of materials and in subcontracting. (These motivations came together in the case of UIE (UK) Ltd., who, having taken over the Marathon oil rig construction yard at Clydebank, shed the outfitting trades but assisted the redundant outfitters to set up on their own and gave them subcontracts.) Thirdly, private sector development organisations provide a training-ground for future top management and a suitable final posting for those approaching the end of their career. Fourthly, they can provide a use for spare resources, and thus a relatively inexpensive way of securing favourable publicity. Finally, firms benefit from the economic health of the communities in which they are located in terms of the morale of their labour force and labour relations; and local initiatives can make a substantial contribution to that health.

There is also, and despite the Marxian critique, room for altruism, although it is often impossible to define where commercial considerations end and altruism begins. In evidence to the Environment Committee, the Committee of London Clearing Banks noted that 'the distinction between the banks' commercial activities and their social responsibilities is not totally clear cut', and suggested that even their charitable donations can be a commercial investment since 'the long-term interests of the community are our long-term interests'.[3]

The centralisation of decision-making in areas other than those in need of help has, however, limited the scope for altruism and self-interest to prompt firms to involve themselves in local economic recovery. Decision-makers in the City of London may not perceive the benefits of action in the provinces, a theme stressed in Mr Heseltine's letter to the financial institutions following the Merseyside riots.[4] Charles Newman, writing in the *Investors Chronicle*, notes that 'It has been St Helens' good fortune that Pilkington's has retained its head office there. If it had moved to London, it is unlikely that it would have accepted more than grudging responsibility for the effects of lengthening dole queues on the town, brought about by new capital-intensive production techniques.'[5] And in a message to the Prime Minister following its 1982 conference, the Association of British Chambers of Commerce suggests that Chambers would welcome 'Prime Ministerial ex-hortation of top managers to take a direct and personal interest in the well-being of the communities in which their firms exist. This would be particularly valuable where a high proportion of employment and output is provided by branches of large firms with headquarters elsewhere.'[6]

Despite the problem of centralisation, however, enlightened self-interest has led to a number of private sector initiatives, involving varying degrees of collaboration with the public sector, and leading to the establishment of local Enterprise Trusts and Agencies, the establishment of Business in the Community and its Scottish counterpart, and the development of a 'wider role' for Chambers of Commerce. In addition, private sector firms are becoming involved in the management of renewal projects, and, following American experience, the Government has experimented with 'pump-priming' grants to stimulate private sector investment in marginally viable projects of benefit to the inner urban areas. Finally, as we shall note in considering the initiatives on Merseyside and in Scotland, private sector managers have been seconded into public sector bodies concerned with economic regeneration in order to inject their own expertise.

1.   Enterprise Trusts and Agencies

Private sector led Enterprise Trusts had, by mid-1983, been established in well over 100 localities to stimulate local economic development. There is no single model; they vary considerably in size and scope; and most enjoy support from the local authorities in their area. (They should be distinguished, however, from the local authority led Enterprise Boards which we considered above.) Here we shall consider, as an example of such private sector led bodies, the St Helens Trust, founded by Pilkington's (with the support of other local private and public sector bodies) in 1978.

The Trust's role has been described by its first director, Mr W. E. G. Humphrey, as 'that of a catalyst in an effort by a community to pull itself up by its own boot straps'.[7] Its objective is 'to attack unemployment'; the means is 'to marshall the resources of the community to create an environment favourable to growth of business enterprise, in particular new small business'.[8] Humphrey stamped a characteristic style on the Trust which has profoundly influenced similar bodies elsewhere. In his view, too many employment creation initiatives were imposed from the top downwards by hierarchical organisations which believed that they could create jobs through planning and through the establishment of employment-creating projects of their own. But it is entrepreneurs, and not public agencies, who create jobs, and entrepreneurs require the help of an organisation which can mobilise the resources of the community to provide advice and assistance and to relieve the 'loneliness of the small businessman'. Such an organisation would function most effectively if it were small, elusive, and under-resourced, since only thus could it retain the necessary flexibility and avoid becoming another bureaucracy. It should, to use a favourite phrase of Humphrey, be modelled on the 'poor friar'.

The St Helens Trust, then, has a lean organisation and is run on a shoe-string. Its staff consists of a director and two or three managers seconded for a year—typically, a Pilkington's executive, a bank manager, and someone with experience of small business—together with secretarial help. The total cost of the organisation has been estimated at £100,0000 per year, met partly by income from loans made by the Trust, partly by urban aid grants and donations from supporters, and partly in kind by Pilkington's, who provide offices and meet secretarial and administrative costs, and by the companies who second staff on full salary. Because the Trust has few resources of its own (a fund of £50,000 from Pilkington's and £40,000 from other sponsors) it must rely on the help of other organisations to achieve its ends; Humphrey has noted that 'even the most efficient organisation at any given moment has some surplus resources under-utilised. It is this which is tapped.'[9] Also tapped is the expertise of professionals who provide advice to the clients of the Trust on such matters as marketing, accounting, and business plans. A major task has indeed been the establishment of links with those who can help. Its governing body, which includes representatives of the major influences in St Helens—industry, banks, the local authorities, and the Chamber of Commerce—has clearly been of help here; but the Trust maintains a sturdy independence from its governors and sponsors, who appear to be very much on tap rather than on top. If, however, the Trust's success is to be judged by its ability to get others to use spare resources to achieve its objectives, it does not rely on charity. As Humphrey put it, it seeks 'to appeal to supporters' self interest and not simply to social conscience or charity. If, for example, premises were to be constructed, then the rentals should be economic.'[10]

To its sponsors and other supporters the Trust is, then, pro-active: it seeks to encourage them to act in support of its objectives and clients. It has, for instance, encouraged property owners to subdivide factories for small businesses, and persuaded Pilkington's to provide small factory units—in the event, a profitable activity.[11] To clients, by contrast, it is reactive. It sees its function as helping the businessman to solve his problem, 'whether it be in areas of finance, premises, general business advice or training'.[12] It does not promote grandiose plans to generate employment and does not even publicise its address: those seeking its assistance have to search it out. The assistance which it offers ranges from minor help with business plans to advice on premises and opportunities and assistance with finance: the Trust has, for example, helped a young graduate with a good idea but no business experience to raise £250,000 of equity. Its own finance is severely limited, and is generally applied to short-term loans to tide clients over particular emergencies or longer-term loans at concessionary rates to those who find it impossible to raise money elsewhere—the sixteen-year-old school-leaver with a good idea. It does administer, on behalf of Merseyside County Council, the Council's grants for small businesses, but most of the financial help provided by the Trust consists of pointing small businessmen towards appropriate sources of funding. It had access to Rainford Venture Capital Ltd., a £2m. fund, run on a commercial basis and now fully invested, set up by Pilkington's with support from BP, ICFC, the National Westminster Bank, and the Prudential Assurance Company; and David Boult, the new director of The Trust (Humphrey retired at the end of 1982), is seeking to secure the establishment of a venture capital fund to invest on Merseyside.

The general consultancy services offered by the Trust involve using existing firms; and the presence of Pilkington's headquarters in the town, with its full range of functions and close links with the Trust, has clearly facilitated the provision of such services. Through a subcommittee the Trust seeks to co-ordinate public and private sector factory provision in the area to secure an adequate supply of suitable premises: particular attention has been paid to the provision of so called 'seed bed' premises, where the small businessman can begin operations. Advice is given on business opportunities, with particular attention to trading opportunities within the town. The Trust also makes a particular contribution to the training of entrepreneurs, both through arranging placements with other businessmen working on a similar activity, and through what Boult describes as 'tutorial style' assistance with the development of business plans. A small business club sponsored by the Trust attracts some eighty members to its monthly meetings: a particularly well attended meeting dealt with the subject of credit control![13]

How successful has the Trust been in its first four years of life, and what general conclusions can be drawn from its activities? Accepting Humphrey's point that the Trust does not create jobs itself, and that all it can do is to make it slightly easier for the businessman who, 'by undertaking economic activity, creates permanent viable employment',[14] the Trust has undoubtedly been an effective catalyst for business development in the area. Through providing 'one stop shopping' for the potential entrepreneur and a bridge between the small man and the large firm, impersonal financial institutions based elsewhere, and local and central government, the Trust has succeeded both in tapping resources for the small businessman and in generating a new self-confidence in the district. This is reflected in the generation of new business activity. In the four years to February 1983 the Trust received enquiries from 1,450 individuals and was involved in 186 new starts (eleven of which were part time), 117 expansions, and 235 consultancy cases. While the Trust declines to put employment figures onto this activity, it does modestly concede that unemployment in St Helens, which has suffered some 13,400 redundancies since 1978, would be 'much worse but for the effect of Trust clients'.[15]

The Trust has succeeded, moreover, in changing the attitude of the whole community. In 1978 a press conference to launch the Trust was cancelled because its sponsors did not wish to be associated with possible failure.[16] Today the Trust is an accepted part of the St Helens industrial scene, and its activities have contributed to a marked change in people's perceptions. As Humphrey has pointed out,

People in authority in the District started thinking differently. Things which at one time would not have been considered as being of concern, for example, to the local authority became of concern. The implications of rates for small business survival resulted in rates being kept down as much as possible. Building and conversion programmes were instituted. A flexibility of approach to planning, and to a variety of local authority activities became the order of the day.[17]

It was not only in St Helens that perceptions were changed. Following a visit to St Helens in March 1980, Mr Heseltine realised the potential of such trusts for the regeneration of local economies and put the weight of the Department of the Environment behind them. The North West Regional Office of the Department has devoted considerable effort to encouraging the establishment of Enterprise Trusts and Agencies in the Region; and DOE publishes a guide to such Agencies.[18] Enterprise Agencies had found a home.

Enterprise Trusts and Agencies provide a model of community involvement in economic regeneration, and they have demonstrated both the potential for community self-help and the benefits to local industry of such activity. They have made a major contribution to filling the 'management gap' through securing the provision of financial advice (often more important than finance itself) and the other professional help required by small businesses. Highly professional consultancy can be obtained from the Trusts' supporters. But, despite their obvious successes, they are not a panacea. Essential prerequisites for success appear to be a relatively thriving business community whose talents can be tapped, and an absence of major environmental and physical constraints on development which require a concerted programme of physical investment. Where such constraints inhibit economic activity, the public sector must play a greater part than Humphrey, quite properly in St Helens, has been prepared to accord it. But the public sector has much to learn—and indeed has learnt much—from the St Helens experience in relation to the tapping of private sector initiative and enthusiasm, the need to facilitate enterprise, and the benefits of a flexible and non-bureaucratic approach. Above all is the lesson that the regeneration of the local economy is of benefit to the whole community, including in particular private sector companies already operating there. Action is not charity: it can benefit industrial relations, public realtions, and purchasing, and it can secure further business opportunities for the firms in the area. As the St Helens Trust puts it, 'It is to enlightened self interest that the Trust appeals for support. Social conscience is a bonus.'[19] Seen in this light,

Home's assertion of the incompatibility of the best return on investment and the social objectives of inner city policy does not ring true.

2. Business in the Community

A similar appeal to enlightened self-interest led to the establishment of Business in the Community (BIC) in 1980 and its Scottish counterpart in 1982. Sir Alastair Pilkington, chairman of BIC, expresses the matter pithily in his introduction to *Handbook for Action* produced by the organisation for the guidance of participants: 'It is our first responsibility as managers to improve the efficiency of our own firms, but it is in our own interests and that of our firms to support the well-being of the community.'[20] BIC was formed, therefore, to develop ways of aiding the communities on which business depends for its success, and to stimulate action by member firms throughout the country. Pilkington's experience of the St Helens Trust no doubt played a major part in its development. But another strand was the experience of US companies and Chambers of Commerce in supporting community development in partnership with the public sector, an activity which had taken off following the American urban riots of the late 1960s.

BIC's Governing Council includes the chairmen of many of the country's blue-chip companies, and the executive (in November 1982) consisted of a part-time director on secondment from the DOE and five secondees from large companies. Scottish BIC's Governing Council similarly includes the chairmen of twenty of Scotland's leading companies under the chairmanship of Sir Hector Laing of United Biscuits (the moving force in its establishment), together with representatives from the CBI (Scottish Branch), the Scottish Council (Development and Industry), the STUC, the Convention of Scottish Local Authorities, the Scottish Council of Social Service, the Scottish Office, and the MSC. The somewhat smaller staff consisted of a director and a secretary-cum-research assistant seconded from United Biscuits, and an assistant director seconded from the Scottish Office.

The encouragement of Enterprise Trusts forms much of the work of both organisations. BIC's October 1982 newsletter comments that 'In the last 3 months 22 further agencies have been established and another 30 new initiatives are in formation or being actively discussed';[21] and SBIC saw the development of further Enterprise Trusts in Scotland as a major part of its role:[22] at the time of its establishment, only the Ardrossan, Saltcoats and Stevenston Enterprise Trust (ASSET) was in being. But their work goes wider than the encouragement of such Trusts and Agencies, involving both the provision of advice on practical issues and on action which might contribute to the organisations' aims, and raising the consciousness of business at national and local level as to their responsibilities to the community. BIC and SBIC aim, in brief, to encourage business to involve itself more fully in the community using its special skills and strengths, to build on current initiatives by supporting existing organisations working to this end, to help in the creation of new local organisations where they do not exist, and to disseminate information about good practice so that firms and local organisations can learn from the success of others.

BIC's *Handbook for Action* and its newsletters illustrate the range of activities involved: translating ideas, such as those developed in university laboratories, into marketable products; helping to set up new businesses; investing in premises suitable for small businesses; buying from small firms and assisting their cash flow by prompt payment; providing work experience places or supporting training workshops to prepare young people for business; and developing closer links between business and education to ensure an adequate supply of skilled personnel and an understanding of 'industry's essential role of wealth creation'. In addition to activities which are relatively closely linked to the health of business, the *Handbook* also considers more general contributions to the well-being of the locality, for example through support for community projects and environmental improvement.

Much of the work undertaken by BIC and SBIC parallels activities of central government departments, which have also been concerned to encourage Enterprise Trusts, translate the results of research into products, develop closer links between education and industry, support training, secure the provision of premises suitable for small firms, and improve the environment. But it would be a mistake to regard the activities of BIC and SBIC as capable of substituting for central government initiative. Sir Hector Laing comments in the newsletter that 'Instead of looking to central government to solve the problems of economic decline, inner city decay and environmental blight, I believe that more could be achieved more quickly and probably at less cost if companies and their people tackled these problems in a local context'.[23]

Such sentiments chime in well with current thinking about rolling back the frontiers of the state, and Sir Hector is right about the importance of private sector action to solve local economic problems and about the need for action at the local level. But in areas like Merseyside, the East End of Glasgow, and Dundee the environmental and infrastructure investment required to remove constraints on development is such as to make action by central government or its agencies essential. Even in Glengarnock (which, as we shall see,[24] presented a far more localised problem), the necessary environmental improvements and infrastructural investment could in no way have produced a sufficient return to attract private sector finance; in any case, the private sector was insufficiently represented in the area to make reliance on it a feasible option. Even where the private sector is well represented, it may be too concerned with efforts to stay afloat to be able to spare resources for community regeneration. One cannot quarrel with IBM's comment on social responsibility:

These activities should not be considered a drain on or alternative to profit. The long term profit-making potential and continued survival of industry will be jeopardised unless companies substitute for their token handouts a heavier investment in the community. These responsible actions are therefore part of a company's survival kit.[25]

But not if a company is about to collapse. The squeeze on profitability over recent years which has made investment in the community so much more necessary has been the very thing which has made companies in the UK less able to make that investment. Business in the Community has performed a useful role in emphasising what the private sector can do, and it is stimulating much useful activity. But it cannot be the whole answer.

3.   The 'Widening Role' of Chambers of Commerce

Chambers of Commerce also have begun to play a more active part in local economic regeneration. Traditionally concerned with providing services for their members (for example export documentation) and with lobbying local and central government on behalf of industry and commerce in their area, they have become increasingly involved in the development of local Enterprise Agencies, in urban regeneration, and in training. The 1982 conference of the Association of British Chambers of Commerce considered this 'widening role' of Chambers, and the Association urged its members to emulate the activities of the more imaginative. The establishment of Enterprise Agencies was singled out as 'probably the most effective way in which a Chamber can contribute to the future prosperity of its business community': Chamber involvement could give the Agency a degree of trust not necessarily enjoyed by financial institutions, government bodies, or large firms; and an Enterprise Agency could be 'an important practical arm for a Chamber' through enhancing its claim to be an organisation capable of delivering results and through giving the Chamber a clearer idea of local problems and constraints on development. But in addition Chambers were encouraged to liaise closely with local authorities on the Urban Programme to ensure that funds were applied to projects which had 'a realistic possibility of becoming commercially viable' or which were necessary for the commercial and economic well-being of an area. They should take the initiative by pressing for suitable projects; and in certain cases there was scope for practical participation, as with the Bradford and Manchester Chambers, which were involved in promoting the conversion of old mill buildings for use by small firms.[26]

The Merseyside Chamber of Commerce and Industry provides an example of a Chamber which has adopted this wider role. The Chamber has been heavily involved in the establishment of Business in Liverpool and other Enterprise Agencies in the region, in particular through encouraging its members to provide support; in the case of Business in Liverpool this involved letters to forty companies and banks in the region and close collaboration with the DOE's North West Enterprise Unit. The Chamber seeks to provide a 'signposting service' for firms seeking assistance (it could be argued, indeed, that there are too many such services in Liverpool[27]), and its director suggests that, through such activities, it is learning far more about the needs of small firms than hitherto. It maintains close links with the Merseyside Task Force and other arms of central government in the region, and with the industrial development units of the City and County Council, and it has clearly contributed to the greater understanding of industry's needs which has developed on Merseyside over recent years. But (unlike

Continental Chambers) it relies entirely on subscriptions and charges for its funding; and the 'wider role' has clearly stretched the resources of the Chamber.[28] Nevertheless, the Merseyside Chamber's activities do demonstrate the potential for Chambers to bring together local firms and public bodies 'to make a practical contribution to solving the major problem of unemployment'.[29]

4. Private Sector Management

Apart from consultancy work, private sector involvement in local economic renewal has, in general terms, been on a non-commercial basis, although as we have seen firms do see long-term commercial advantage in such activity. The private sector has, however, become involved in the regeneration of local economies in a more directly commercial way through the management of certain renewal projects. The model for such direct involvement sprang not from the private sector itself, but from British Steel, through its subsidiary, BSC Industry Ltd., which was formed to create new jobs in steel closure areas.

BSC Industry tackled its formidable task through a policy of providing advice and support for small businessmen and those wishing to set up on their own, through provision of premises (often redundant buildings on the steelworks offered at less than market rentals), through offering help with applications for financial support, and through the development of small workshop or nursery units (of which Clyde Workshops at Tollcross in Glasgow is an outstanding example). In this way, BSC(I) helped to create some 3,000 jobs in its first year of full operation and over 6,000 in its second. Its experience led directly to the creation of Job Creation Ltd., a private company established by some of the senior staff of BSC(I) to provide a job creation service for local authorities, while the former manager of Clyde Workshops established his own company, Clyde Management Ltd., now absorbed into PA, to perform a broadly similar role.

Initially Job Creation Ltd. concentrated on two approaches to job creation in the local context: the development of nursery units like Clyde Workshops, where the new businessman could obtain suitable small premises on flexible terms together with advice and support services from a resident manager; and helping to overcome constraints on expansion by the already existing small businessman.

Subsequently, as we shall see, it became responsible also for the administration of the Belfast Enterprise Zone.[30] The company provides both a consultancy service to advise on appropriate action by other bodies and direct action to create jobs through a small team based in the area, as at Corpach in the Highlands, where it was employed to alleviate the impact of the closure of a pulp mill.

What place is there for such private sector initiatives? Job Creation Ltd. is adamant that it does not seek to duplicate the activities of other bodies involved in economic regeneration; rather it seeks 'to key in with regional authorities and government agencies, to supplement and enhance their efforts, while making its own unique contribution to the process of job creation'.[31] With its private sector base and experience it can provide many of the things required by a small businessman working to establish himself or expand: an appreciation of the difficulties, assistance in negotiations with public authorities, financial institutions and other sources of finance, and the co-ordination of the various strands of support which the small businessman requires. But none of this is unique: Job Creation Ltd. is, indeed, providing much the same sort of service as is offered by Enterprise Trusts (although without, initially at least, some of the local contacts which help the Trusts, and for a fee charged to the local authority rather than at the expense of the local business community), or by the industrial units of some of the larger local authorities. Nevertheless, there is clearly a role for Job Creation Ltd. and its like. The local business community in some areas is simply not strong enough to support an Enterprise Trust. Not all local authorities have the resources or experience to undertake the work, and when faced with a 'one-off' problem, such as the closure of a major plant in a remote area, they may be quite understandably reluctant to establish a team of their own. For some small businessmen, moreover, the private sector has a credibility which the public sector simply cannot acquire. Private sector companies have a useful role in stepping into these gaps.

5. Urban Development Grants

While the Government's attempts to involve the private sector in local economic regeneration have relied to a considerable extent on exhortation and administrative support (as with the North West Enterprise Unit's encouragement of Enterprise Trusts), in 1982 the Government added financial assistance for appropriate projects which are on the verge of viability. Urban Development Grant

(UDG) and its Scottish equivalent, Local Enterprise Grants for Urban Projects (LEG UP), were among the first fruits of a visit to the US by the Financial Institutions Group, a group of 26 managers from banks, building societies, pension funds, and insurance companies established by Mr Heseltine in the wake of the riots of summer 1981 to advise on means of securing increased investment by the institutions in inner city areas. The American model which so impressed the Group, Urban Development Action Grant (UDAG), provides 'pump-priming' grants for private sector projects of benefit to deprived inner city areas. In the four years to 1982 it attracted a private sector investment of $13bn. through federal grants of $26m. to some 1,300 projects, and created, it was claimed, over 250,000 new jobs. Originally it was hoped that the scheme would attract three private sector dollars for every one federal dollar. In the event, the scheme has secured a gearing of double that.[32]

Like the American scheme, the British schemes are designed to attract private sector money into projects which require an element of funding to make them viable and which will contribute to the relief of social needs—and particularly unemployment—in the inner urban areas. They have been criticised for being another piece of 'tinkering and fine tuning' and for taking decisions out of the hands of the local authorities[33]; it is central government and its Agencies (in Scotland the scheme is administered by the Scottish Development Agency) which take the final decision on which projects to support. Not all projects supported, moreover, are directly relevant to economic renewal. But they have succeeded in attracting substantial private sector support for inner city projects as the figures for approval starts in 1983-84 demonstrate—

Table 3. *Urban Development Grants 1983–4*

	Projects	Total Investment	Public Contribution	Gearing
England	72	£153 m.	£31 m.	1:4.9
Scotland	35	£32 m.	£6 m.	1:5.3
Wales	13	£40 m.	£6 m.	1:6.7

source: SDD

UDG is beginning to make a modest contribution to encouraging development in deprived areas. Despite the criticisms it appears to be a useful addition to the battery of measures available under the Urban Programme.

6. Conclusions

How successful has the Government been in involving the private sector directly in the regeneration of local economies and how important is such a private sector contribution? It seems clear in the first place that the private sector has become more aware of their responsibilities to the community. The experience of Enterprise Trusts and the proseletysing work of Business in the Community and of the Association of British Chambers of Commerce have done much to bring this about. Mr Heseltine's encouragement of the private sector to play a greater part in the regeneration of Merseyside, and the pressure which he has put on the financial institutions, have also played a part; in January 1983 the Institutions went so far as to establish a small company, Inner City Enterprises, to work up inner city development projects to a stage where the large pension funds and other institutions can invest in them.

This change in attitudes is being translated into useful activity on the ground—in particular in assisting the development of small firms—and in a more sensitive approach to inner city needs on the part of the institutions. The National Westminster Bank for instance, has appointed Inner City Development Officers in Merseyside, Manchester, and London to act as a link with the local communities and to provide advice and support for those wishing to set up in business.[34] But the involvement of the private sector can add to the difficulty of concerting action: we shall comment below on the organisations, public and private, concerned with the regeneration of Merseyside.[35] And it is significant that the major developments are taking place where there is no public sector body to take on the responsibility: Enterprise Trusts, for example, are far more prolific in England, where there is no Development Agency, than in Scotland, where a local economic problem inevitably leads to demands for action by the Scottish Development Agency. Public sector activity can drive out private sector involvement. Since the private sector has skills and an ethos which are highly relevant to the rehabilitation of declining areas, care needs to be taken to counteract this tendency. The attempts by the SDA to attract institutional capital to such major inner city projects as the National Exhibition Centre at the Queen's Dock in Glasgow are the more important for that. For the answer cannot be the withdrawal of the public sector. The removal of constraints on development requires a considerable investment in infrastructure and in the improvement of the environment; and however far the frontiers of the state are rolled back, the funding of such public social capital cannot in general be a commercial proposition for the private sector. The public sector will continue to bear the major burden. But the public sector will work in the context of a fuller understanding by private firms of their role in regeneration and of the benefits which they may gain from it, and from the increased co-operation over recent years the public sector itself will have a greater appreciation of the private sector's needs.

Notes

1. A similar approach was tried in the 1930s. At that time, orthodox belief held that 'local self-help and initiative must be keynotes to any efforts to bring new industrial activities into the depressed areas' (CAB 58-112); and in 1930-1 the Government discussed with business and financial groups a proposal that 'disposal and development corporations' should be set up to sell surplus industrial premises and attract industry. See Bush, H., 'Local, Intellectual and Policy Responses to Localised Unemployment in the Inter-war Periods: the Genesis of Regional Policy', Oxford 1980 (unpublished D. Phil. thesis, Nuffield College, Oxford).
2. Home, Robert K., *Inner City Regeneration*, E. and F. N. Spon, London 1982, p. 70.
3. Evidence, p. 58, memorandum submitted by Committee of London Clearing Banks, para. 2.
4. See below, chapter 5.1, and Evidence, q. 189.
5. Newman, Charles, 'St Helens Trust: Success on a Shoestring', *Investors Chronicle*, 1 February 1980.
6. Quoted in *The Widening Role of Chambers*, report of the 1982 Annual Conference of the Association of British Chambers of Commerce, ABCC, September 1982.
7. Community of St Helens Trust, unpublished paper.
8. Humphrey, W. E. G., 'Enterprise Trusts: Looking Back and Looking Forward', talk delivered to DOE seminar, Manchester, 14 December 1982.
9. *Guardian*, 12 October 1979.

10. Humphrey, W. E. G., op. cit.
11. Interview with director of St Helens Trust, March 1983.
12. Community of St Helens Trust, unpublished paper.
13. Interview, March 1983.
14. Community of St Helens Trust, unpublished paper.
15. *Outline of Community of St Helens Trust*, Community of St Helens Trust, February 1983.
16. Humphrey, W. E. G., op. cit.
17. Ibid.
18. DOE, *Local Enterprise Agencies—a Guide*, second edition, London 1982.
19. Community of St Helens Trust, *Features and Lessons*, Community of St Helens Trust, October 1981.
20. Business in the Community, *Handbook for Action*, London 1982.
21. BIC Newsletter, October 1982.
22. Interview with assistant director, SBIC, November 1982.
23. BIC Newsletter, op. cit.
24. See below, chapter 7.1.
25. Quoted in *Handbook for Action*, op. cit.
26. See *The Widening Role of Chambers of Commerce, report of the 1982 Annual Conference of the Association of British Chambers of Commerce*, ABCC, September 1982.
27. See below, chapter 5.1.
28. Interview with Mr H. M. P. Robinson, director, Merseyside Chamber of Commerce and Industry, who provided the information in this paragraph.
29. Submission to the Prime Minister by Mr C. J. Risk, chairman of the ABCC, quoted in *The Widening Role of Chambers*, op. cit.
30. See below, chapter 4.1.
31. Job Creation Ltd., *Job Creation in the Local Context: the Immediate Option*, brochure, London 1981.
32. Pauley, Robin, 'How America Created Jobs', *Financial Times*, August 1982.
33. 'Two Cheers for UDG', *Town Planning Review*, vol. 53, no. 4, October 1982, p. 363.
34. Evidence, p. 47, memorandum submitted by the National Westminster Bank PLC, para. 2.
35. See below, chapter 5.1.

4

'A New and More Adventurous Approach': Enterprise Zones and Freeports

In the previous chapter we suggested that private sector initiative, by itself, was unlikely to secure the regeneration of areas requiring substantial investment in land renewal and infrastructure to bring them into a developable state. Enterprise Zones were, however, designed to encourage the private sector itself to make just such an investment in land renewal. As we shall see, it is doubtful whether they have succeeded in this particular aim. They have stimulated a lively debate. Bennet Harrison has described them as 'a number of old ideas, about statecraft... resuscitated and sold to the public as bold new initiatives'.[1] For Sir Geoffrey Howe, by contrast, they represent 'a new and more adventurous approach to the whole question of industrial and commercial renewal'.[2] But, whichever view one takes, the experiment has had a marked impact on a number of the more disadvantaged areas of the United Kingdom, and it has some important lessons to teach, not only about the effectiveness of particular measures to regenerate local economies, but also about the translation of political vision into policy prescription and its subsequent implementation.

1. Policy Drift or Learning Curve: the Concept and its Development

Enterprise Zones originated in a belief that bureaucratic controls and high taxation are central to the malaise of the private sector and to inner city decline. The Department of the Environment's *Guide to Enterprise Zones* notes that their aim is 'to restore vigorous private-sector activity to these zones by removing certain tax burdens and by relaxing or speeding up the application of certain statutory or administrative controls'.[3] They were conceived as an exercise in non-government, and they are presented in such terms.

In their development, however, they have arguably been transformed into 'an exercise in government intervention and public subsidy', so that for Keating they present 'an object lesson in the translation of opposition rhetoric into government reality'.[4] Professor Denman argued that 'the bureaucrats have succeeded in frustrating the government's original plan',[5] and Stan Taylor talks, more temperately, of 'policy drift'.[6] But a comparison of the proposals made by the future Chancellor in his Isle of Dogs speech with the British Enterprise Zone experiment as it finally emerged suggests that commentators have overemphasised the differences. It is arguable also that the British form of zone, in the way it is administered, is far more suited to the needs of the inner cities than its prototype, for while both tax burdens and bureaucratic controls may be inhibitions on the growth of productive industry, they are by no means the most important constraint on development in the inner cities. Nor did the bureaucrats have it entirely their own way. Stuart Butler comments that 'the distribution of the British Zones reflects a strong political as well as economic rationale':[7] in the case of the Invergordon zone designation was apparently a direct political response to a major industrial closure; and the Freeports experiment, announced in the 1983 Budget speech, represents a reversion to an idea associated with the original proposal. Whitehall perhaps stole the Emperor's clothes, but the Empire struck vigorously back.

The origins of Enterprise Zone policy have been treated fully elsewhere[8] and need only be sketched briefly here. The germ of the concept was outlined by Professor Peter Hall at the 1977 conference of the Royal Town Planning Institute, when he argued that in some parts of the inner cities decline had gone so far that it was virtually impossible to secure regeneration through conventional means. Here 'highly unorthodox measures' would be required: 'Small, selected areas of inner cities would be simply thrown open to all kinds of initiative, with minimal control. In other words, we would aim to recreate the Hong Kong of the 1950s and 1960s inside inner Liverpool or inner Glasgow.' Such 'Freeports', as Hall termed them, would be based on 'fairly shameless free enterprise'. They would be outside the scope of UK taxes, customs duties, social services, and industrial regulations, and residence within them would be 'based on choice'. They would be 'most appropriate to inner city areas that are largely abandoned and denuded of people, or alternatively areas with very grave social and economic problems'.

Sir Keith Joseph took up the theme at a conference arranged by the Adam Smith Institute, when he announced that the next Conservative government would establish a number of 'demonstration zones' in which 'the Queen's writ shall not run', and in which it would be possible to see what could be achieved if the market were freed of virtually all government regulation.[10] The theme was endorsed and elaborated in a speech by the future Chancellor, Sir Geoffrey Howe, in the Isle of Dogs on 26 June 1978.[11]

In his speech Sir Geoffrey unravelled three different concepts to be found in Professor Hall's proposals: the 'Crown Colony', which would be exempt from most legislation and taxes but denied all state benefits; the 'Freeport', where goods could be imported, processed, and re-exported free of tariffs; and the Enterprise Zone, where substantial areas of land in four or five places would be given 'as much freedom as possible to make profits and create jobs' in order to stimulate redevelopment. Sir Geoffrey rejected the 'Crown Colony' (a point which has been overlooked by some subsequent diagnosticians of policy drift) and favoured the Enterprise Zone, which could, however, be combined with a Freeport. In such Enterprise Zones, detailed planning controls would cease to exist, subject to 'very basic anti-pollution, health and safety standards', and public authorities would be required to sell land to private bidders within a specified time scale. Firms in the zone would be exempt from certain legal obligations, such as some or all of the Employment Protection legislation, and entrepreneurs moving into the zone would be granted exemption from Development Land Tax and 'perhaps exemption from rates, in whole or part'. Conversely, no government grants or subsidies would be payable in the zone. The conditions would be guaranteed for a 'stated and substantial' number of years, and the Enterprise Zone would be managed, not through the local authority, but through a 'new model of authority... with *some* of the qualities of a New Town Corporation'.

Sir Geoffrey was careful to stress that his proposal was tentative and that its details would require to be worked up. But he warned that 'of course the grey men whose job it is to consider the "administrative difficulties" of any new idea would be ready enough to start manufacturing the small print that could stop the initiative in its tracks'. This, according to many commentators, is precisely what the grey men did to it. What finally emerged from their ministrations into the Local Government, Planning and Land Act 1980 and the Finance Act 1980 was a mixture of fiscal benefits and adminstrative simplifications available for ten years from the date of designation of the zone. Local authorities, New Towns, or Urban Development Corporations were to be invited to prepare an Enterprise Zone scheme for a site in their area. (It was indicated that the Government intended to issue six or seven invitations: in the event, invitations were issued to secure the establishment of eleven zones, in Clydebank, Belfast, Swansea, Corby, Dudley, Speke, Salford/Trafford, Wakefield, Hartlepool, Tyneside, and the Isle of Dogs.) The scheme would, in particular, provide for the planning regime within the zone to be greatly simplified, so that developments conforming to the published scheme would not require individual planning permission. It would, however, specify certain conditions governing development—for example health and safety requirements—and could reserve specified types of development for decision by the zone authority. Such controls as remained would, however, be administered more speedily, as would applications for inward processing relief and customs warehousing (which allow goods to be imported, processed, or stored, and subsequently re-exported, without payment of duty). New and existing commercial and industrial enterprises within the zones would be exempt from rates and Development Land Tax and could offset expenditure on buildings against Corporation Tax. Finally, the powers of Industry Training Boards to impose levies on employers and to demand information would be removed, and government requests for statistical information would be substantially reduced.

It is readily apparent that some of the more radical elements of the original proposal—for example removal of protection under the Employment Protection Acts—have disappeared entirely, and other have been transformed almost beyond recognition. There were often severely practical reasons for this transformation. The entry of the UK into the European Community and the availability of Inward Processing Relief and customs warehousing had removed the advantages of the Freeport status (although this was not an essential part of the original EZ concept). The benefit of location in the zones was not regarded as sufficient inducement, of itself, to permit the abolition of other government grants and incentives.

The creation of tax havens was ruled out on the grounds that it would be impossible to prevent abuse, for example by multi-plant firms shifting profits into the zones through transfer pricing. But Sir Geoffrey's original proposals for tax and rates relief were in fact enhanced in the development of the policy. What finally emerged into legislation did, indeed, contain the two fundamental elements of the original proposal: a reduction in planning and bureaucracy, and a reduction in fiscal burdens in a more extensive form than originally envisaged. The first of these elements was, however, to be substantially modified in the course of implementation.

To what extent, then, did the schemes which emerged in the UK Enterprise Zones match up to the original prescription of a simplified planning regime, administered by a new model of non-bureaucratic authority, private sector based, and subject to rigorous assessment of its results? It is convenient to consider these elements in turn.

'*A Simplified Planning Regime*'

A major theme of the Isle of Dogs speech was the allegedly disastrous effect of development control on economic activity and prosperity. Sir Geoffrey quoted with approval the words of one frustrated planner that

One is forced to question the current priorities of a system of planning which spends so much time and energy exercising strict controls over the extensions of individual houses and minor changes of use, while allowing whole areas to be demolished and laid to waste for years, even decades, at the heart of the most populous cities in the country.[12]

The answer was a simplified planning regime, in which only the most basic anti-pollution, health, and safety standards would apply. The Enterprise Zone schemes do indeed provide for deemed planning consent to be granted in a great many instances, and for a speeding-up of the administration of the remaining controls. But a glance at any of the schemes will illustrate that development planning in the zones is as elaborate as planning elsewhere, if not more so. Instead of the most basic anti-pollution, health, and safety standards we have those applied nationally. Particular types of activity are reserved entirely or restricted to particular parts of the zones. Even where planning permission is deemed to be granted it is necessary for the developer to obtain other statutory consents, such as building consent. Some authorities, such as Swansea, even suggest that anyone contemplating development in the zone should consult them about their plans, so that they can ensure that the proposals conform to the scheme.

Nowhere is the departure from the original concept brought out more clearly than in the case of retailing. The Government had conceded during the passage of the legislation in the House of Lords that restrictions on hypermarkets would be accepted as part of the planning regime. Zone authorities remained very worried, however, at the impact of subsidised competition from other shops in the zone on shopping facilities elsewhere. Within Clydebank, for example, a major shopping development was in the course of construction just outside the zone boundary. The District Council lobbied vigorously for a total reservation on retailing, so that all proposals for retail development would require individual planning consent. Such a total reservation was unacceptable to the Government; but in the event the Scottish Office accepted that the scheme should permit control of retail developments over 400 square metres—considerably less than the Government had originally proposed. Similar agreements were struck in most of the other zones, though there the reservations are somewhat less restrictive.

The planning regimes thus contain a number of provisions designed to meet the circumstances of individual zones. Many zones contain 'a sensitive boundary sub-zone in which the grant of planning permission is restricted to certain specified uses and design details require approval'. There are health and safety sub-zones in which no development is permitted without normal planning permission: in Clydebank, for example, the site of a former asbestos factory is protected in this way. Corby has a 'highway safeguarding area' where no development may take place without prior approval. Hartlepool and Wakefield have 'landscape sub-zones'. All the zones reserve the Special Industrial Use classes (covering such noxious processes as blood boiling, the storage and processing of hazardous substances, explosives manufacture, development or use requiring licensing under the Nuclear Installations Act 1965, and storage and treatment of waste). Perhaps the most intriguing reservations are Corby's exclusion of casinos, fun fairs, bingo halls, and betting shops, and Clydebank's exclusion of Space Invader parlours.[13] In the words of the Chief Executive of Corby District Council, 'The existing planning permissions were less limiting than the scheme which was approved. Hong Kong did not arrive in Corby.'[14]

'A New Model of Authority'

A second theme emphasised by Sir Geoffrey was the failure of public authorities to deal with the problems of the urban wilderness. The public purse was unable to provide either the funds or the enterprise to match the aspirations of the planners. All attempts at reform, moreover, seemed only to multiply the bureaucracy. The solution was to create a 'new model of authority... with *some* of the qualities of a new town corporation'. The problems associated with organisational solutions to local economic decline have been noted above; but it is in any case a lot easier to criticise bureaucracy than to abolish it. Instead of a new model of authority a variety of organisational arrangements was developed to administer the zones, and while private consultants are closely involved in the management of the Dudley zone and are responsible for the administration of Belfast, Enterprise Zones are in the main administered by local authorities or other public sector bodies (the SDA in Clydebank and the LDDC in the Isle of Dogs).

If, however, the public sector has retained its hegemony, it does appear to be the case that, with one possible exception, all the responsible authorities have sought to cut through red tape, speed decision-taking, and facilitate development, often using their own development powers rather than relying on the private sector. A striking feature of the zone authorities is their enthusiasm. While Sir Geoffrey has not succeeded in unhorsing the bureaucrats, he has encouraged them to ride in a different way—and this is a major achievement.

'Private Sector Based'

The new Agencies proposed by Sir Geoffrey would have some of the qualities of a New Town Corporation, but in one important respect they were to be entirely different. Instead of acquiring property for the public sector they would be required to dispose of it to the private sector, and within a specified time limit. Private sector entrepreneurship was to replace public sector planning.

The reality turned out to be somewhat different. Public authorities were not required to dispose of their land to the private sector; and in the case of Dudley, of which over 98 per cent was privately owned, the Secretary of State for the Environment insisted, before designation, that the owners should undertake to sell their land to the local authority, at a discount, if it were not brought forward for development by a specified date. As we shall see, initially the speed of development depended crucially on public ownership of land. Those zones which had a high proportion of land in the ownership of public development agencies—the SDA, English Industrial Estates, and local authorities—were the zones which saw the greatest increase in factory space, activity, and employment in the first year, for many of the privately owned sites were derelict, large, and requiring substantial investment in reclamation and infrastructure before they could be brought forward for development. Also, a high proportion of the private sector owners were relatively unprofitable manufacturing companies, without the scope to benefit from the tax advantages of development, and without the expertise to undertake it.

The fact was that the original analysis had failed to distinguish two sorts of public sector and two sorts of private sector owner. The public sector includes both statutory undertakings and nationalised industries, notorious for their tenacity in holding onto underused land, and the public development authorities, which had the remit, and were provided with the resources, to ensure that development took place. The private sector includes both production and service companies, lacking the expertise and often the resources to recycle land, and development companies, who have both the necessary skills and the profitability to take advantage of incentives for development within the zones, provided that the zones are in the right place to meet their other requirements.

At first, changes of ownership in the zones were in the main within the public and private sectors rather than across boundaries. Public development authorities acquired land from the statutory undertakers, and private developers acquired land from manufacturing and service companies. Thus, while the Enterprise Zone experiment did not lead initially to a massive transfer of land from the public to the private sector, it encouraged the shifting of ownership to those parts of both the public and the private sectors which have the powers and the resources to develop it. Subsequently there have been further transfers of land from public and private developers to production companies building for their own occupation.[15]

An Experimental Approach

Although it is urged upon the policy-makers in the text books, the vigorous testing of the impact of policy is fairly unusual. It was therefore refreshing that the original proposal should embrace the concept of 'test market areas' or 'laboratories' in which to assess the potential of fresh policies to stimulate economic activity. Sir Geoffrey even suggested that it would be worthwhile making parts of the zone available to non-commerical groups who might wish to establish workers' co-operatives. 'If the Tribune Group or the Socialist Workers Party wanted parts of an Enterprise Zone to themselves—well, why not?'[16]

In two respects at least the concept of laboratory experimentation was retained. The monitoring arrangements are highly developed, and in principle are such as to make possible an objective assessment of the success of the experiment. Also, the choice of a variety of zones with different characteristics would in principle enable comparative judgements to be made on the effectiveness of zone incentives in different kinds of places. The geographical spread of the zones, and the increase in their number from the five or six announced in the budget statement to eleven, did, however, reflect political and economic considerations[17] as well as the wish to construct a well-designed experiment—perhaps more so. They were spread throughout the older industrial areas and distressed parts of formerly prosperous areas. They included both inner city areas (as with the Belfast Inner City Zone and the Salford part of the Salford/Trafford zone), areas on the periphery of the large conurbations (as with Speke and Clydebank, although the latter has many inner city characteristics), areas in need of major servicing and land reclamation (as with Dudley and Salford), and areas where services were in place (as with the Team Valley part of the Tyneside zone). Stan Taylor has criticised this 'haphazard choice of zones' as causing the experiment to lose its inner city characteristics.[18] But the experiment was not conceived as an inner city measure; and, whatever the motivation for their choice, a variety of zones would be of benefit to its evaluation.

And yet, in the definition of objectives, and in the Enterprise Zone scheme adopted for each zone, there were significant departures from test conditions. In the first place, it was not entirely clear from the outset what the objective of the policy was. The consultants appointed by the government to monitor the experiment concluded from official statements that 'the EZs aim to stimulate industrial and commercial activity', but they noted that this objective required to be clarified in one particular respect—'what size of geographical area should be regarded as the target of the policy'.[19] It had, indeed, never been stated explicitly whether the aim was to regenerate the economy of a zone itself, or the wider region in which the zone was located, or the country as a whole. Other objectives, moreover, might also be of importance—encouraging a greater private sector role in the regeneration of the inner city, or tackling the environmental problems associated with derelict and vacant land. Indeed, as the consultants pointed out, policy objectives might vary from zone to zone. Where there is a depressed inner city within an otherwise prosperous region (as is arguably the case with the Isle of Dogs zone) it might be sufficient to transfer jobs within the region; where, however, unemployment is high throughout the region (as in the case of the Belfast and Clydebank zones) the aim might be to attract work from other regions.

By the third year of their study the consultants had concluded, by induction, that the general objective of the policy was to promote development and productive use of the sites by the private sector in order to generate such broader benefits as a net increase in economic activity in the wider area in which the zone was located as well as 'contributing to town and country planning and other objectives'.[20] But even this formulation begs a number of questions, and it is open to the criticism that it defines the objectives against which the experiment is to be monitored by its results.

There were, then, to be significant difficulties in monitoring the experiment. But these were compounded by the variety of the regimes adopted within individual zones. Objective evaluation of the Enterprise Zone concept would, in an ideal world, require a uniform set of conditions in each zone; and this would of course preclude variations in the schemes to meet local circumstances. But, as we have noted, the local authorities who negotiated the schemes with the territorial departments were determined that local circumstances should be taken into account. The fact was that the local authorities saw the zones as an additional arm in the battery of powers available to them to deal with the increasingly intractable problems which they were facing. For them, variety was essential. The laboratory technicians lost out; but the zones might be the better for it.

Nor did all the elements of the original experiment survive. Some, as we have seen, were refined almost out of existence. Others disappeared altogether. No zone is run by the Socialist Workers' party, and the zones concentrate almost exclusively on economic development. There is, as Stuart Butler points out, no social experimentation in the zones, no encouragement of variety in housing tenure, no particular support for workers' or community co-operatives. Thus the primary aim of the zones appears to be 'to encourage industrial and commercial redevelopment in derelict or cleared areas of cities'.[21]

Liberation Transformed

Enterprise Zones had, then, undergone a sea change. From being an experiment in the liberation of free enterprise, they had become assimilated into the range of spatially biased governmental incentives to encourage economic activity. Many of the elements of the Enterprise Zone package were, indeed, part of more traditional forms of regional or industrial policy. As early as 1937 the Special Areas (Amendment) Act had empowered the Commissioners for the Special Areas to make contributions, for a limited period, to rents, rates, and taxes; and an easing of bureaucratic restrictions is an important feature of the Thatcher adminstration's policy towards the small firm.

But, whether or not Enterprise Zones should be seen as part of traditional regional or urban policy, the transformation which they have undergone has arguably made them more fitted to their purpose than their prototype. Bureaucratic controls and tax burdens, as we have noted, are by no means the most important constraint on development. The incentives offered within the zones, moreover, do little to address the real causes of decline. Rates form only a small proportion of the costs of most firms. Development Land Tax, which is payable only when a change in permitted use increases the value of land, is unlikely to be of help in the kind of areas chosen for the zones, where much of the land is already zoned for industry. The Corporation Tax concessions are of benefit only to profitable firms; and because of the allowances already available to manufacturing industry in the assisted areas they are far more favourable to service industry in zones in such areas (although, as we have suggested, the attraction of service industry may be an appropriate aim). Training provision is an important element of inner city regeneration; yet the writ of the Industry Training Boards does not run within the zones, and, although they are empowered to provide services for firms based there, the arrangements give them no encouragement to do so. (Indeed, the Construction Industry Training Board has withdrawn its services from firms in the zones.) If the incentives did not address the real problem, nor did the relaxation of planning controls, for planning control was not seen as a constraint in many of the areas which became Enterprise Zones. Development planning may have inhibited industrial development in the inner city areas, but by the mid-1970s the inner city planning authorities were for the most part so keen to attract industrial development that they applied development controls in a relatively relaxed way. Rather it was the preference of manufacturers for greenfield sites on the periphery of conurbations, the decline of the traditional industries on which many of the inner city areas had depended, the increasing space requirements of modern industry, the policy of many authorities in the 1950s and 1960s of shifting industry and people to the periphery, and grandiose and often incomplete redevelopment programmes, that had caused the problem. Its cure, therefore, was not in a relaxation of planning controls—indeed, some developers have been worried about the effect of relaxed planning on their investment—but in its redirection.

Enterprise Zones have nevertheless created two very powerful aids to regeneration. First, while rates are a small proportion of firms' costs, they are a most unpopular tax, particularly for industrialists. The rates concession (which is in effect a central government subsidy)has become a highly visible incentive to locate within a zone. Indeed, for entrepreneurs (as opposed to property developers) it is the most important incentive of all. Thus designation has given the zone authorities an effective promotional tool. Secondly, the prospect of designation provides local authorities and other public agencies with a strong incentive to plan for industry's needs, and to use their own powers positively to meet them. In this sense, Enterprise Zones have become an exercise, not in non-planning, but in good planning. Those who had framed the policy had moved along the learning curve; and in doing so they had encouraged the development authorities to do likewise. How effectively this has secured regeneration we shall consider in the following section.

2. The Impact of the Zones

The experiment which emerged from the cocoon of Whitehall was open to criticism from both right and left and on both philosophical and practical grounds. For the right, it had become an essay in government subsidy and public sector planning. For the left, it was a charter for property owners and capitalists. Critics argued that the zones were unlikely to lead to any general resurgence in economic activity; that they would encourage relocation and boundary-hopping, harming adjacent areas; that they would benefit property owners and developers rather than entrepreneurs (although the benefits were arguably insufficient to encourage redevelopment by the owners of the more derelict areas); and that they would damage other programmes designed to assist the inner city.

These concerns were given forcible expression during the debate on Mr Heseltine's statement on the location of the second round of zones, which took place on 15 November 1982.[22] Allan Roberts, the Member for Bootle, put the matter thus:

As so many Hon. Members want enterprise zones, will the Secretary of State consider moving one from Speke to one of their constituencies? In Merseyside it is taking industries from docklands to Speke so they can get the benefit of the cheaper rates and is not creating any new jobs.

Ken Eastham (Manchester, Blakely) alleged that 'in the Manchester Area the local authorities feel that they [Enterprise Zones] have been damaging to the inner city programme', and Edwin Wainwright (Dean Wells) argued that 'instead of creating new jobs he [Mr Heseltine] is transferring jobs from one district to another'. To what extent have the concerns of such critics been borne out in practice?

A Resurgence of Economic Activity

In the first place, there has been a considerable amount of development in many of the zones. In the year to 31 May 1982, 297 firms employing 2,975 people established themselves in the zones: of these just over half were new openings.[23] Between designation and September 1984 the number of jobs increased by about 45 per cent (14,400) in GB first-round zones excluding Corby; by then there were 1,486 establishments in the GB first-round zones, employing in total 37,300 people. The experience of the individual zones has, however, varied considerably. Those which at the time of designation were enjoying major programmes of land reclamation and development hardly surprisingly progressed the most at first, headed by Clydebank, where the Scottish Development Agency was in course of the major renewal project begun 15 months before designation.[24] Subsequently, private sector led development has attained increasing importance. It is worthwhile, therefore, to consider in somewhat greater detail the experience in a number of the zones.

The Clydebank zone has benefited both from the attention which it was already receiving from the SDA at the time of designation and from the concentrated and professional effort which the SDA has subsequently put into its promotion and development. The zone has seen a considerable amount of activity, all the more remarkable given the very depressed state of the local economy as recently as 1979. In the year 1981–2 a total of 8.8 hectares of land was brought into use, and 8,136 metres of floor-space were completed; on 31 May 1982 a further 13,000 square metres of floor-space were committed or under construction. The greater part of this activity was funded by the public sector: £7.7m. by contrast with a private sector contribution of £2.7m. In the year, there was a net increase of 49 firms and 549 jobs, increasing the number of firms within the zone to 254 and the jobs to 2,801. The firms are generally small: 82 per cent of the new firms in fact employed ten people or fewer. By September 1984 there had been a slight fall in the number of establishments to 236, but an increase in employment to 5,500, over 65 per cent of whom were in manufacturing.

In the view of the consultants, it was the public sector which was the driving force behind the regeneration of the area, and designation as an Enterprise Zone did not alter the situation. District Council officials interviewed in 1983 indeed considered that the sole benefit of designation was promotion. The planning regime had in their view had little effect, and the incentives were insufficient to attract private sector, and in particular institutional, capital to any great extent. They acknowledged, however, that in time that might change: the National Westminster Bank was, for example, investing in an office block in the zone (although with the help of a rent guarantee from the SDA).[25] And in 1982–3 the balance of investment in development swung to the private sector: in that year the public sector contributed £2.6m. and the private sector £3.5m.

Corby, too, saw, in the words of its Chief Executive, 'a vast amount of economic activity' in its first year.[26] Fifty-six new companies were attracted to the zone in the period to March 1983; 50,000 square feet of factory space were let; almost 1,500 new jobs had been created; and 1m. square feet of factory space was under construction. Unlike Clydebank, investment in Corby was weighted towards the private sector from the start: of a total investment of £345m. by March 1983, £225m. was private, £70m. was from the European Community, and £50m. was GB public investment. The high level of activity and private sector investment continued thereafter: by September 1984 there were 91 establishments operating in the zone, employing 4,100 people.

Like Clydebank, Corby benefited from infrastructure planning and organisational arrangements predating the designation of the zone. Following the announcement in 1979 that the Corby Steel Works was to close with a loss of 12,800 jobs, the area was made a Development Area, and a committee of Corby District Council, Northamptonshire County Council, and the Commission for the New Towns was established to co-ordinate remedial measures. Regional assistance, the availability of aids from the European Coal and Steel Community and the European Commission, unity of ownership of the land in the zone, and political acceptability all increased the attractiveness of the area before the establishment of the Enterprise Zone. Proximity to London has clearly been of major importance, and the zone has been particularly successful in attracting food and distribution companies.

Dudley is of interest in that it has been almost entirely funded through the private sector, and thus is close to the Chancellor's original conception. It also has some of the worst problems of land reclamation: toxic waste had been dumped on part of the site; a geological fault runs through it; underground workings make development difficult and costly; and a coal seam approaches the surface at one point. Major investment in access roads and sewers has also been necessary. Hardly surprisingly, Dudley secured development and won jobs more slowly than some of the more fortunate zones. Nevertheless, by mid-1982 land preparation and development was taking place. New industrial buildings were being constructed on part of the site. A temporary road had been built to allow tipping in an area which was undermined. The coal seam had been sold to a private mining company, who will in due course render the site fit for development. All of this will, in time, lead to new jobs. In the view of the consultants advising the District Council on the development of the zone, designation has been a catalyst which has enabled 250 acres of dereliction to be reclaimed, developed, and in due course occupied. In other words, it has played a major part in the recycling of derelict land. This has, over time, led to the creation of new jobs. Seventy of the 112 establishments existing in the zone on designation were still in existence in September 1984, employing 1,900 people; and a further 75 firms which had moved in employed a further 900.

Despite its lack of Dudley's acute physical problems, Speke was one of the slowest zones to take off. The zone is founded essentially on the sites of two closed businesses, British Leyland and Dunlop, together with part of Speke airport and a site owned by English Industrial Estates. At the time of designation, 25 August 1981, four firms were operating in the zone, employing about 400 workers, and English Industrial Estates were in course of supplementing their five large advance factories on the site with 68 'beehive units' of from 500 to 5,000 square feet. By 6 December 1982, 22 further firms had located in the zone, bringing with them 343 jobs. Ten of these firms were from elsewhere on Merseyside (and eight from Liverpool itself), four from elsewhere, and eight were new. Thus for the City Council the main effect of designation was the redistribution of existing activity by prompting short-distance transfers.[27] Nevertheless, it could be the case that the jobs moving into the zone would have been completely lost without it. For both the City and the County Council, however, the most important elements in the experiment are the increased public expenditure which it has engendered, together with increased forward planning. Neither sees the zone as an experiment in free enterprise.[28] Modest progress has continued since 1982: by September 1984, 59 establishments were operating in the zone, employing 900 people.

There is, then, a considerable amount of new activity in some of the zones; increases elsewhere are gathering momentum as the experiment proceeds. But to what extent has economic policy generally been stimulated by the policy? After two years the consultants found very little evidence of firms locating in the Enterprise Zones achieving higher output and employment than they would have elsewhere.[29] By Year Three, however, the consultants estimated that 'between 4% and 12% of the wholly new firms might not have been started but for the EZ' and that some 10 per cent of firms have achieved higher levels of output than they would have in the absence of the EZ. They judge, however, that this is likely to have been at the expense of activity elsewhere.[30] The critics' assertion that the zones would not lead to a substantial increase in activity nationally seems to have been borne out in practice, although there has been a measure of increased activity and it has to be acknowledged that it is too early to reach firm conclusions yet.

Relocation and Boundary-Hopping

While the encouragement of activity in particular locations may not be of any great benefit to the national economy, at least in the short term, it can in principle benefit the locations where activity is engendered, particularly if it comes from another region. The evidence is, however, that the majority of moves are of a short distance. In the period to May 1982, 87 per cent of the firms moving into zones from elsewhere came from the same district or county, as did 90 per cent of the jobs. In the following year 86 per cent of firms came from the same district or county, and 92 per cent from the same Economic Planning Region. Corby, with its proximity to London and its assisted area benefits, attracted by far the greatest proportion of long-distance moves. The performance of the districts, still less the regions, in which the Enterprise Zones are located seems so far to have been little affected by the existence of the zones.

There have, however, been few 'frivolous' moves of firms simply seeking the financial advantages of location within a zone. Virtually all the firms moving into the zones had decided to relocate before finding the site which they were now occupying, because for example of shortage of space or dissatisfaction with the layout or design of their existing premises. The main benefit of the zones was, moreover, seen to be the availability of suitable accommodation rather than the incentives as such: incoming employment was 'systematically related to vacant modern floorspace'.[31] But, other things being equal, the incentives were of importance in influencing the location of firms which had decided to move, and of these rates relief 'is the most important incentive in attracting firms'.[32]

Damage to Adjacent Areas

On the face of it, it seems likely that the encouragement of activity within the zones in preference to a relatively small area around them would damage the surrounding areas. Job-seekers there might be disadvantaged; property owners and developers might be harmed by reduced demand for their services; and firms might suffer from subsidised competition from within the zones. In fact, in the first year of operation, apart from the property sector, such fears did not come to pass.

Given the short distance of many of the moves, it seems unlikely that the zones have had a major effect on the labour market in their areas. Many of the firms establishing themselves in the zones would have set up somewhere in the same travel to work area; and jobs within the zones can of course be filled by commuters. Indeed, it is one of Stuart Butler's criticisms of the UK zones that they do nothing to favour deprived inner city residents.

The experience of the property sector varied from zone to zone. Rents fell around the Dudley zone by as much as 90p per square foot, and around Trafford by some 50p. Institutional investors were discouraged from activity adjacent to the zones, although they were active in very few areas before designation. But the experience was not all one-sided: the consultants reported that the publicity generated by the zone had in some cases attracted development to an adjacent site outwith the zone, a point reiterated by the Chief Executive of Corby District Council.[33]

Some of the most vehement fears were expressed about subsidised competition in retailing (which is, of course, subject to some control) and warehousing. The evidence is, however, that the measures did not lead to a distortion of either activity, or harm the competitive position of other firms. None of a sample of external firms interviewed by the consultants felt that they had been damaged by firms competing from within the zones, although a quarter of them were in direct competition.

In sum, then, designation seemed in the first year of operation to have had little adverse effect on adjacent areas. In the words of Mr Heseltine, 'many of the most heartfelt concerns about the areas outside the zones have not been manifested'.[34] In their subsequent study the consultants were unable to draw firm conclusions on the matter. They do, however, comment that, given the restricted nature of many of the activities undertaken in the zones, 'offsetting reductions in activity are likely to have occurred on a significant scale'.[35]

Who Benefits?

Initial analysis suggested that the main beneficiaries of the Enterprise Zones were likely to be landowners and property developers. The rates and tax concessions, it was argued, would push up demand for space, leading to an increase in rents and the price of land in the zones and a decrease in adjacent areas. Thus there would be a shift of benefits from one set of property owners—those outside the zone—to another; and from the taxpayer—who funds the incentives—to property owners and developers within the zones. The entrepreneur had somehow been missed out of the process. Since, moreover, the tax incentives were in the main of benefit only to profitable companies, they were more likely to benefit mature companies than the small entrepreneurs who offered the best hopes for innovative ideas and jobs.[36]

We have seen that a transfer is, in fact, taking place between property owners within and outwith the zones; but the evidence so far is that the incentives have been divided between landowners and developers on the one hand and firms on the other so as to benefit both. Rental levels have risen within the zones, but not so high as to remove the benefits of the rating concessions and capital allowances in their entirety. Small entrepreneurs are establishing themselves within the zones, although they may well be attracted there by the availability of suitable premises provided by the public authorities rather than the future prospect of tax allowances. The real question, however, is not whether too high a proportion of the benefits is going to private developers and landowners, but whether the benefits are sufficient to encourage them to reclaim and develop land in their ownership.

Experience to mid-1985 suggests that the incentives are insufficient in themselves to secure the reclamation of large derelict sites needing considerable expenditure if they are to be brought into use. Such sites can be recycled only through public sector intervention. It was, indeed, the activity of the public sector which was most crucial to the success of the zones in their ,initial stages. Of the firms moving into Enterprise Zones between June 1981 and May 1982, 26 per cent set up in Clydebank and 14 per cent in Swansea, both zones where there had been major land assembly and site preparation programmes, funded by the public sector, immediately prior to designation. Subsequently there has been an increase in the proportion of private sector investment in development, but this has to a great extent been undertaken by producer firms building for their own occupation on land restored by the public sector. Enterprise Zones have provided a focus for concerted public sector activity; and it is this, above all, which accounts for the high level of activity within the zones.

Impact on Other Programmes of Regeneration

Does such public sector interest harm other programmes designed to tackle spatial economic problems? Local authorities in particular have been concerned that it does. As we have seen, local authorities in the Manchester area were concerned that the zones would damage the inner city programme. Liverpool City Council received the invitation to submit for a zone on the outskirts of its territory with marked lack of enthusiasm. During 1983–4 Salford received considerably more in Derelict Land Grant than all the other local authorities in the region. Yet in other areas the presence of an Enterprise Zone is seen as complementary to other programmes designed to tackle the problems of urban decline. In Scotland, as Keating *et al.* have observed, Enterprise Zones have been assimilated into local planning and renewal policies.[37] In Dundee both the District Council and the Scottish Development Agency regarded designation as essential to the success of the Integrated Project which they had established to attempt the renewal of Dundee's economy.[38] In Clydebank a zone was seen as a useful adjunct to the work of the SDA's Task Force; and Glasgow District Council supported the establishment of a zone there despite its potential effect on economic activity in other areas of urban renewal in the conurbation. Enterprise Zones, in other words, can be complementary to other central and local government activities aimed at economic renewal, or they can distort them. What happens in any particular case depends on circumstances.

Conclusions

What contribution have Enterprise Zones made to solving problems of implementation and to the process of regeneration itself? They have not side-stepped the need for collaboration among a number of authorities: no new model of authority has emerged, the private sector has not in general been induced to take over the whole responsibility, and success in most cases has depended on collaboration between a number of public sector bodies, in particular the local authorities or New Towns, public development agencies such as the EIE or SDA, and the central government departments concerned with industrial support and infrastructure development. But if they have not created an institution to facilitate such collaboration, they have engendered a style, an approach to the problems of recovery, which does. They have transformed the attitudes of the participants in a way which is likely to have wider benefits.

While the existence of the zones has to date had little effect on employment and economic activity nationally or even in the regions or districts in which they are located, it has generated a considerable amount of development and activity within the zones themselves. Rather than stimulating development through the freeing of entrepreneurs from bureaucratic controls and burdensome taxes, they have largely owed their success, so far at least, to the acceleration of publicly funded site assembly and development in the zones, the focusing of the activities of public sector agencies on the area, and the use of Enterprise Zone status as a promotional tool.

Enterprise Zones have become associated with success; and it is this, rather than their potential impact on the national economy, that explains their popularity with local authorities which might, on doctrinal grounds, be expected to oppose them. For developers, they are attractive because of the availability of tax allowances and the prospect of early lettings; but the crucial factor is the location of the zone. Thus Enterprise Zone status might be seen as removing the final obstacle to development: if the overall picture did not seem right, a developer would not operate there. While the speedier handling of planning questions is an advantage, a relaxed planning regime could be a discouragement if it permitted investment to be harmed by a nearby development of poor quality. For entrepreneurs, the most important Enterprise Zone incentive as such is the prospect of rates relief, but other regional incentives, such as rent-free periods, are of greater importance; help from the public authorities is vital; and the most important factor of all is the availability of suitable premises.[39]

Enterprise Zones have, then, succeeded in the UK almost despite their philosophical origins. That is not to denigrate them as a tool for the regeneration of hard-hit areas; fortuitously, they have begun to tackle some of the basic causes of inner city decline which we considered in chapter 1. But whether the Enterprise Zone package as it has emerged in the UK is the most effective means of securing this result is another question.

3. Freeports and the Reassertion of Enterprise

UK Enterprise Zones are but one model of zone; and some commentators have suggested that they are more about zones than about enterprise.[40] Elsewhere more radical experiments are being prepared. An American model, for example, the Urban Jobs and Enterprise Zone Bill (HR7563), places far more emphasis on meeting the needs of disadvantaged inner city residents and urban neighbourhoods with high unemployment and poverty: thus there will be incentives for housing as well as business, and priority will be given to businesses employing disadvantaged residents.[41] The Belgian experiment is far more like the British 'Crown Colony' prototype: taxes on employment, profits, and dividends were abolished in six or seven zones designated during 1983; labour market inflexibilities, such as the right to redundancy payments, were abolished; no government subsidies or grants are payable in the zones; and the zones are managed by a separate authority, funded by voluntary levy, to which both local and central government have transferred many of their powers. All the sites proposed for designation have, however, already been serviced for industry by the Belgian government.[42] In Britain the original concept reasserted itself in the campaign for Freeports, enclaves treated as being outside the customs territory of the host state, where goods might be imported, stored, processed, and re-exported without becoming subject to customs duties.

Freeports were seen by some as the key to rapid development of the Far Eastern economies. Worldwide, they were host in 1981 to six million jobs and handled 9 per cent of world trade, rising to as much as 20 per cent by 1985. Thus for the Adam Smith Institute it came as 'something of a surprise' that the UK made no use of Freeports.[43] For others, however, Freeports represented a threat as potent as that of the Enterprise Zone, if not more so. Their success was attributable to 'the ability of quasi-totalitarian regimes to reproduce cheap docile labour operating under barbaric conditions'.[44]

Much of the success of Freeports has, however, little to do with the customs regimes operating within them. Other benefits are often added, such as remission of taxes and local rates, grants towards capital expenditure, and removal of requirements to comply with certain legislation. It is in the latter, rather than in the customs regime, that the implicit threat to labour lies. The influence which a Freeport has on the local level of economic activity within the host state will clearly depend on the availability of customs and other incentives elsewhere in the economy, and the openness of the economy to foreign trade. Thus Freeports have far more to offer developing countries which have imposed highly protective regimes to help infant industries than developed economies with liberal regimes. In the case of the UK, over 80 per cent of industrial imports already enter free of duty; membership of the European Community limits both the need for and scope of free trade zones; and such incentives as are permissible under UK law—customs warehousing and inward processing relief—are already available throughout the UK. It was considerations such as these which led to the abandonment of Freeport incentives as part of the Enterprise Zone package. And it was an examination, not of measures to stimulate local economies, but of the future of Prestwick airport, which caused the Government to rethink its position.

The Scottish Affairs Committee, in the course of an enquiry into the underuse of Prestwick airport,[45] received much evidence to the effect that Prestwick should be designated a Freeport. The concept was supported by, among others, the British Airports Authority (who did, however, suggest that other incentives would be necessary if it were to succeed), the District Council, the Institute of Directors (somewhat paradoxically in view of its express opposition to 'any distortion of trade by specific regional or sectoral aids and tax advantages'), and the SDA, who thought that the Freeport concept was 'highly marketable'. But the evidence was not entirely one way: HM Customs and Excise, who received something of a grilling at the hands of the Committee, argued that as the full range of relief available under EC law was clearly offered throughout the UK, 'there would be no purpose in setting up enclaves which would merely duplicate existing arrangements'.[46]

Faced with such conflicting evidence, and the scepticism of most of its members who felt that Freeports would simply attract jobs at the expense of Glasgow, the Committee compromised. Although the existing regimes in the UK might compare favourably with those elsewhere, their promotion and marketing left much to be desired. To bring all the facilities together in an area designated a Freeport and promoted and managed through specially constituted development agencies could, it argued, be 'a very valuable marketing tool'. Thus it recommended a 'limited experiment involving the establishment of two or three Freeports or zones'.[47]

The Government's response was to establish a working party under the chairmanship of the Economic Secretary to the Treasury, which received much the same conflicting advice, and came to the same conclusion.[48] Despite the 'aggressive caution' with which the Chancellor was said to approach the subject,[49] he announced in his 1983 Budget speech that Freeports would be introduced in the UK on an experimental basis.[50] In the subsequent debate the Economic Secretary, Mr Bruce-Gardyne, added a note of caution:

I wish to add a word or two of warning. I get the impression sometimes that a good many eminent authorities, and even perhaps some Hon. Members, look on Freeports as a sort of cross between a status symbol and Shangri-La, a place of hash and dancing girls and cut-price videos, where the Humphrey Bogarts of the 1990s will come together to do business from the corners of the globe—places in whose reflected glory adjoining civic leaders will bask.

The reality, he stressed, would be a 'good deal more prosaic': simply a large measure of exemption from basic customs control, unless or until their products enter community territory, together with a 'potentially alluring style and title, although even there there is no copyright'.[51]

Notwithstanding the Economic Secretary's scepticism, the announcement stimulated much the same kind of interest as the announcement of the creation of Enterprise Zones. The Government made it clear that the Freeports would receive no special assistance in the form of infrastructure investment, but 45 applications for designation were submitted, prompting further waspish comments from Lord Bruce-Gardyne (as he had now become): 'why traders should flock to meet the cost of building warehouses and assembly plants and perimeter defences to make goods, for export outside the European Community... when they can do the same with Customs supervision at existing factories and warehouses remains a mystery'.[52]

In the event, six sites were chosen, at Southampton, Liverpool, Birmingham, Cardiff, Prestwick, and Belfast. Four were to be administered by private sector companies, but, despite the emphasis on the private sector, the Merseyside Freeport is to be run by a public utility, the Mersey Docks and Harbour Company, and the Prestwick Freeport by the District Council. The choice, moreover, demonstrates much the same sort of horse-trading as Enterprise Zones: Felixstowe, perhaps the front runner on purely economic grounds, was not chosen, and the successful applicants inevitably included one each from Scotland, Wales, and Northern Ireland.

Progress since designation has been relatively slow. In Liverpool by mid-1985 the Freeport had handled goods worth some £16m., and some 45,000 square feet of warehousing were available. But elsewhere the Freeport authorities have been largely engaged on economic evaluation and preparatory work and construction.[53] Indeed, the consultants appointed to monitor the experiment observed that the operators saw the present regime as of limited attractiveness and had suggested additional concessions in order to ensure that the zones were treated as far as possible as being outwith UK customs territory.[54]

Freeports are a much more limited experiment than the right had hoped or the left had feared; and their main purpose, like that of the Enterprise Zone, appears to be promotion and marketing. On their own they have little to offer areas of industrial decline and the inner city: indeed, given the absence of government funding the choice of an area with potential seems even more important than in the case of Enterprise Zones. Even the concept is not exclusive; and the Scottish Development Agency has used the generally available incentives to market Clydebank as the Clydebank International Trade Zone. If Enterprise Zones have failed to bring Hong Kong to Corby, it seems even less likely that Freeports wiill recreate Taiwan in Prestwick. But that remains to be seen.

Notes

1. Harrison, Bennet, in Hall, P., Harrison, B., and Massey D., 'Urban Enterprise Zones: a Debate', *International Journal of Urban and Regional Research*, vol. 6, no. 3, 1982.

2. Sir Geoffrey Howe, Budget speech 1980, OR, vol. 981, col. 1487.
3. Department of the Environment, *Enterprise Zones*, London 1982.
4. Keating, M., 'Enterprise Zones, from Rhetoric to Reality', *Municipal Journal*, 21 August 1981.
5. *Daily Telegraph*, 20 April 1981.
6. Taylor, S., 'The Politics of Enterprise Zone', *Public Administration*, winter 1981, vol. 59, p. 421.
7. Butler, S. M., *Enterprise Zones: Greenlining the Inner City*, Heinemann Educational Books, London 1982, p. 125.
8. See Butler, op. cit.
9. Speech to RTPI, 15 June 1977. See also Hall, P. *et al.*, 'Urban Enterprise Zones: a Debate', op. cit.
10. Cited in Butler, op. cit., p. 99.
11. Sir Geoffrey Howe, 'Liberating Free Enterprise: a New Experiment', speech delivered at the Waterman's Arms, Isle of Dogs, 26 June 1978.
12. Ibid.
13. DOE/COI, *Enterprise Zones*, London 1982.
14. Discussion at Enterprise Zone Workshop, Preston, March 1983. See Building Design Partnership, Roger Tym and Partners, *Enterprise Zone Workshop 1983: Report of Proceedings*, London 1983, p. 8.
15. Roger Tym and Partners, *Monitoring Enterprise Zones; Year Three Report*, London 1984, p. 30.
16. Sir Geoffrey Howe, op. cit.
17. See Butler, op. cit., p. 111.
18. Taylor, S., 'The Politics of Enterprise Zones', op. cit.
19. Roger Tym and Partners, *Monitoring Enterprise Zones: Year Two Report*, London 1983, introduction.
20. Roger Tym and Partners, *Monitoring Enterprise Zones: Year Three Report*, op. cit., p. 10.
21. Butler, op. cit., pp. 107-9.
22. OR, 15 November 1982, vol. 32, col. 20 ff.
23. The information in the following section, except where otherwise indicated, is drawn from Roger Tym and Partners, *Monitoring Enterprise Zones: Year Two Report*, London 1983; Roger Tym and Partners, *Monitoring Enterprise Zones: Year Three Report*, London 1984; and Department of the Environment, *Enterprise Zone Information 1983-4*, London 1985.
24. See below, chapter 7.1.
25. Interview with officials of Clydebank District Council, November 1982.
26. Enterprise Zone Workshop, Preston, March 1983; see Proceedings, op. cit., p. 9.
27. Interview with officials of Liverpool City Council, March 1983.
28. Interviews, March 1983.

29. Op. cit., p. 87.
30. Roger Tym and Partners, *Monitoring Enterprise Zones: Year Three Report*, op. cit., pp. 144–5.
31. Roger Tym and Partners, *Monitoring Enterprise Zones: Year Two Report*, op. cit., p. 57.
32. Ibid., p. 119.
33. Discussion at Enterprise Zone Workshop, March 1983.
34. OR, 15 November 1982, vol. 32. col. 32.
35. Roger Tym and Partners, *Monitoring Enterprise Zones: Year Three Report*, op. cit., p. 145.
36. See Massey, D., in Hall *et al.*, 'Urban Enterprise Zones: a Debate', op. cit., and Butler, op. cit., for a fuller exposition of these criticisms.
37. Keating, M. *et al.*, *Enterprise Zones and Area Projects*, Glasgow 1983, p. 33.
38. See below, chapter 7.2.
39. Discussion at EZ Workshop, Preston, March 1983.
40. E.g. Roy Adams, EZ Workshop, Preston.
41. See Butler, op. cit., pp. 130 ff.
42. Van Notten, M., EZ Workshop, Preston, see Proceedings, op. cit., pp. 45–6.
43. Adam Smith Institute, *Freeports in the UK*, 1982.
44. 'Free for Some', John McIroy, *New Statesman*, 15 April 1983, p. 11.
45. Scottish Affairs Committee, *Prestwick Airport*, first report of the Committee on Scottish Affairs, session 1982–3, HMSO, London, vol. 1.
46. Ibid., Evidence, vol. 2, qs. 44 and 123 and pp.. 40, 100, and 130–2.
47. Report, vol. 1, para. 53.
48. HM Treasury, *Freeports in the United Kingdom*, March 1983.
49. *Financial Times*, 4 March 1983, p. 8.
50. OR, 15 March 1983, vol. 39, col. 154.
51. OR, 17 March 1983, vol. 39, cols. 437–8.
52. *The Times*, 25 January 1984.
53. *The Economist*, 17 August 1985, p. 22.
54. Roger Tym and Partners, *Monitoring the Freeport Experiment: Progress Report 1985*, London 1985.

5

Deus Ex Machina:
the Merseyside Task Force

The Merseyside Task Force, established in October 1981, presents a charismatic solution to problems of implementation. Despite early indications that it would offer a comprehensive and strategic approach to tackling Merseyside's problems, it has deliberately eschewed co-ordination, strategic planning, and the provision of new large-scale resources. It operates largely on the basis of bilateral transactions designed to secure specific *ad hoc* objectives, and it derived its initial impetus principally from the enthusiasm of one man, Michael Heseltine. Nevertheless, it does bring together many of the kinds of activity appropriate to the regeneration of local economies which were considered in earlier chapters; it has gone some way towards developing a structure for interdepartmental co-operation in the English regions; and it has made a hitherto unprecedented attempt to bring the private sector into the heart of the process both of policy-making and of implementation. In this chapter we shall review the origins and nature of the Merseyside Task Force, the relevance of its work to the task of economic regeneration, and the extent to which its approach overcomes problems of implementation, so that we may judge how far its organisation and activities may be applicable elsewhere.

1. Background and Diagnosis

The Merseyside Economy

Merseyside suffers to a marked degree from the general causes of regional decline. It relies heavily on declining industries; there is a high proportion of large branch firms, many of them attracted to the periphery of the conurbation in the fifties and sixties; and there has been considerable net loss of jobs. The economy has been heavily reliant on industries with poor prospects, such as textiles, food and drink, motor vehicles and components, and port activities, while growing activities such as banking and financial services, basic chemicals, and process plant and information technology are under-represented.

The figures speak for themselves. After a loss of some 100,000 jobs in the ten years to 1976, Merseyside County lost a net 59,730 jobs between June 1977 and March 1981, a decline of 9.7 per cent. Manufacturing lost 47,000 jobs, nearly 25 per cent of employment in that sector. In 1975, 86 per cent of Merseyside's total manufacturing employment was controlled from headquarters outwith the Region, and less then 20 per cent of the employment in the 29 firms which in 1976 employed more than 2,000 was controlled from within the County. Fifty-six per cent of the manufacturing workforce and 28 per cent of the total workforce in 1976 was employed in companies of over 1,000 employees, by contrast with 22 per cent of the manufacturing workforce and 18 per cent of the total workforce in the country as a whole. Merseyside, in short, is highly vulnerable to the investment and disinvestment decisions of external firms.[1]

The area suffers also from extensive environmental decay. Redevelopment in the fifties and sixties has left large areas of derelict and unused land, which had been augmented through plant closures in the seventies and eighties. In 1977 just under 10 per cent of the land area of the county was vacant and unused.[2] Much remained undeveloped because of expenditure constraints and political differences within and between the local authorities. A shift in port activity downstream, and away from the Mersey altogether, had left much empty land. Many of Liverpool's splendid Victorian buildings were in need of refurbishment.

Employment decline and environmental decay were associated with population loss, which in turn threatened services catering for the local population and increased the costs of providing such services. Nor is migration likely to reduce unemployment significantly, since it is generally the more skilled who migrate. The inner areas had been particularly hard hit, but the problem was by no means confined to such areas. As in Glasgow, the decanting of the population to peripheral estates during the fifties and sixties had created pockets of high unemployment in the outer areas also, and many of the large firms attracted to these areas had closed. Kirkby, for instance, had become

notorious as standing illustration of the mistakes of post-war planning; many of its houses stand empty, falling victim to vandalism and, eventually, demolition by the local authority; it has a registered unemployment rate of one third of the workforce, among the highest in the country; over the last ten years the population of this new township has fallen by 15 per cent, a greater fall than in many inner city problem areas.[3]

Merseyside had, then, been in decline for many years before the establishment of the Task Force. Both local and central government had made strenuous efforts to alleviate its problems; and two initiatives of the pre-Task Force era stand out in particular and to some extent foreshadow it: the strategic Targets for Merseyside, adopted by the County Council in January 1977, and the Inner City Partnership arrangements.

Targets for Merseyside and the Partnership Arrangements

Merseyside County Council's *Targets for Merseyside* outlined the Council's assessment of the policies necessary to tackle the economic and social problems of the area. The overall strategy was to

concentrate investment and development within the urban County and particularly those areas with the most acute problems, enhancing the environment and encouraging housing and economic expansion on derelict and disused sites. It would restrict development on the edge of built-up areas to a minimum.[4]

The strategy relied on a familiar mix of action to stimulate the creation of new jobs and bring unemployment down to the national average, to make land available for development, to improve the environment and bring vacant land into productive use, and to improve the housing stock. New jobs were to be encouraged through enhanced incentives for both manufacturing and service industry. Advice and initial funding was to be offered to the potential entrepreneur. A 'nursery environment' would be provided to encourage the growth of small and medium-sized enterprises and to generate indigenous growth. The skills of the unemployed, and particularly the unskilled inhabitants of the inner area, would be improved by doubling training opportunities and increasing the number of apprenticeships.

Land was identified as a particular problem, and the County proposed the establishment of a land bank to enable land which was currently needed for development to be brought into a marketable state and the remainder to be managed positively as 'green space' until it was required. Steps would be taken to encourage the statutory undertakings to release the large amounts of sterile land which they held, and environmental improvements were to be secured through the treatment and planned maintenance of derelict land funded by 100 per cent derelict land grant. Steps would be taken also to improve the quality of housing through new building, mainly in the public sector, and through improvement to older private property by the housing authorities and housing associations.

Essential to the whole strategy was additional public expenditure on Merseyside. It was considered, for instance, that expenditure on economic measures would require to be increased by some 60 per cent over the following decade if the targets were to be met. Many of the strands of the strategy were the responsibility of other bodies; and the Council noted that 'The combination of proposals and programmes... will require close working between central and local government and voluntary and private agencies. Co-ordination would be required to achieve success and this may need changes or adaptations to existing institutional arrangements.'[5]

The possibility of such co-ordination and co-operation was provided by the Liverpool Inner City Partnership, established in 1978 with responsibilities extending over 40 per cent of the city's land area and half its population. Partnership represented 'a formal recognition that the scale of the problem required a co-ordinated approach by all the agencies of government';[6] and this, rather than additional resources as such, was seen as crucial to a solution. Additional resources were, however, to be provided, amounting to some £10m. in 1979, rising to £22m. in 1982, and directed at a combination of economic, environmental, and social objectives.

Despite early hopes the Partnership arrangements were not an unqualified success. Under the Partnership Committee, chaired by the Minister and representing all the public sector bodies with interests on Merseyside, was constructed a Byzantine structure of boards and sub-boards—as many as 40 at one stage[7]—to concert action by the different agencies concerned. Mr Heseltine acidly describes the Partnership Committee itself as follows:

You would turn up in the area concerned, and there would be perhaps 40 people involved in the discussion, most of whom represented one of the spending agencies of the public sector... all looking for the little bit of their programme that they had not been able to get out of the traditional budget from the local authorities. That was then broadly parcelled up and there would be a general discussion about the problems of the area... After a couple of hours people would go away and that would be that end of the partnership for another three months.[8]

The private sector was not involved, and participants did not, in Mr Heseltine's view, take the real decisions which would have a major impact on the area. Nor was the substructure much more successful. The City Council, who chaired most of the boards, argued that in the early days a 'real dialogue' developed between the parties; but others were not so sanguine. The County Council considered the boards bureaucratic and hampered by their reliance on officials of the City Council; there was little consideration of how central government programmes could be adapted to meet the special needs of Merseyside; and one of the most important of the central government departments, the Department of Industry, was not closely involved in the work.

It was small wonder that the arrangements had little impact on the problems of the area. The elaborate structure of boards and sub-boards atrophied (the City Council disbanded the officer working parties in 1980); and in his statement of 9 February 1981 Mr Heseltine announced that he had taken steps to simplify partnership procedures.[9] Meanwhile the area's social problems intensified; and in April 1981 occurred the Toxteth riots.

A New Form of Machinery

It is not clear whether the riots prompted or simply accelerated the establishment of the Task Force. Mr Heseltine, giving evidence to the Environment Committee, suggested that his department had been considering an initiative of this kind before the riots; but one of his officials conceded that it was 'fair speculation' that the Task Force would not be in existence had it not been for the disturbances.[10] The Government's response was, nevertheless, virtually unprecedented. Not since Lord Hailsham had been made Minister for the North East in the 1960s had the Conservatives appointed a Minister with specific responsibilities for a particular conurbation, and the Task Force which resulted from his visits over the summer represents, on the face of it, a very considerable concentration of governmental effort on the area.

Mr Heseltine's visit highlighted a number of barriers to the solution of the conurbation's problems, in particular the structure and political balance of Merseyside local government, a plethora of overlapping organisations, a poor image, lack of self-confidence, and the flight of private sector initiative.

The political situation on Liverpool City Council, which was controlled at the time by a minority Liberal administration, was not such as to encourage an aggressive response to the area's difficulties; and relations between the two tiers of local government left a good deal to be desired. The Dean of the Faculty of Social and Environmental Studies at Liverpool University put it tactfully in written evidence to the Environment Committee:

Merseyside County Council has enjoyed conventional two-party politics with changing control, but a clear and certain political direction, permitting a good deal of officer initiative and experimentation. Liverpool in contrast has had no firm control and has had minority government since reorganisation. The result has been uncertainty and delay in decision-making and a heated and public political debate inhibiting officer initiative and experimentation. When two such systems seek concerted action at either member or officer level there must be severe difficulties.[11]

An example of these 'severe difficulties' is the case of the Anglican Cathedral precinct, which lay vacant for twenty years while the City Council debated with itself, the County, and a Housing Association which owned part of the land whether the site should be developed for public housing, private housing, or public open space. With official understatement the Chief Executive of the City Council observed that 'the decision-making process as to exactly how to redevelop that site was not an easy one for a council politically composed as the Liverpool Council is'.[12] So far as relations between the two tiers were concerned, the County Council did not agree with the City on priorities and felt that its strategic role was inhibited by the actions, or inaction, of the City. The City Council felt that its offers of co-operation were rejected.[13] In the light of these difficulties one might be tempted to conclude that the Task Force is simply an expensive and labour-intensive way of remedying the shortcomings of a particularly bad example of conflict between two tiers of local government.[14] This is an over-simplification: the two tiers do manage to co-operate on particular projects; there are a good many other actors on the Liverpool stage; and it was not in any event clear to the Environment Committee that the Task Force involvement had solved problems of joint working.[15] But there is an element of truth in it none the less.

The other actors add a further degree of complexity. Merseyside County Council has suggested that 'Merseyside is perhaps unique in the variety of mechanisms that have been created to tackle urban problems';[16] but whether this is an advantage must be open to doubt. In brief, there were in the early 1980s:

(i) Merseyside Chamber of Commerce, which is in particular concerned with the health of the private sector on Merseyside;

(ii) Several Enterprise Trusts, including the St Helens Trust, Business in Liverpool, and In Business Ltd. (Birkenhead), whose main function is to foster small private sector initiative through self-help and co-operation between large and small firms;

(iii) The Merseyside Development Corporation, established in March 1981, with responsibility for the redevelopment of 865 acres of derelict and underused docklands on either side of the Mersey;

(iv) The Speke Enterprise Zone;

(v) MERCEDO (the Merseyside County Economic Development Office), the industrial promotion arm of the County Council (to be abolished from April 1986), which is responsible for marketing the area, encouraging tourism, liaising with business, and stimulating the development of small firms. MERCEDO claims that its grants scheme CHASE (County Help for Active Small Enterprises) created 8,000 jobs over four years;[17]

(vi) The Liverpool Development Agency, the promotional arm of the City Council, and 'your one stop shop for all the support you need to start a new business or expand in Liverpool'.[18] The LDA pioneered land registers on Merseyside; and it claims to have saved or created 3,700 jobs between April 1979 and November 1982 through grants of £4m. to companies investing in the inner area, stimulating investment of £30m. on their part;[19]

(vii) The four other District Councils on Merseyside, described in evidence to the Environment Committee as 'the Districts against the County';[20]

(viii) English Industrial Estates, who are responsible for the development and marketing of individual factories and of industrial estates;

(ix) The Manpower Services Commission, which is responsible to the Department of Employment for the delivery of employment services and training in the region;

(x) The Department of Industry, which is responsible for the administration of regional policy in the area, and for support and advice to individual firms;

(xi) The Department of the Environment, which is responsible for inner city and urban policy.

Organisational confusion was mirrored by geographical complexity. The region is a 'patchwork quilt' of different priority areas, including Industrial and Commercial Improvement Areas, Housing Action Areas, General Improvement Areas, Conservation Areas, Environmental Improvement Areas, Intensive Housing Management Areas, an Inner City Partnership area, and an Enterprise Zone. It was small wonder that the Merseyside Council perceived a clamant need for co-ordination.

Also of concern to the Secretary of State were the poor image of the region, which both sapped local initiative and discouraged inward investment, and the flight of top managers and decision-makers. In a letter to the financial institutions seeking support for his initiatives on Merseyside, Mr Heseltine wrote:

one of the key problems of Merseyside, and this applies to some of our other conurbations, is the loss of business leaders. Most of the larger firms are controlled from London or abroad. Locally the proprietors and managers no longer live in the cities... I think there is a danger... that with the concentration of wealth and power in London the needs of the less fortunate parts of the country which nevertheless provide the markets and savings for the big national business tend to be forgotten. I realise of course that some institutions already look consciously at the social implications of their commercial and investment decisions, but I believe that many more companies could do so, and much more systematically.[21]

These problems were not new, nor were attempts to tackle them. But despite the large sums of public money which were being spent in the region and the new initiatives which sprang to life to deal with individual problems, the situation grew worse. New attempts to solve them through an elaborate all-embracing strategy imposed from the top downwards had done little more than create new levels of bureaucracy. A different approach was needed. And that approach was to be provided through the Task Force.

2. The Nature of the Task Force

The establishment of the Task Force was announced in a Press
Notice issued from 10 Downing Street on 9 October 1981. The
Task Force, it was said, would assist the Secretary of State in his
work on Merseyside; it would collaborate with the local authorities,
the private sector, and other organisations in order to promote the
best use of central government resources; it would make proposals
for the modification of policies or the switching of resources; it
would generate new initiatives; and it would consider how further
resources could be used 'for the reduction of unemployment
and the improvement of the economic and social life of the
conurbation'.[22] This raised considerable expectations, particularly
with the County Council, to whom it was presented as 'building
on partnership'.[23] But in the event the Task Force was to concentrate
almost exclusively on two aspects of its remit: assisting the Secretary
of State, and developing specific initiatives.

It is not hard to see why the Task Force should have developed
in this way. Mr Heseltine's appointment as Minister for Merseyside
carried with it no new responsibilities and did not affect the structure
of central government. His function has indeed been described as
that of a 'high powered friend at court';[24] and on matters outwith
his own statutory responsibilities his role was limited to advice
and consultation. The Task Force, too, involved no shift of
responsibilities: it is not an agency in its own right; it has no
financial resources of its own; and to secure its objectives it must
rely very heavily on pre-existing agencies. It is very small; and
perhaps two-thirds of its thirty or so civil servants (costing in total
some £400,000 a year) would be working on the area's problems
anyway. The majority of these civil servants came from the
Department of the Environment, reflecting that department's lead
role in matters of urban renewal. Thus in November 1982 the
staffing of the Task Force was as follows:

Director (from DOE)	1
Other DOE	17
Manpower Services Commission	7
Department of Industry	5
Private sector secondees	8

Such a slim-line organisation, with no additional responsibilities and finance and heavily dominated by the Department of the Environment, was likely to be better at sorting out individual problems than developing a corporate approach to the use of government resources on Merseyside; and there was, moreover, a pressing political need for action. The development of an overall strategy involving the other bodies in the area would be too time-consuming; Mr Heseltine himself was sceptical about the value of strategic planning and favoured an *ad hoc* and empirical approach. For him, the role of the Task Force was 'getting results', which involved 'specific decisions in specific programmes'.[26] If particular ideas worked in practice, they would be extended; if they failed, they would be dropped.

Despite this *ad hoc* approach, certain themes have emerged from the work of the Task Force, which have been summarised by its director as follows. First, it aims to 'build upon the strengths of the local community' through maximising private sector involvement and mobilising voluntary effort. Secondly, it seeks to 'utilise every asset in urban areas' through upgrading and bringing into use unused land and industrial infrastructure, improving housing, and bringing key sites into use. Thirdly, it proposes 'making Merseyside a better place in which to live and putting right some of the mistakes of the past', particularly in relation to housing schemes. Finally, it seeks to 'create better conditions to rebuild the local economy and encourage economic investment'.[27] The overall approach is to demonstrate that things can happen on Merseyside and to improve its image.

These themes were not, however, clearly defined at the outset, and the Secretary of State's close personal involvement created some initial confusion about the Task Force's objectives. Nevertheless, his enthusiam was crucial in encouraging people to have a further attempt at tackling the problems of Merseyside. Many of the more imaginative projects pursued by the Task Force were originated by Mr Heseltine himself: examples are the Garden Festival and the Wavertree Technology Park. His regular visits to Merseyside—as much as once or twice a fortnight—encouraged the local politicians and the private sector to collaborate and kept up the pressure on officials; he inspired those who worked with him with his genuine enthusiasm. His charismatic leadership was crucial to the success of the Task Force, and has invested it with its characteristic style.

In the words of one of his officials, 'The Task Force is dominated by the man, not by the strategy'.[28]

Like the man, the Task Force is innovative, pro-active, private sector orientated, anti-strategic, and anti-bureaucratic. Its lack of funds prevented it inventing another bureaucracy, the result being, according to one commentator, 'an inventiveness that more money could have spoiled'.[29] Suspicion of the grand strategy caused the Task Force to concentrate its attention on *ad hoc* solutions to particular problems rather than on overall solutions to the overall problem: hence the programmes of the Task Force are built 'bottom up' from an aggregation of specific projects rather than 'top down' from an ideological definition of the causes of urban decline; successful ideas are duplicated, and the unsuccessful dropped. This approach has been criticised, in particular by the County Council, which conceived of itself as having the strategic role and was disappointed at not being given the chance to exercise it.[30] And, as the Environment Committee has observed, it is far more modest than the 'far-reaching' remit announced in October 1981.[31]

The absence of an overall strategy removes the need for an all-embracing machinery to implement it. Thus there is no mechanism to bring all the interested parties together, and Task Force officials advance particular projects on a bilateral basis. The partnership arrangements have been allowed to wither. Mr Heseltine argued to the Environment Committee that in a sense there was a 'permanent Partnership meeting now';[32] but the Task Force is not what the County Council understood by the concept.

In all of these ways the Task Force differed from previous attempts to tackle the problems of particularly hard-hit areas, but it was in the involvement of the private sector that the Secretary of State was most innovative. Mr Heseltine's analysis suggested that the loss of decision-makers to the centre had blunted company awareness of the needs and the potential of the areas in which they were operating. Their departure contributed to the general decline of the area. If local companies, and national companies with subsidiaries on Merseyside, could be persuaded to play a part in the regeneration of the area, their responsiveness to its needs might be enhanced and that decline might be halted.

Mr Heseltine accordingly encouraged companies to second managers to work on the Task Force, and over the period to December 1982 13 companies made staff available. After initial confusion about their functions the secondees were integrated into the work of the Task Force on particular projects, and they have worked on such diverse activities as the promotion of the Speke Enterprise Zone, the development of a maritime museum, the refurbishment of the Knowsley Industrial Estate, and support for small firms. Mr Heseltine has commented thus on their involvement:

These seconded managers have made a tremendous contribution to the development of the Task Force's projects, and have shown that the experiment of joint public/private sector working can be a resounding success. The response of Merseyside companies is part of what I believe is a new wave of cooperation between public and private sectors, in the business of regenerating our cities. I have repeatedly said that Government, either local or central, can't do the job on its own; and I am very pleased that so many companies, large and small, are shouldering a share of the responsibility.[33]

The secondees have, indeed, played a major part in the success of many of the projects. But whether their participation has increased company awareness of the problems and potential of the areas where they are operating is a different question. Most of the companies which have participated could be said to have been socially aware before they were invited to participate, and many, through the Chamber of Commerce, were already involved in encouraging the development of the local economy. Others were too preoccupied with difficulties elsewhere in the country to be concerned with the activities of the secondee whom they had provided as a matter of conscience, or to have their consciousness raised as the Secretary of State had hoped. It needs more than a dozen or so seconded managers to raise the consciousness of the private sector; and of major importance must be the development of areas of local decision-making and the strengthening of the indigenous economy.

3. Lessons and Achievements

The Secretary of State for the Environment, then, acquired no new powers when he assumed his responsibilities for Merseyside—a fact which the Environment Committee regarded as both surprising and unsatisfactory[34]—and the Task Force had few staff (in addition to those who would have been there anyway), no specific powers, and no funds. It would be a mistake, however, to conclude that this rendered either the Secretary of State or the Task Force ineffectual. Mr Heseltine's position in Cabinet enabled him to argue the case for Merseyside, and his colleagues recognised that his frequent visits to the area exposed him to its problems, so that they were prepared either to consult him or to take advice from him on their own programmes. The backing of the Secretary of State and the intimate involvement of staff at a relatively senior level in particular projects was a powerful catalyst for action, for example in persuading other, often more junior officials to accelerate programmes for which they were responsible, or to 'bend' programmes to the advantage of Merseyside. Thus the Department of the Environment argued in its written evidence to the Environment Committee that 'generally, in the absence of the Task Force, the projects would not have started at all, or proceeded much more slowly'.[35]

Task Force officials were then able to package projects requiring the co-operation of two or more agencies, and to arrange for joint funding. While no finance as such was available to them, they were able to secure additional resources for the derelict land programme on Merseyside, enabling virtually all the projects capable of going ahead in 1983-4 to proceed, by comparison with some 10 per cent in the North-West region as a whole. They secured additional finance for other programmes also, and housing, the Manpower Services Commission, the Merseyside Development Corporation, and the Urban Programme all showed increases in their allocations greater than might have been expected in the absence of the Task Force,[36] even though funds for many of the programmes are allocated according to national formulas. What happened was that recognition of Merseyside's problems provided some leeway, and the perceptions of the Task Force helped to shape the application of the national formulas. In short, ministerial interest and the involvement of senior officials can be a powerful catalyst for action.

This catalyst has secured a good deal of activity on the ground, and a large number of imaginative projects have been set in train.[37] Assistance has been provided to small firms through, for example, English Industrial Estate's programmes of small factory building and the establishment of a businessmen's association in the Liverpool Industrial Improvement Areas. Secondees to the Task Force have sought to identify imported products which might be produced on Merseyside and to publicise the Department of Industry's support for small firms and innovation. High technology developments, particularly among small and medium-sized companies, are being encouraged through the Plessey Industrial Park. The Merseyside Innovation Centre provides an 'interface' between the academic and commercial world in order to bring together the scientific skills and ideas of local academics with companies who need their skills and might develop their ideas commercially. A Merseyside Enterprise Fund has been created to provide risk capital for smaller businesses in the Merseyside Development Area. Through Sapling Enterprise (Merseyside) Ltd., a joint venture of Collinson Grant Associates Ltd. and the British Technology Group, it will provide up to £50,000 for investments in new or existing ventures, especially those involving technological innovation.

In the training field, Merseyside secured a greater number of the Information Technology Centres designed to give training in computing skills to unemployed school leavers than might have been expected given its share of school-leaver unemployment. Three Commercial Business Training Centres, unique to Merseyside, were pioneered in the area. Government-funded apprenticeships and one-year traineeships for the young unemployed were expanded to a greater extent than in the country as a whole, and local companies were encouraged to make a large contribution to these projects through financial sponsorship, the provision of training places, management expertise, and help with premises.

Derelict land clearance has been accelerated, both to prepare new industrial sites and to clean up the environment more generally. In Operation Groundwork, which received particular mention in the Conservative manifesto of 1983, derelict land and countryside management programmes were linked in an unprecedented way to advance the reclamation of land on the fringes of the conurbation, and local people and industry were closely involved.

The Ellesmere Port Boat Museum is designed to stimulate tourism in the area, which the Task Force has identified as of major growth potential; and the International Garden Festival 1984, a major project of the Merseyside Development Corporation, attracted over 3.3 million visitors.

Housing tenure is being diversified through encouraging developers to build for sale and for shared ownership in the inner city on difficult sites which would otherwise remain undeveloped:

by October 1982, builders had shown interest in sites sufficient for 400 houses. The private sector was encouraged also to refurbish run-down housing estates. Knowsley Borough Council, for example, sold Cantril Farm, an outer housing estate of 3,500 houses, to the private Stockbridge Village Trust, who have upgraded houses, improved the area generally, and sold sites to private builders for owner occupation.

Thus action has been taken over the whole range of functions relevant to the needs of Merseyside: assistance to industry, particularly small firms and high technology industry, training, environmental improvement, tourism, and housing. The Task Force sorted out 'log jams', and while red tape has not been abolished, it speeded up the procedures and accelerated action on the ground. Superficially, the Task Force has a record of considerable achievement.

It is, nevertheless, pertinent to consider how original the Task Force's approach was and whether it has indeed planned or achieved anything which would not have happened anyway. Its impact on Merseyside does appear to be considerably greater, in terms both of projects brought to fruition and of improved self-confidence, than the local authorities are prepared to admit (the City Council spoke of 'sticking plaster'[38]). But despite the packaging of the Task Force as an entirely new approach to the problems of Merseyside, the overall thrust of its activities is very close to the overall thrust of 'Targets for Merseyside'. Both aimed to improve the environment, bring land into productive use, and encourage the growth of small and medium-sized firms, particularly in areas of high technology. Both sought to upgrade the skills of the workforce through increasing opportunities for training and retraining. Both identified a need to improve the housing stock. Indeed, the only fundamental difference of approach appears to be that 'Targets for Merseyside' makes a virtue of being a strategy, while the Task Force makes a virtue of not being one.

It is of course possible that the piecemeal approach resulting from the Task Force's rejection of strategy could be counterproductive. In its evidence to the Environment Committee the County Council argued that concentration on individual projects might divert attention from the need for action over the whole range of relevant policies—housing, social policy, and regional policy—and for increased resources for the main programmes with which local authorities tackle the totality of urban problems, which, it argued, had been savagely cut by Mr Heseltine. The conflict between special initiatives and main programme spending was in its view 'nowhere more apparent than in the work of the Merseyside Task Force'.[39]

Whether a more strategic approach on the part of the Task Force would have encouraged central government to release further resources for main programmes is a moot point; but its *ad hoc* approach did, as we have seen, secure a good deal of activity on the ground. But how much of this activity would have occurred anyway? The Environment Committee was in some doubt as to the extent to which the Task Force had stimulated initiatives which would not have happened in due course.[40] The leader of the Merseyside County Council conceded that the Task Force had been of assistance in encouraging co-operation by the private sector, and that some of the local initiatives had 'moved on in bureaucratic terms', but he argued that 'its successes have been very limited'. Certain initiatives, he claimed, had indeed been delayed through the actions of the Task Force, and others which had been claimed by the Task Force had in fact been initiated by other organisations. The Chief Executive was even more damning: so far as the Lime Street station improvement was concerned, 'The question is whether the Task Force as a Task Force did anything to speed the process up or whether it merely acted because it was there. It seems to me that it was the latter . . . I cannot see that it had any impact at all. The system should work without a Task Force.'[41] The City Council was more complimentary: it considered that the Lime Street project would not have proceeded without the intervention of the Task Force, and saw considerable benefits in the stimulus which the Task Force had given to co-operation between the local authorities and the private sector.[42] The Environment Committee noted that 'Where the Task Force has not initiated projects, it appears to have played a role in the progress-chasing, in facilitating decision, in providing a catalyst for new thinking and as a broker between institutions.'[43]

Underlying these questions about the benefits and drawbacks of strategic planning and the contribution which the Task Force has made to new initiatives there lie more fundamental questions which are relevant to the possibility of generalising operations such as the Merseyside Task Force. These concern the effectiveness of multi-departmental organisations in resolving policy conflict and role confusion within and between different levels of government, their skill at cutting through organisational confusion, and their capacity to concert the activities of the different organisations with an input to the regeneration of local economies. In all these respects the Merseyside Task Force may be found wanting.

As we have seen, the statement which announced the establishment of the Merseyside Task Force gave it a virtually universal remit, and raised expectations that it would establish a corporate approach. In the event, such an approach did not emerge. Merseyside County Council, for example, considered that government policies were not being 'co-ordinated as a total package'.[44] Statutory responsibility for the relevant programmes remained with the traditional departments. Task Force officials retained their allegiance to their parent departments and are responsible both to the head of the Task Force in Liverpool and to their superiors in their department's regional office. Thus Department of Industry officials answer both to the Task Force Director in Liverpool and to their Regional Director in Manchester. The DI regional office has, moreover, retained responsibility for most of the relevant functions of that department, including the granting of Selective Financial Assistance and industrial promotion. Conflict can clearly arise over individual cases, where the Task Force, closer to the ground, may take a view different from that of the Regional Office on whether assistance should be given to a particular company; and there is potential conflict also over promotion of Merseyside rather than the region as a whole, which includes areas of considerably greater attractiveness to the inward investor than Merseyside itself. Even within the Department of the Environment itself there is the possibility of conflict. The Environment Committee noted the 'area of policy conflict' involving 'the Government's policies with regard to the inner cities on the one hand and the control of public expenditure on the other'.[45] And the leader of the Merseyside County Council argued that sometimes 'the Minister for Merseyside has no influence on the Secretary of State for the Environment'.[46]

More fundamentally, there are potential areas of conflict between the philosophies of the departments involved on the Task Force. The Department of Environment sees its role as combining the economic, the social, and the political and favours a fine-grained and pro-active approach. The Department of Industry is almost exclusively concerned with the industrial and economic aspects of the work and is very much more reactive. Financial assistance is a demand-led operation; and philosophical objections to involvement with 'lame ducks' encourage a somewhat aloof stance. These different approaches naturally create the possibility of conflict. An industrial secondee to the Task Force has suggested indeed that the Department of the Environment was more attuned to the needs of industry on Merseyside than the Department of Industry.

The potential for conflict with the Manpower Services Commission is perhaps less: the Commission, like the Department of the Environment, favours a fine-grained approach to individual firms and problems, and it is geared to be pro-active. But there are tensions none the less. Traditional MSC doubts about the value of training for stock run across the Task Force's concern to improve the quality and quantity of training on Merseyside; and the Commission decided to transfer its regional headquarters from Liverpool to Manchester during the first year of the Task Force's operations. While the MSC was perhaps the most active partner in the early days of the Task Force, its role appears to have diminished very considerably since.

Nevertheless, too much can be made of such potential conflict. It would be impossible to remove the possibility of interdepartmental conflict without major change in the structure of government— something which the Environment Committee appears to think desirable.[47] But this would inevitably create fresh areas of boundary dispute. Departmental reorganisation cannot in any case remove the problem of policy conflict within departments which we noted in chapter 1, and the activities of central government are so diverse that tension between policies is at times inescapable. The measures operated by the different departments do give different degrees of priority to urban regeneration and the inner city, but underlying the work of the MSC, DOE, and DI is the collective responsibility of Ministers, who have mechanisms for reconciling the claims of conflicting policies when the tensions between them become too acute. Economic revival is clearly in the interest of the inner city. And, while the policies of the DOE and the DI can be criticised for their lack of synchronisation,[48] informal co-operation on the Task Force can reconcile the differences and provide an approach to synchronisation.

The Task Force organisation can, then, provide an approximation to the corporate approach by central government sought by the local authorities in the area; and certainly the involvement of officials from different departments in a common task is likely to encourage the evolution of such an approach. But the Task Force has not tackled the fundamental problem of organisational confusion. It has in fact been added to the patchwork quilt of organisations charged with the regeneration of Merseyside, and it has augmented the number further by its own activities, for example through encouraging the establishment of further enterprise agencies and bodies such as the Merseyside Enterprise Fund.

Such a profusion of bodies is not necessarily a disadvantage. Given the wide range of functions which they must discharge, it is hard to conceive of a single organisation which could effectively perform their responsibilities. But in certain areas—particularly in that of industrial support and promotion—proliferation of bodies can be positively harmful. The Liverpool Development Agency, for example, presents itself as the 'one door' which an entrepreneur must enter for all the support he needs to establish himself on Merseyside. But so do MERCEDO, and the Speke Enterprise Zone, and the New Towns in the area, and the Chamber of Commerce, and the Enterprise Trusts. Having spoken to one or more of these, the potential industrialist, if he is not weary, must approach the Department of Industry, and possibly the Department of the Environment and the Manpower Services Commission as well. One-stop shopping is still remote from Merseyside.

Nor is there any single way to bring all the relevant parties together. Mr Heseltine argued to the Environment Committee that this did not matter: the Task Force was not about securing an improved degree of co-operation because there was no problem about co-operation; and there was indeed nothing to stop the parties getting together if they wished.[49] But, while co-operation may not have been a problem in the early days—the Task Force's director was, indeed, 'pleasantly surprised' at the co-operation at both political and officer levels from other organisations in the area[50]—it may be necessary to improve co-ordination against the day when high-powered officials and a determined Secretary of State are no longer on tap to badger other organisations into action. The Environment Committee took the view that 'the attitudes of those involved in the management of urban renewal in

Merseyside fall far short of the joint working necessary for the effective co-ordination of effort'.[51]

Finally, the Task Force failed to secure any overall approach to government funding. Witnesses told the Select Committee that there was no bending of government programmes to meet the needs of Merseyside, and the Task Force director conceded that 'it would be wrong to ascribe to the Task Force the bending of programmes'.[52] Such adjustments as were made were very much at the margin, and the Task Force provided no real opportunity to consider the totality of government programmes for Merseyside from a zero base. As Merseyside County Council's Director of Development and Planning put it, there is no mechanism for bringing the budgets of the implementing agencies together to see what the total picture looks like.[53]

Conclusion

Mr Heseltine was reluctant to be drawn by the Environment Committee on the question of whether new Task Forces on the Merseyside model would be established in other English cities;[54] the so-called Task Forces which were subsequently established at Smethwick and Brixton were on a very much smaller scale and led by local and not central government; later central government initiatives have also been of smaller compass. It seems clear that the Merseyside Task Force is a one-off operation. Mr Heseltine argued that his own experience on Merseyside suggested that 'given the will to make this present system work, it can'.[55] But the successes of the Task Force have relied heavily on charismatic leadership by Mr Heseltine himself, which has, to some extent, made up for the lack of a corporate approach.

Charisma does not, however, translate readily into the bureaucratic environment of the regional offices of central government. But to replace charisma by the corporate approach which the Task Force's original remit suggested it would adopt requires institutional change. Nor is charisma readily exportable, although, as the Environment Committee noted, Mr Heseltine's activities on Merseyside have demonstrated the extent to which the close involvement of a Minister can accelerate existing initiatives and generate new ones.[56] Thus the Merseyside model, as it stands, is not repeatable, and its limitations cannot readily be overcome. But it has nevertheless taught lessons which are transplantable to other soils.

In the first place, the presence of senior central government officials within the conurbation is regarded by many as a major benefit. Unlike most officials of central government in the regions, the members of the Task Force are concerned with the formulation of policy as well as its implementation, and their local knowledge and experience enable them to design or respond to initiatives appropriate to the local situation in a way arguably denied to their Whitehall-based colleagues. Aloofness and closeness to the Treasury and the Cabinet Office are not necessarily the best prescription for solving the problems of the regions. The co-operation of central and local government officials on the implementation of specific projects is, moreover, one way through a basic dilemma of central/local relationships, that of how to reconcile the wish on the part of central government to regulate expenditure and encourage good practice with the desire to delegate more to local decision-makers.[57]

Secondly, many of the specific initiatives pioneered on Merseyside could be introduced elsewhere. Commercial Training Centres might, for example, be developed in other conurbations, and there is clearly scope for the introduction elsewhere of private sector capital and skills into the renovation of both industrial and housing estates, as indeed is happening on Clydeside.

Thirdly, the Task Force demonstrated the benefit of co-operation between the central government departments primarily concerned with the economic well-being of the inner cities, the Department of the Environment, the Department of Industry, and the Department of Employment and Manpower Services Commission. The City Action Teams established in February 1985 for the Inner City Partnership Areas of Birmingham, Liverpool, London, Manchester/Salford, and Newcastle/Gateshead have consciously built on the Task Force experience; indeed, the Government's publicity material on the Liverpool City Action Team explicitly states that

The decision to establish City Action Teams in all the partnership areas is less of an innovation for Liverpool. The idea builds on the experience of the Merseyside Task Force, which has already shown some of the benefits that can flow from better co-ordination of government programmes.[58]

The teams bring together the regional directors of the three departments in order 'to secure improved cooperation between

Departments in developing and implementing their policies and programmes reflecting local circumstances in partnership areas'.[59] Leadership of the Teams varies in order to emphasise the inter-departmental approach: two of the Teams are led by DOE (Liverpool, where the Team Leader also leads the Task Force, and London), two by the Department of Industry (Birmingham and Manchester/Salford), and one by the Department of Employment/MSC (Newcastle/Gateshead). The Teams will draw on the experience of other central departments with relevant programmes, and the Government has indicated that it wishes to consider in due course how their remit might be widened to cover the programmes of DHSS, DES, and other departments responsible for policies relevant to the inner cities. The objective is to develop co-operation not simply among Government departments, but also with the local authorities, voluntary organisations, and the private sector. Teams are charged specifically with developing priorities for their areas (an activity which is likely to lead to a more strategic approach than that adopted by the Task Force), establishing arrangements for co-ordinating departmental programmes, monitoring projects, developing joint funding opportunities, and providing a point of contact for external sources of finance.

But perhaps the most important lesson to be drawn is the value of co-operation between the private and the public sectors, and the extent to which there are underutilised resources in the private sector which might be devoted to helping solve the problems of the conurbations.

The Environment Committee concluded that 'the creation of an integrated approach by the Departments of the Environment, Industry, Employment, Education and Science, Health and Social Services [*sic*] and the Home Office at a conurbation level would... be a valuable development in other areas.'[60] The Merseyside Task Force has made some moves towards such an approach, and the City Action Teams have extended it to other areas. As we have seen, however, the Task Force's efforts have been hindered both by potential conflicts of policy and by the structure of government, and the City Action Teams will have a formidable task in overcoming such problems. Structural problems at the central government level are, by contrast, avoided to a considerable extent in Scotland; it is to the Scottish experience that we shall now turn.

Notes

1. For a fuller description of the Merseyside economy, see *The Merseyside Economy: Performance and Prospects to 1986*, Merseyside County Council, Liverpool December 1981, from which the information in this section is drawn.
2. See *Targets for Merseyside in the 1980s*, Merseyside County Council, Liverpool January 1977.
3. 'Final Report of the Kirkby Study Team'; quoted in evidence to the House of Commons Environment Committee, session 1982-83, 'The Problems of Management of Urban Renewal'; Minutes of Evidence, p. 109 (hereafter referred to as 'Evidence').
4. *Targets for Merseyside*, op. cit., para. 1.3.
5. Ibid., para. 1.20.
6. Evidence, p. 87; memorandum by Liverpool City Council.
7. Evidence, p. 82, q. 208.
8. Evidence, p. 148, q. 341.
9. OR, 9 February 1981, vol. 998, col. 603.
10. Evidence, p. 145, q. 330; p. 37, q. 13.
11. Evidence, p. 163.
12. Evidence, p. 94, q. 213; interview with Liverpool City Council, March 1983.
13. Evidence, p. 104, q. 244.
14. Interview with Scottish Office official.
15. House of Commons, Environment Committee, *The Problems of Management of Urban Renewal* (*Appraisal of the Recent Initiatives on Merseyside*), HMSO, London 1983, vol. 1, p. xxiv.
16. Evidence, p. 57; memorandum submitted by Merseyside County Council.
17. Evidence, p. 67, q. 139.
18. Merseyside Enterprise Newsletter no. 1, December 1982, p. 11, Merseyside Task Force, Liverpool 1982.
19. Evidence, p. 88; memorandum by Liverpool City Council.
20. Evidence, p. 61, q. 108; p. 67, q. 138.
21. Letter from Secretary of State for the Environment to chairmen of financial institutions, 13 August 1981.
22. Press Notice issued by 10 Downing Street, 9 October 1981; quoted in Evidence, p. 33.
23. Letter from Secretary of State for the Environment to leader of Merseyside County Council, cited in interview with MCC, March 1983.
24. Evidence, p. 141, q. 316.
25. Evidence, p. 39, q. 28.
26. Evidence, p. 157, q. 390.

27. Evidence, p. 43, q. 48.
28. Interview with officials of the Merseyside Task Force.
29. Charles Moore, 'It will take more than money to save Merseyside', *Daily Telegraph*, 10 February 1983.
30. Evidence, p. 59.
31. House of Commons, Environment Committee, report, op. cit., pp. xxxvii–xxxviii.
32. Evidence, p. 156, q. 386.
33. Merseyside Enterprise Newsletter no. 1, p. 2.
34. House of Commons, Environment Committee, report, op. cit., pp. x and xxxvii.
35. Evidence, p. 6; memorandum by the Department of the Environment, para. 20.
36. Evidence, pp. 149–50, qs. 348–50.
37. See in particular the Merseyside Enterprise Newsletters and the Progress Logs produced by the Task Force.
38. Evidence, p. 105, q. 247.
39. Evidence, pp. 58–9, memorandum by Merseyside County Council, para. 3.
40. House of Commons, Environment Committee, report, op. cit., p. xxxviii.
41. Evidence, pp. 70–1, qs. 155–61.
42. Evidence, p. 98, q. 224; p. 93, q. 212.
43. House of Commons, Environment Committee, report, op. cit., p. xxxix.
44. Evidence, pp. 58–9; memorandum by Merseyside County Council, para. 3.
45. House of Commons, Environment Committee, report, op. cit., p. xxvii.
46. Evidence, p. 77, q. 193.
47. House of Commons, Environment Committee, report, op. cit., p. xl.
48. Evidence, p. 526, q. 1220.
49. Evidence, p. 157, q. 390.
50. Evidence, p. 39, q. 29.
51. House of Commons, Environment Committee, report, op. cit., p. xxi.
52. Evidence, p. 45, q. 59.
53. Evidence, p. 66, q. 133.
54. Evidence, pp. 538–9, q. 1283.
55. Evidence, p. 156, q. 379.
56. House of Commons, Environment Committee, report, p.. xxxvi.
57. See Evidence, p. 143, q. 322.
58. DOE, DTI, MSC, DE, *City Action Team: Your City and Your Government*, London 1985.
59. OR, 26 February 1985, vol. 74, WA col. 98–9.
60. House of Commons, Environment Committee, report, op. cit., p. xli.

6

'Multi-organisational Sub-optimisation'? Area Initiatives in Scotland (I)

In Scotland, a single Department of State has responsibility for most of the functions exercised by the various central government departments concerned with the regeneration of local economies in the South; at local level too there are significant differences in the organisational arrangements, although, as in the South, a variety of bodies are involved. The first major attempt at local economic regeneration in Scotland, the Glasgow Eastern Area Renewal project, did indeed come up against major difficulties in concerting the activities of the participants despite the advantages which a unified central government organisation might be expected to present. Subsequently, however, strategies to secure collaboration have been developed which appear to offer means of overcoming many of the problems of implementation. In this chapter we shall consider the economic background, the extent to which structures of government at national, regional, and local level in Scotland are likely to facilitate the regeneration of local economies, and early attempts to tackle the problem through the Glasgow Eastern Area Renewal project. In the next we shall explore the co-ordinated approaches offered in later Scottish economic development projects.

1. Problems, Structures, and Functions

Scotland in the past suffered from many of the disabilities of a declining economy—heavy reliance on uncompetitive older industries, under-representation of the post-war growth industries, high emigration, and some of the worst urban deprivation in Europe. In addition it was disadvantaged by its remoteness from the markets of the South and Europe, and it possessed a number of one-industry towns highly vulnerable to changes in demand and to investment and disinvestment decisions taken elsewhere.

Over the past two decades, however, Scotland's economic fortunes have been remarkably transformed. The Scottish Council (Development and Industry) recently ran an international forum on the subject of the renaissance of the Scottish economy; and while Charlotte Lythe and Madhavi Majmudar thought it necessary to add a question mark to the title of their book on the same subject, they end on a confident note:

Provided that the current view that future developments lie in fields like micro-electronics and bio-engineering is accurate, Scotland now has an industrial structure very well suited to the demands of the future. If the 1990s are going to be a decade in which those who are in work are farmers, scientists designing new microchip circuits and new genetic engineering programmes, and people working in personal service industries and administration, Scotland should by then be if not the most prosperous region of the UK, at least the region with the most fully employed workforce.[1]

It is not necessary to consider the causes of this transformation in detail here. Regional policy, which attracted to Scotland in the sixties many of the firms involved in high technology which give the Eastern Midlands of Lothian, Fife, and Angus a claim to be Britain's silicon valley; the restructuring forced upon the Scottish economy through the contraction of the coal, steel, shipbuilding, and heavy engineering industries; the discovery and development of North Sea oil; and government policies to disperse central government activity to the regions—these have all played their part. But while the transformation has enabled Scotland to weather the present recession rather better than the UK as a whole (hitherto Scotland has always pulled into recession first and come out last), unemployment has increased substantially, prospects over the immediate future are not good, and the location of the new activity in the East and North has not helped those areas in the West which were most affected by the decline of steel, shipbuilding, and heavy engineering.

Scotland, then, no less than England, requires the kind of measures to tackle localised unemployment and regenerate local economies which we have considered in relation to Merseyside. But there are likely to be differences both in prescription and in delivery, reflecting the nature, strengths, and potential of the Scottish economy and the structure of government at both the national and the local level.

In England, the central government responsibility for the relevant programmes is divided among the Department of the Environment, the Department of Industry, and the Department of Employment, with smaller contributions from the Departments of Transport and Education. Witnesses appearing before the Environment Committee criticised the apparent failure of these departments to develop a corporate approach to the solution of Merseyside's problems; and we have seen the tensions to which different departmental philosophies can give rise. While the Scottish Office has been described as a 'framework for the discharge of certain functions' rather than a comprehensive Scottish administration,[2] and while in the economic sphere the Secretary of State's capacity to develop independent policies is strictly limited, delivery of the relevant programmes is very largely his own responsibility.

Thus, through the Scottish Economic Planning Department (SEPD) (subsequently retitled the Industry Department for Scotland (IDS)), he is responsible for regional policy (and in particular the granting of selective financial assistance and, following the new Regional Aid package announced on 28 November 1984, the administration of Regional Development Grants), and for the activities of the Scottish Development Agency and the Manpower Services Commission in Scotland. Through the Scottish Development Department (SDD) he oversees the activities of the Scottish local authorities, the Housing Corporation and Housing Associations, and the Scottish Special Housing Association; the SDD is also responsible for physical planning and infrastructure and for the urban programme and urban renewal in Scotland. The Scottish Education Department oversees the Scottish education system, and was in the past involved, for instance, in the Educational Priority Areas which were an early attempt to tackle inner city deprivation.

These Scottish departments do not necessarily work to the same junior minister (in the Conservative administration of 1979–83 the Scottish Economic Planning and Education Departments answered to a Minister for Industry and Education, while the Scottish Development Department answered to a Minister for Home Affairs and the Environment), and, as we have seen, tensions can arise within as well as between organisations. But the Scottish Departments do collaborate closely on the development and delivery of policies addressed at urban decline and economic recovery. This has produced advantages for the agencies working at the local level: the leader of Strathclyde Regional Council, for example, told the Environment Committee that the existence of a Minister for Scotland was an appropriate way of ensuring co-ordination of government departments in the field of urban renewal: 'You are dealing with, virtually . . . one man. If you had to deal with several Ministers it makes the problem of co-ordination and co-operation much more difficult.'[3]

There are, of course, limitations. While the Secretary of State has responsibility for the activities of the MSC in Scotland, he is one of a triumvirate of ministers to whom the Commission is answerable (and a junior one at that): the opportunity to 'bend' Commission policies to meet the special needs of Scotland is accordingly limited. There has been considerable criticism of the Commission in Scotland, as elsewhere, for its failure to meet the needs of the more disadvantaged inner city residents through its training policies. The Depute Chief Executive of Strathclyde Regional Council, for instance, has criticised the MSC for the length of time it took to appreciate the need to discriminate in favour of the Glasgow Eastern Area project (GEAR).[4] Even where the Secretary of State has what appears to be a sole responsibility, as in the case of local government finance, he is constrained by the general policy of the Government and the political difficulty of taking a markedly different line north of the border. So the conflict between expenditure on mainline programmes and special initiatives can arise in Scotland just as it does in the South. Strathclyde Regional Council, for example, has criticised the Secretary of State for reducing Rate Support Grant and commented that its budget cannot cope with the need for additional expenditure on infra-structure, education, or social work within GEAR.[5] Thus, while the structure of central government within Scotland can make solution of the problems easier, it does not resolve all the difficulties. Nevertheless, whatever the limitations, as the *Scotsman* has put it, 'undoubtedly true is that the structure of Scottish administration has been able, over the past two decades, to nurture the economy almost in spite of what has been happening elsewhere in Britain.'[6]

Organisational benefits at the level of policy-making are paralleled in Scotland by benefits at the level of execution. The Scottish Development Agency, as we have seen, is an organisation with the dual purpose of 'furthering the development of the Scottish economy and improving its environment'[7]—the two interrelated keys to the rehabilitation of local, as well as national, economies. In England the equivalent powers are diffused among no less than six different organisations—English Industrial Estates, the Department of the Environment, both tiers of local government, the British Technology Group, and the Small Firms Service of the Department of Industry. Small wonder that the leader of Strathclyde Regional Council got the impression that 'down south there seems to be an awful "guddle" between the different agencies'.[8]

On the face of it, differences in the distribution of responsibilities between the two tiers of local government might make for a more coherent approach to local economic regeneration than is possible in England: the Regional Councils in Scotland have more extensive responsibilities than the Metropolitan Counties in England, and District Councils in Scotland are now inhibited from promoting their area as a location for inward investment other than within their own boundaries. But the possibility of conflict remains: both tiers in Scotland, for instance, have powers to assist industry— albeit on a relatively small scale—and both tiers are keen to secure the political kudos of securing major projects in their area. The leader of Glasgow District Council suggested in evidence to the Environment Committee that the split in functions between the two tiers of authority in Scotland 'does make it difficult to deliver the goods to the people of the different areas';[9] and development of the Integrated Project in Dundee was, as we shall see, inhibited to a certain extent by differences of view between the Region and the District. Thus, when the District Council appointed a professional director for its grandiloquently named Centre for Trade and Industry, the leader of the Tayside Regional Council felt obliged to challenge the assertion that he would be 'leading the fight to save Dundee from industrial devastation'. Instead, he would be 'joining an established team of fellow-professionals from the Scottish Development Agency, Tayside Regional Council and Dundee District Council as a member of the Dundee Project Team'.[10]

Nevertheless, Scotland has avoided many of the difficulties which have arisen south of the border, and the distribution of responsibilities between the two tiers of local government has clearly been of some benefit. Of perhaps more importance, however, is the Scottish Development Agency's capacity to hold the ring between the two tiers. The relative closeness of central government and its agencies to the other institutions is also important. As the *New Statesman* has suggested,

Through bodies like the Scottish Development Agency, central government plays a much bigger part than it does in England, and Ministers— Conservative or Labour—gain a good deal of credit for that. They and their senior officials know the people and places they are dealing with; and they have a sharper sense of responsibility for the human impact of their decisions.[11]

Kellas and Madgwick note that the tendency for the local - central boundary to 'soften and shift' at the regional level is more apparent in the Scottish (and Welsh) Office than in the English regional offices.[12]

Structure, functions, and style all, then, facilitate a more integrated approach to area renewal in Scotland than south of the border; but at the same time they limit the scope for translating Scottish experience elsewhere. The integrated approach did, moreover, take some time to develop: the early initiatives were broadly based responses to political pressures or economic disasters very much akin to the Merseyside Task Force. But more recent initiatives offer a solution to many of the problems of implementation which bedevil attempts at regeneration.

2. The Glasgow Eastern Area Renewal Project

Origins and Objectives

The Glasgow Eastern Area Renewal project (GEAR) has been described as 'probably the most comprehensive and advanced urban renaissance scheme in Western Europe'.[13] It was the first of the geographically focused projects co-ordinated by the Scottish Development Agency and it remains the most ambitious in terms of both the scope of its objectives and the extent of the investment in the area. It is seeking the comprehensive regeneration of 4,000 acres of what was in 1976 the area of worst multiple deprivation in Europe[14] through a concerted attack on its economic, physical, and social problems.

By 1983 the project had achieved a considerable degree of success. In 1976 the community was hostile and contained large numbers of disadvantaged groups, population was in decline, there was a large acreage of vacant and derelict land, the traditional economic base had collapsed, and new firms were not springing up in sufficient numbers to replace jobs which had been lost. By 1983 the community was creatively involved in the regeneration of the area, the first private housing in the area for fifty years had been sold, dereliction was being systematically tackled through Agency environmental improvement activities, new industrial floor-space had been provided, and new small firms were springing up.

GEAR originated from a reappraisal of the thrust of regional policy in West Central Scotland. Boyle and Wannop suggest that its political origins lay in the Scottish Office's dissatisfaction with the speed and quality of urban renewal achieved by the former Glasgow Corporation in comparison with the perceived successes in development of the New Towns.[15] In fact, its origins stemmed more from concern at the impact of the New Towns on the inner city areas. The Strathclyde Regional Report 1976 had noted the impact of the New Towns on inner Glasgow and recommended that Stonehouse should not proceed;[16] and while the traditional view, reiterated by the Secretary of State in 1974, was that inner city regeneration and the development of the New Towns was not incompatible,[17] by 1976 the Government, announcing the abandonment of Stonehouse New Town, stated unequivocally that the decision 'endorses a change of emphasis by both central and local government, in social and economic policies towards urban renewal in West Central Scotland, by recognising the need to give priority to older urban areas, in the allocation of increasingly scarce resources.'[18] The 'scarce resources' freed by the abandonment of Stonehouse were to be diverted to the renewal of the Eastern area of Glasgow under the overall direction of the Scottish Development Agency. On 31 May 1976 the Secretary of State announced

proposals for comprehensive concerted action by Strathclyde Regional Council and Glasgow District Council, the Scottish Special Housing Association and the Agency to tackle the renewal of a major sector of the inner city of Glasgow. The co-ordinating management of the project was to be handled by the Agency though each of the parties was to retain its own statutory responsibilities.[19]

The GEAR area, as it came to be known, included the site of the closed Clyde Iron Works together with the communities of Tollcross, Fullarton, Sandyhills, Shettleston, Parkhead, Camlachie, Bridgeton, Dalmarnock, Calton, and Cambuslang. Between 1961 and 1976 its population had fallen from 105,000 to some 45,000, largely as a result of demolition and rehousing in peripheral estates. The younger and more highly skilled had moved out to the New Towns and other areas where prospects were better as the older industries of the area contracted or relocated, leaving a significantly greater proportion of the unskilled, the old, the chronically sick, and the single homeless than in Glasgow as a whole. Vacant and derelict land encouraged vandalism; and the population 'was losing confidence, interest and hope'.[20]

To tackle this battery of problems the GEAR project had objectives as broad as those defined for the Merseyside Task Force, if not broader. A Working Document on Organisation defined the overall aims of the project as being the securing of 'The social, economic and environmental regeneration of the East End, creating the conditions for the development of a balanced and thriving community . . . the undertaking cannot succeed simply on the basis of physical planning and redevelopment . . . social and community services are vital.'[21] The project, which was to have a budget of £120m., was to be overseen by a Governing Committee, meeting two or three times a year under the chairmanship of a Scottish Office Minister, and including elected members from the Regional and District Councils and members of the Agency and the Council of the Scottish Special Housing Association. Under the Governing Committee was to be a Consultative Group of senior officials (including also officials from the Greater Glasgow Health Board) who would be responsible for co-ordinating day to day matters and handling the scheme on the ground.

Despite the favourable publicity which attended its launch, the project did not have a particularly auspicious start. It was plagued by much the same difficulty in defining how to achieve its objectives and securing co-operation among the participants that we have noted in the case of the Merseyside Task Force. The statutory powers of the participants were unaltered; each was expected to make its own contribution. Two bodies which had a major potential input to the project were not included at the outset; it was not until later that the Manpower Services Commission and the Housing Corporation were added to the co-ordinating team. The Scottish Development Agency itself was at first somewhat lukewarm towards the project. It was only six months old at the time that the additional responsibilities for GEAR were imposed, and was still heavily engaged in defining its role and negotiating with the government the guidelines governing its activities. At that time, moreover, it regarded its main function as the regeneration of the Scottish economy through the exercise of its powers of industrial investment, not the regeneration of inner Glasgow through the use of its far less glamourous powers of environmental improvement and factory building. Glasgow District Council was sceptical; and while the Regional Council was more enthusiastic—the concept had, after all, originated in its Regional Report and the area included some of the 52 areas of multiple deprivation which the Region has itself designated for priority treatment within Glasgow District[22]—it had not itself fully recovered from the traumas of local government reorganisation. It took some time, therefore, to achieve the necessary approach on the part of all the participants. Lewis Robertson, Chief Executive of the Agency at the time, commented in 1979 that 'the organisational structure of the project has tended to inhibit action and promote discussion ... Putting together a programme involving several authorities has taken time.'[23] The subsequent chairman of the Agency commented in evidence to the Environment Committee that 'We went through two years of considerable difficulty in relating all these people together and had the same kind of problems as I think they have probably had in other areas in trying to co-ordinate the various bodies that are involved.'[24]

The GEAR project was, then, hampered at the outset with many of the difficulties of implementation which Pressman and Wildavsky noted in the Oaklands project, and which have caused problems on Merseyside. It was imposed on the area by ministerial dictat (although one of the parties had been urging action of a similar kind); it involved the participation of a number of agencies with different political and policy objectives and differing views of priorities; little thought had been given to objectives, targets, and termination and there had certainly been no attempt to reach a broad agreement among the participants on strategy. Small wonder that the project took some time to bed down: indeed, on the basis of Pressman and Wildavsky's probability calculus,[25] one might have predicted that the project would simply fail. But simple probability analysis does not take account of the political pressures for success; and agreement on joint action was helped by three things. Firstly, unlike the Merseyside Task Force, the SDA had resources of its own which could be used to secure the co-operation of the other parties. Secondly, the Agency enjoyed the goodwill of the other parties: the fact that it was not a central government department or overtly political body meant that it avoided some of the inter-organisational rivalries which inhibited the work of the Merseyside Task Force. Thirdly, it was not precluded, as the Task Force appears to be, from devising strategies to tackle the problems of the area in a comprehensive way. Thus the Agency's annual report for 1978 notes that

Working groups of officials... have reached an advanced stage in their examination of policies, making full use of existing expertise and available knowledge of the area. The Agency is drawing together the various submissions of the Working Groups and providing a report on key issues and courses of action . . . It is expected that overall proposals for the area will be produced by the end of 1978.[26]

On the Working Groups were officials from all the participating Agencies; this was of course a powerful means of securing the commitment of their parent organisations to the strategy which emerged.

It was not, however, necessary to reach agreement on a co-ordinated and strategic approach to regeneration before work could start. There was an obvious task of physical rehabilitation to be done, whatever strategy was ultimately adopted, and the Scottish Development Agency had both the powers and the resources to undertake it. In the meantime, therefore, work proceeded on physical rehabilitation in very much the *ad hoc* way favoured by Mr Heseltine on Merseyside, both to secure progress on the initiative as a whole and to boost the confidence of the area by giving early and visible physical evidence that action was being taken. Confidence was boosted also by the involvement of the local community, which was seen as essential if the project were to succeed. Some commentators have suggested that community involvement was simply a cynical exercise in public relations.[27] But experience in Maryhill, where environmental improvement projects had been vandalised almost as soon as they were completed, had pointed to the folly of imposing solutions which failed to take account of the wishes or make use of the skills of the community. Therefore early in the project's life the Agency launched a major consultation exercise to determine the wishes of the local community; it also established a 'GEAR centre' in Bridgeton in 1977 (followed by a second in Shettleston in 1980) to provide a focus not simply for the dissemination of information about the project, but also to gather ideas from the residents themselves about what might be done. The Agency has commented that these centres 'have convinced residents that their suggestions are not merely received politely and forgotten promptly, but considered carefully and, if practicable, implemented'.[28]

What, then, was the nature of the strategy developed for the project? It has been criticised for the vagueness and breadth of its objectives, but it is important to recognise that it was not all-embracing. The participants acknowledged that a number of fundamental problems affecting the area, such as low wages or lack of support for the single homeless, were beyond their scope. There was no commitment to an all-embracing review of government policies in relation to the East End of Glasgow on the lines of that offered—but not, in the event, followed through—for Merseyside. Secondly, the approach was not to be uniform throughout the GEAR area. Certain parts of the area were to be singled out for special treatment, either because they had a particular concentration of disadvantage, or because they were seen to have particular potential for economic development. Vulnerable groups were also to receive preferential treatment. Thirdly, the participants recognised that they could not provide a total solution themselves. It was essential to engage the interest of the private sector; and particular attention was to be given to the creation of conditions in which private investment would return to the area.

Nevertheless, the prescription was very broad, involving not simply economic and environmental recovery, but also social measures. The participants defined six 'basic objectives' for their work in the GEAR project:

(i) To increase residents' competitiveness in securing employment;
(ii) To arrest economic decline and realise the potential of GEAR as a major employment centre;
(iii) To overcome the social disadvantage experienced by residents;
(iv) To improve and maintain the environment;
(v) To stem population decline and engender a better-balanced age and social structure; and
(vi) To foster residents' commitment and confidence.[29]

These basic objectives (which, following a review by consultants in

1982 and further examination of priorities by the Agency in the course of 1983, were refined to cover three broad categories—economic development, social development, and management and resources[30]—subdivided into 19 priority topics) have been criticised for being so broad as to make it impossible to judge to what extent they have been achieved. They do, however, serve as both a definition of the problems afflicting inner Glasgow and a prescription for their solution. Inner city areas generally, as we have seen, suffer from a socially disadvantaged population, uncompetitive in the labour market and lacking in confidence, from high unemployment and a high rate of job loss, from environmental decay, and from unlocked potential. The problems are interrelated, and require concerted action. What action then has been taken on these fronts in the GEAR area?

Competitiveness in the Labour Market

A superficial examination of the area's problems might encourage one to place as the first objective not an increase in the competitiveness of residents in securing employment but the reversal of economic decline and the release of its economic potential. The provision of new jobs in an area like the GEAR will not, however, do much for the residents of that area unless it is coupled with positive measures to help them secure those jobs. Many new inner city jobs are, as we have seen, taken by commuters travelling in to work from more favoured parts of the conurbation; if one is concerned with the prosperity of people in the inner city areas it becomes essential to take steps to improve their competitiveness through raising their level of skill. Thus the SDA notes in its annual report for 1981 that there is 'a need for longer term training or retraining initiatives to equip people for the range of jobs which will develop in the future'.[31] Such steps involve both the education service and the Manpower Services Commission. It is perhaps easier for the Education Authority, with its local administration and local political control, to take positive steps to discriminate in favour of the residents of a particular area than it is for the Manpower Services Commission, with its national programmes and its aversion to 'training for stock', but action is being taken on both fronts. The Regional Council, for example, in collaboration with a national voluntary organisation, has increased opportunities for final-year school pupils to participate in work experience and residential training courses; and the MSC, the Regional Council, and the Agency have established a GEAR Employment Centre, which provides short courses in basic skills for unskilled GEAR residents. The MSC has also been active in the area on its own account. In 1980-1 over 200 separate manpower programmes offering over 550 places for young people and 90 places for adults were under way: these programmes were expanded during the following year, and the targets for 1983 included the provision of places under the Youth Opportunities Programme 'for every unemployed school-leaver and long-term unemployed youngster'.[32] Activities on this front have been continued and expanded subsequently. The SDA, in collaboration with the MSC, has sought to encourage the employment of local labour in public programmes and in environmental improvement projects. Strathclyde Regional Council has introduced training in computer-based skills into its Adult Education Unit, and has appointed a schools/industry liaison officer to assist school-leavers in the transition from school to work. Two ITECs have been established, and other training opportunities expanded.[33]

It must be asked, however, whether such provision can make sufficient impact on the problems of an area which in 1979 had about 4,000 unemployed, a figure which by May 1985 had increased to some 13,000, half of the economically active population.[34] Most of the MSC's activities in the area are under national programmes not directed specifically at the needs of GEAR residents. The Youth Opportunity Programme Targets, for instance, were national targets for the programme as a whole, not an example of positive discrimination in favour of residents of the GEAR area. While residents have access to the Queenslie Skillcentre, which provides places for 266 adults and 20 young people for good-quality craft training, places here are not restricted to GEAR residents and the Centre is scheduled to close in March 1986. Nor is the Training Opportunities Programme (TOPS), which supports about 300 GEAR residents a year in skill training, mainly in further education colleges, specific to the needs of GEAR. The GEAR Employment Centre, which is more closely focused on the needs of residents of the area, provides places for only about 100 people a year. Measured against the scale of the problem, such provision—necessary and welcome though it is—seems very slight. It is hard not to conclude that, if residents' disadvantage in the labour market is to be overcome, further steps must be taken to discriminate in favour of the area. MSC philosophy and financial constraints both militate against this.

Arresting Economic Decline

No such constraints have inhibited action on the second objective. To arrest economic decline involves action to sustain existing jobs, to encourage indigenous growth, and to attract new investment from elsewhere—all functions well within the remit and financial resources of the Scottish Development Agency, and all functions which appropriately have a local focus. The Agency accordingly formulated a 'Business Development Package' including incentives for potential new employers, the provision of workshops for the very small firm, new factory building and renovation of existing premises for the larger firm, land assembly, promotion and the provision of advice and information. Considerable progress has been made on these fronts. Over the period 1977-82 the Agency assembled some 190 hectares of land and 62,000 square metres of buildings. Agency factory building had by mid-1982 brought the total of new factory floor-space in the area to 50,000 square metres, including 107 units of under 1,000 square metres and ten larger units. Thirty-six older premises have been refurbished to provide offices, workshops, and small factories. At the Templeton Business Centre (a former carpet factory in a splendid Victorian-Venetian building) over 6,000 square metres of factory floor-space have been made available, and demand was such as to cause the Agency to advance the second phase of the project. Opening Phase I, Robin Duthie, the Agency's chairman, said that he believed that it would provide a 'focal point' to attract business of all kinds back to the area.[35]

Work on provision and marketing of sites and premises has subsequently proceeded apace: for example, 20,000 square feet of industrial floor-space is due for completion in Cambuslang by late 1986, bringing the total industrial floor-space in Cambuslang to 250,000 square feet; in addition, the Cambuslang Investment Park has been extensively promoted.[36] A wide range of support and advisory services is provided by the Agency to the area's business community. In February 1982 two Business Development Areas, in which environmental improvements are linked with an intensive marketing campaign and assistance for business development for both new companies and the 160 or so companies already active in the area, were launched in Bridgeton. This initiative has subsequently been extended to other parts of the GEAR area. New premises and the provision of advice do not necessarily mean new jobs. Extensive promotion has, however, meant that demand for factory accommodation in the area is high; and there has been particularly high demand for the smallest units.

Overcoming Social Disadvantage

At first glance, the alleviation of social disadvantage might seem of slight relevance to the regeneration of an area's economy; and most of the current British projects do not seek to tackle social disadvantage directly. But such activity is of importance for a number of reasons. Social disadvantage destroys morale, it encourages crime and vandalism, it contributes to the poor image of the areas which it afflicts, and, as the research of the 1960s suggested, it is self-reinforcing. The mistake then was to think that action to alleviate social disadvantage would solve the problems of the inner cities. It is, however, equally mistaken to suppose that these problems can be solved if it is ignored.

The GEAR partners resolved on a six-point plan to 'improve the quality of life for the whole community', involving action over the whole range of the social services. Steps have been taken to make people aware of the benefits to which they are entitled: the Department of Health and Social Security had in 1985 a new office under construction in Bridgeton and plans for a further office in Shettleston; Strathclyde Regional Council has strengthened community support and, with the District Council, is developing spatial frameworks for the delivery of public sector services. Facilities for young people and access to educational facilities are being improved: nursery schooling has been expanded under the Urban Programme, additional teachers and youth leaders have been employed, and sports facilities and meeting places are being provided for unemployed youngsters. Leisure facilities more generally are being upgraded, including the provision of District Parks and sports centres. Crime and vandalism is being tackled through putting more policemen on the beat and through the Strathclyde Police's Community Involvement Branch. The leader of the Regional Council has indeed expressed the view that Strathclyde Police were ahead of the Scarman Report in community policing and community education.[37] Health and social service provision is being expanded, for example through the provision of new Health Centres in Parkhead and Shettleston, the employment of additional community health and paramedical staff, and provision of sheltered housing. Finally, local transport and shopping facilities are being upgraded to improve local residents' access to employment and services.

It is not easy to form a quantitative judgement on this nexus of activity: a lot has been done; much remains to be done. Qualitatively, however, the activity of the various agencies concerned in the work appears to have made a major contribution to the improvement of morale in the area, and consequently to its capacity to generate self-sustaining economic growth.

Improving and Maintaining the Environment

Environmental improvement also works indirectly; but it is perhaps through its work on the environment that the GEAR project has had the greatest immediate impact on the area. Activity has ranged from clearing up the back courts of tenements to major landscaping, local traffic management improvements, pollution control, and the relocation, with SDA assistance, of one of the major industrial polluters of the area from a residential quarter to the heavily industrialised Cambuslang section. Between 1977 and 1983 some £8.3m. was spent on general landscaping, treatment to buildings, and backcourt improvements, and £2.1m. on traffic management. Further major projects have continued subsequently, and arrangements are being made to provide for the continued maintenance of all environmental improvements.

Stemming Population Decline and Engineering a Balanced Age and Social Structure

The provision of jobs, assistance for the socially disadvantaged, training, and the improvement of the environment will all pay a contribution to the fifth objective; but the GEAR team has taken direct steps to stem decline and build a balanced population through its housing policies. A symptom, and a cause, of decline in the GEAR area was the loss of population to peripheral areas, leading to large-scale clearance, vandalism, sub-standard housing in both the public and the private sectors, and further loss of population. No new private housing had been built in the area for fifty years.

The GEAR housing policies accordingly were addressed at both public and private sectors, and at both renovation and new building.

Renovation involved the modernisation of some 4,000 public sector houses and apartments and the rehabilitation of 1,800 privately owned tenements, mainly by housing associations, in the period 1977 to 1982. In the same period, 1,668 new public sector dwellings were completed, at a cost of some £30m., about half of them by the District Council and half by the Scottish Special Housing Association, with a small contribution by housing associations. Work both on modernisation and new building has continued subsequently, although the District Council's programme has been reduced as a result of funding restrictions.

As in Merseyside, the private sector has been encouraged to build houses for sale, and the first new private houses in the area for two generations have been completed. At Calton, over 300 dwellings for private occupation were under construction in 1982, and there were other such developments elsewhere in the GEAR area. Further sites were being sought, and Glasgow District Council was considering the possibility of a homesteading scheme. It was estimated in 1985 that, since the project began, 2,000 private sector dwellings were completed or under construction, with firm plans for a further 1,250. In total, over 13,000 new or improved dwellings had been completed in the area, and 60 per cent of local residents lived in new or fully modernised dwellings. A survey by Glasgow University[38] showed that purchasers generally had close connections with the area but were younger than the average for GEAR residents, had higher incomes, and included a high proportion of first-time buyers. Over time, the strategy could, therefore, lead to the desired result in terms of social mix; and population expansion generally will lead to new demands for retailing and other services. Indeed, GEAR registered an increase in population of 2 per cent between 1981 and 1985, compared with a fall of 3 per cent in the population of Glasgow as a whole.[39]

Fostering Residents' Commitment and Confidence

In addition to other work in the GEAR area, which will clearly affect the perceptions of local residents, the District Council is endeavouring to involve its tenants in decisions through the decentralisation of housing management. The GEAR Community Fund makes funds available to community organisations: during

1981–2 it received 315 applications and made awards totalling £13,000, and regular meetings are held, not only with the national and local politicians who represent the area, but also with representatives of local groups. Local residents assumed responsibility in 1984–5 for two Community Environmental Schemes. Stringent efforts are made to inform local organisations and residents at large about plans and progress.

Conclusions

How successful has the GEAR approach been, and what lessons are to be drawn from it? Visiting the area, it is difficult to challenge the words of the then Scottish Minister for Industry and Education, Alec Fletcher, who when opening the Templeton Business Centre spoke of the 'transformation of the area'. Robin Duthie, chairman of the Agency, claimed on the same occasion that 'we are well on the way to seeing a remarkable reconstruction and resurgence of industry and commerce in the East End'.[40] The consultants appointed by the SDA in 1982 to review the GEAR strategy commented that 'potential outside investors now consider GEAR to be on a par with competing locations in terms of environment'.[41] The GEAR has been greened; and a considerable amount of the credit is due to the Scottish Development Agency.

Yet very severe problems remain, and both the claims made for the GEAR project and its structure have been the subject of criticism. Booth, Pitt, and Money have argued that most of the results claimed for the project would have been achieved anyway by statutory authorities already in the area: 90 per cent of the dwellings planned for completion by 1984, for example, would have been built without the project. Much of the work of the SDA has, they suggest, been frustrated by central government action, in particular national economic policies, which have led to the loss of far more jobs in the area than have been created. There has been 'frustration in training and basic skill development',[42] and the measurement of success has, in any event, been 'an ephemeral concept in GEAR owing to the vagueness of basic goals and the difficulties of monitoring and co-ordination'.[43]

If the results claimed for the GEAR experiment were open to question, so, claim Booth *et al.*, was its organisation. The 'GEAR constellation of organisations', they suggest, 'is in a category of organisations which might best be described as a "mango", a mutually non-effective group of organisations'.[44] Such an animal, they argue, is characterised by decision-making unrelated to clear goals, the engagement of organisations for cosmetic purposes, the imposition on existing functional authorities of a 'new organisational network' without real powers or resources, the establishment of new hierarchical layers, the retention of old allegiances by officials working in the new structure, and the resort to symbolism and ritual jargon to legitimise the new organisational form. GEAR is, they suggest, 'an organisation unfitted in real terms to the multiplicity of Glasgow urban renewal'. It was established not because it is functional, but because of the initial need to be seen to be doing something quickly, the 'administrative and political fashionability of the area approach' (which avoided the need for legislation to create 'powerful united organisations to cope with urban problems'), and the need to be seen to generate 'consensus among the different parties involved'. It survives because termination would be seen as an admission of failure; 'stakeholders' in the organisation expect and are in a position to secure growth; growth, in any case, is regarded as a fact of official life. GEAR accordingly 'raises a question about the utility of the concept of the "area approach" '.

It is difficult to do justice to Booth *et al.*'s critique in the space of a few paragraphs: certainly there is an element of truth in their analysis of the organisational difficulties raised by the project and of its lack of success in some areas. Between 1979 and 1982, for example, manufacturing employment, always the mainstay of economic activity in the area, fell by 40 per cent. Mobile investment is scarce, and the area still suffers acutely from deficiency in demand (which is, of course, largely determined by the state of the national economy). But none of this calls into question the utility of area approaches. The performance of local economies depends crucially on the state of the national economy; but how well particular areas do depends on a range of factors which can be influenced by local initiatives.

Experience of the GEAR does indeed raise questions about its suitability as a model for other area initiatives, and it does have some of the qualities which Booth *et al.* associate with 'Mangos'. Its goals were not clear at the outset, and the six clearly defined goals subsequently adopted were arguably too broad and too unquantified to enable its success, or failure, to be measured.

(The 19 priority topics adopted in 1983 should, however, help monitoring.) But in other respects the charge falls. The Scottish Development Agency, as co-ordinator of the project, has considerable powers and resources relevant to the solution of the area's problems; and the other partners are involved not for cosmetic reasons, but because they too have relevant powers and duties which the SDA can concert, if need be, by the use of its financial clout. The parties are now agreed on broad strategy, so that pre-existing organisational allegiances are no more likely to inhibit the achievement of the project's objectives than in any other joint action. No hierarchical layers have been added, and clearance has been increased only to the extent that collaboration requires participation in decision-making by the various parties involved. Whether the new 'organisational form' has been legitimised by symbolism and ritual jargon depends on one's view of its achievements: another view would be that it has been legitimised by the need to secure concerted action among a number of bodies to tackle the 'multiplicity' of Glasgow's urban renewal problems. GEAR might indeed, as Booth *et al.* argue, be 'a candidate for inclusion in Hood's ... category of "multi-organisational sub-optimisation" '—but the establishment of a new powerful and unitary organisation to tackle the whole range of the problems of the East End would, as we suggest in chapter 1, raise tensions and demarcation problems of equal if not greater difficulty. Hood, indeed, recognises 'multi-organisational sub-optimisation' as a fact of political life.

The 1982 review of the GEAR project tackled at least some of the problems identified in Booth *et al.*'s critique. The consultants proposed a package of measures to stimulate demand, including improved marketing of the area as a location for investment, removing constraints on the growth of local firms, encouraging use of locally produced goods, and involving the private sector more closely in filling the 'management gap' in ways pioneered by the Enterprise Trusts in England. Steps were proposed also to deal with remaining supply-side constraints, including in particular measures to relate training more closely to the needs of residents and firms in the area. Most importantly, the consultants proposed that the SDA should give up its co-ordinating role within three to five years. The Government's acceptance of the review and a pledge of support for a further five years were announced on 10 January 1983.[40]

Subsequent developments have confirmed progress: modest when set against the very considerable problems of the area, but giving some grounds for optimism. In 1984 there was a small fall in absolute terms in the number of unemployed in the area. During 1984–5 some 660 jobs were created in 239 companies, the majority in manufacturing; 269 of the new jobs were in the 64 companies which were new starts. There has been in addition considerable progress in the refurbishment of the area. Nevertheless, unemployment remains significantly above the Glasgow average, much of the property available for occupation is vacant, and there is a considerable surplus of land available for industry. Much therefore remains to be done, though sound progress has been made, and the GEAR area is now well placed to benefit from upturn in demand. But can any general conclusions be drawn from experience of the project?

In its evidence to the Environment Committee the Glasgow District Council suggests that very little could be made of it: it was, it thought, 'by no means certain that general conclusions of any significance can be drawn from the GEAR experience' apart from the 'simple and obvious' benefits of having fewer organisations to co-ordinate than elsewhere, the need for 'extra' money, and the desirability of local commitment to the solution of the area's problems.[46] These conclusions, 'simple and obvious' though they are, are nevertheless pertinent to the management of urban renewal. Contrasting the GEAR experiment with the Merseyside Task Force, GEAR appears to have benefited in particular through the existence of public agencies not available in England. The existence of the SDA and the SSHA enables government to channel resources directly to the GEAR area in a way not possible through the use of generalised controls on local authority capital expenditure and through the Rate Support Grant and Housing Support Grant systems, and has to some extent insulated the project from the impact of public expenditure cuts. The independence of the Scottish Development Agency from government has moreover reduced political conflict; and the Agency has been keen to involve others in its decision-making process and can keep them appraised of its dealings with government. (Merseyside County Council complained, by constrast, that it did not know what action the Task Force had taken on representations it had made about regional policy.) The Agency provides a 'single door' for industrial promotion and advice, avoiding much of the difficulty of proliferation which we noted on Merseyside.

Apart from these institutional advantages, GEAR has benefited from unanimity of objectives on the part of the participants: all of them shared views on priorities, and once the arrangements had been allowed to bed down, there was little of the inter-organisational rivalry which has dogged the work of the Merseyside Task Force to date. (It is too early to dismiss the possibility, however, that the Merseyside Task Force will develop in a similar way, especially since the change of political control on the Liverpool City Council since May 1983, and when the metropolitan tier of local government in England is abolished.) Perhaps most important, the fact that the participants were able to develop a strategy—and adjust it to meet changed circumstances—has enabled the problems of the GEAR area to be tackled in a more systematic way than those of Merseyside.

It was benefits such as these, stemming largely from the different institutional structure in Scotland, which have caused some commentators to argue for the establishment of Regional Development Agencies in England. Some of the private sector participants in the Task Force have, indeed, argued for the establishment of a Development Agency for Merseyside.[47] But the success of the GEAR initiative to date relies as much on the very considerable public resources which have been poured into the project as on institutional factors. Of expenditure in the area to the end of 1982 of some £260m., £200m. or 77 per cent came from the public purse, and over half of the private sector contribution was on private housing.[48] The importance of the public sector to the 'greening' of inner city areas such as the East End of Glasgow cannot be overemphasised. But public sector investment has clearly acted as a catalyst for increased participation by the private sector: by March 1985 total expenditure in the area had risen to £412m., of which 39 per cent was from the private sector.[49]

What then was perhaps underemphasised in the first five years of the GEAR experiment, and what it has learnt from Merseyside, was the role of the private sector. The consultants rightly emphasised this point when they drew attention to the potential of the private sector to fill the 'management gap', especially in enabling small firms to attain their potential for growth, in injecting new ideas for marketing and product development, and in assisting management buy-outs. They also proposed the creation of an Amenity Trust to promote environmental improvements to which firms would contribute management expertise and perhaps funds. LEG-UP, the Scottish scheme for encouraging private investment in urban renewal and environmental projects through covering with grant aid a proportion of the expenditure, should also be of relevance.

Two-thirds of the way through its ten-year span, the Glasgow Eastern Area Renewal project has achieved perhaps half of its remit. It has created the conditions for growth, but it has not yet produced the jobs, or not in sufficient numbers to overcome the effects of the very considerable job losses of the past seven years. It has something to teach us on the handling of large-scale urban renewal projects, as much through the mistakes of its first two years as the successes of its past five. But as unemployment has risen generally the likelihood of securing a general accord on giving a particular area the highest priority has diminished: the institutional arrangements which underpinned the GEAR do not exist in England, and resources are not available for further projects of its complexity and scale. In urban renewal there are no economies of scale, and it seems likely that the majority of future projects will be on a smaller compass.

Notes

1. Lythe, Charlotte and Majmudar, Madhavi, *The Renaissance of the Scottish Economy?*, George Allen and Unwin, London 1982, p. 188.
2. Parry, R., 'The Scottish Office' in Rose, Richard (ed.), *Territorial Ministries in British Government*, Oxford University Press, Oxford, forthcoming.
3. Evidence, pp. 310-1, qs. 754-5.
4. Evidence, pp. 311-2, qs. 762-3.
5. Evidence, p. 316, q. 789; pp. 313-4, q. 770.
6. *Scotsman*, 4 December 1982, leader.
7. Scottish Development Agency Act 1975.
8. Evidence, p. 318, q. 799.
9. Evidence, p. 330, q. 815.
10. Letter to *Sunday Standard*, 13 March 1983.
11. *New Statesman*, 19 May 1983, supplement, p. vi.

12. Kellas, J. G. and Madgwick, P., 'Territorial Ministries: the Scottish and Welsh Offices' in Madgwick, P. and Rose, R. (eds.), *The Territorial Dimension in UK Politics*, Macmillan, London 1982.
13. GEAR publicity material produced by Scottish Development Agency.
14. SDA, *Annual Review of GEAR*, Glasgow 1982.
15. Boyle, R. M. and Wannop, U. A., 'Area Initiatives and the SDA: the Rise of the Urban Project', *Fraser of Allander Institute Quarterly Economic Commentary*, vol. 8, no. 1, Glasgow 1982, p. 55.
16. Strathclyde Regional Council, *Strathclyde Regional Report*, 1976, paras. 9.3 and 9.21.
17. Scottish Office: press release September 1974, cited by Rt. Hon. Judith Hart MP, 18 January 1977 (Scottish Grand Committee).
18. OR, 12 May 1976, vol. 911, WA 194–5.
19. SDA, *Annual Report 1976*, para. 35.
20. SDA, *Annual Review of GEAR*, 1982.
21. Working Document on Organisation; unpublished.
22. Evidence, p. 309, q. 749; Strathclyde Regional Report, para. 4.4; Strathclyde Regional Council, *Urban Deprivation*, Glasgow 1976, pp. 37–40.
23. Cited in Booth, Pitt, and Money, 'Organisational Redundancy: a Critical Appraisal of the GEAR project', *Public Administration*, vol. 60, no. 2, spring 1982, p. 66.
24. Evidence, p. 295, q. 720.
25. Pressman, J. L. and Wildavsky, A. B., op. cit., pp. 87–124.
26. SDA, *Annual Report 1978*, pp. 47–8.
27. For example, Booth, Pitt, and Money, op. cit., p. 66.
28. SDA, *Annual Review of GEAR*, 1982, p. 9.
29. Quoted in SDA, *Annual Review of GEAR*, from which much of the information in the following sections is drawn.
30. SDA, *GEAR Project Report 1985*, Glasgow 1985.
31. SDA, *Annual Report 1981*, p. 50.
32. SDA, publicity material.
33. SDA, *GEAR Project Report 1985*, Glasgow 1985.
34. Ibid.
35. *Scotsman*, 26 October 1982.
36. SDA, *GEAR Project Report 1985*, op. cit.
37. Evidence, p. 310, q. 753.
38. Cited in Deloittes, Haskins, and Sells, R. Tym and Partners, *GEAR Review, Business Development and Employment Strategy*, SDA, Glasgow, October 1982.
39. SDA, *GEAR Project Report 1985*, op. cit.
40. *Scotsman*, 26 October 1982.
41. Deloittes, Haskins, and Sells, R. Tym and Partners, *GEAR Review, Business Development and Employment Strategy*, op. cit.

42. Booth, Pitt, and Money, op. cit., pp. 56–72.
43. Hogwood, B., *Implementation: Glasgow East End Project* Department of Politics, University of Strathclyde, Glasgow 1976, cited in Booth, Pitt, and Money, op. cit., p. 66.
44. Ibid., pp. 56 and 67. The invention of this term seems to owe a good deal to a desire to imitate my kinsman Tony Barker's *succès d'estime* with the word 'quango'. It is, however, hard to envisage Tory MPs going on mango hunts.
45. *Scotsman*, 11 January 1983.
46. Evidence, p. 326, memorandum submitted by City of Glasgow District Council, para. 8.
47. Interview, March 1983.
48. *Scotsman*, 11 January 1983.
49. SDA, *GEAR Project Report 1985*, op. cit.

7

Co-operation and Negotiation:
Area Intitiatives in Scotland (II)

1. The Task Forces: Glengarnock and Clydebank

Glengarnock

The second of the Agency's area initiatives was indeed on a smaller scale than the Glasgow Eastern Area Renewal project. Its objectives were narrowly defined as the replacement of the 800 jobs which would be lost through the closure of BSC's open-hearth furnaces and the run-down of other operations at Glengarnock in Ayrshire. But while the Task Force was smaller in scale and narrower in concept than the GEAR project, the Agency had clearly learnt a great deal from its experience as co-ordinator of GEAR and was able to bring this to bear in administering the Glengarnock Task Force. It is perhaps this which has led commentators to deduce that the Agency's later area initiatives spring from the GEAR project. Boyle and Wannop, for instance, suggest that 'GEAR laid the ground rules for a new style of local planning and development in urban areas ... Four years on, area projects were to figure prominently in the overall programme of the Agency'.[1] Others have suggested that the Task Force was in some way imposed on the Agency by the Scottish Office, giving rise to the risk that the SDA would become 'an agency for distressed areas rather than a force for growth and regeneration',[2] and would 'end up as a "fire brigade" for areas which were hit by major closures and be pushed into projects which it did not consider viable'.[3] As we shall see, neither of these suppositions stands up to examination.

If the origins of the Glengarnock Task Force are to be sought anywhere, they lie, not in GEAR, but in the White Paper of February 1973 on BSC's Ten Year Development Plan.[4] BSC had announced the previous June that open-hearth steel-making would be phased out and that other operations would be curtailed, and the White Paper proposed the appointment of Reconstruction Teams to stimulate economic activity in the closure areas. A team established by the Scottish Economic Planning Board considered two areas in particular—Glengarnock and Cambuslang—and made proposals for environmental and industrial recovery involving the clearance of derelict land, the development of light industry, and the provision of recreational facilities. Work at Glengarnock was to be carried out through a Technical Working Party whose membership would include officials of Ayr County Council, the Scottish Development Department, the Department of Trade and Industry, the Department of Employment, the Scottish Industrial Estates Corporation, and the British Steel Corporation. The working party would produce not only a development brief for the steelworks but also an 'action plan' for development to be undertaken in the short term.

Thus as early as 1973 there was recognition of the need for concerted action to tackle the problems arising from closure, involving both environmental recovery and industrial development, and using the powers and resources of a number of agencies whose work would be planned, if not co-ordinated, through a joint working party. The seeds of the Area Initiative had been planted, and two crucial elements were the concept that all the parties should be involved in the development of broad strategy for the area, and that closure should be followed by early action on the ground.

In the event, steel-making at Glengarnock was reprieved until the early 1980s under the Beswick proposals, and the working party met only once to commission a development brief from the County Council's planners. But the possibility of resuscitating it was kept under review, and interest was revived in 1978 when open-hearth steel-making at Glengarnock came under renewed threat. Because of the remoteness of the area, the importance of steel-making to its economy (the steelworks accounted for 50 per cent of manufacturing employment and 20 per cent of all employment in the local Employment Office Area), and unemployment of twice the national average even before the closure, it was seen as politically essential to alleviate the impact of closure. BSC (Industry) had indicated that it was prepared to give the highest priority to attracting new jobs to the area. But this task was severely hampered by the poor quality of the area's infrastructure.

Just as Glasgow's development had been constrained by its reliance on heavy industry, inhibiting other economic growth in the area,[5] so steel-making at Glengarnock, attracted originally by the proximity of iron ore deposits, had inhibited diversification and growth in the local economy. The run-down of activity had left large amounts of derelict and vacant land—about 100 acres was severely derelict and some 500 underused and available for development—and slag heaps and the open-hearth furnaces themselves dominated the head of the Kilbirnie loch. Road communications with the outside world were not good, though improvements were taking place, and further industrial activity of any kind was allegedly inhibited by the capacity of the Garnock Valley sewer, which had in the past held up industrial development in the valley.[6] There was, in short, a considerable amount of physical reconstruction to be done before new jobs could be attracted.

How best to advance this reconstruction? The Scottish Office's experience in the GEAR project, like the SDA's, had persuaded it of the desirability of securing the advance commitment of all the appropriate parties to a programme of action designed to overcome physical constraints on development and to promote economic activity. The fact that all the parties concerned had, in their present or past incarnations, been considering just such a possibility since 1973 encouraged such an approach. But it was not to be a lengthy and all-embracing exercise aimed at producing the ultimate solution to the problems of the area. It was to identify broad strategies for development only, and it was to report as quickly as possible.

A working party was accordingly convened, under Scottish Office chairmanship, on 30 August 1978; it reported on 31 October. It comprised officials from the Regional and District Councils, the British Steel Corporation, B S C Industry Ltd., the Scottish Development Agency, the Manpower Services Commission, the Scottish Economic Planning Department, and the Scottish Development Department. Its terms of reference required it to consider the impact of the steel run-down on employment in the area, assess development potential, consider steps to encourage further industrial development and other employment opportunities in the area, and 'outline a framework for a development strategy and indicate the priority for action by those bodies with a special interest in the area.'[7] The working party proposed action over the full range of environmental recovery, infrastructure investment, and industrial development. The Government and the SDA were to make funds available and give the highest priority to establishing new industry in the area. The SDA would build a new industrial estate with the potential for 500 jobs and assume responsibility for marketing existing vacant premises. There would be a major environmental recovery programme to tackle dereliction on the steelworks sites in the area, and steps would be taken to ensure that other activity to promote Scottish locations did not conflict with the drive to get industry to Glengarnock. Road improvements were to be advanced, and the link road with Glengarnock was to be upgraded. The detailed proposals were to be incorporated by Cunninghame District Council in a local plan for the Garnock Valley. Finally, and most importantly, a Task Force was to be set up by the Scottish Development Agency 'to take charge of the whole programme'.[8]

The working party envisaged that the Task Force would be small, having an SDA manager and other full-time staff either on secondment from the local authorities, BSC(I), and the Agency, or newly appointed. Their remit would be 'to ensure the purchase of any land necessary for the recommended development, to draw up a phased programme aimed at the earliest practicable completion of the industrial and environmental recovery programme, and to supervise the progress and implementation of such a plan'.[9] It would, as the Minister of State at the Scottish Office commented when announcing his acceptance of the proposals, have 'a strong co-ordinating hand' and 'be in a position to make things work'.[10] But the working party was clear that success would depend on the ready co-operation of all the parties: 'it would be essential', they write, 'that the local authorities and all the public and private agencies involved give the highest priority to carrying through the programme and co-operate fully with the Task Force'.[11] The fact that all the public agencies involved had participated in the working party and subscribed to its conclusions—the report stresses that the conclusions were unanimous[12]—was to be a powerful means of securing that co-operation.

As we have noted, it has been suggested by subsequent commentators that the Task Force was imposed as a 'fire brigade operation' for a distressed area. But the fire brigade had had at least six years notice that the fire would break out. Moreover, the area had potential as well as problems. It lies in attractive countryside; communications with the south and elsewhere could readily be improved; there was considerable scope for improving the environment and amenities of the local communities; and firms moving into the area would qualify for the highest rates of Regional Assistance, as well as support from the European Coal and Steel Community. The working party concluded its report by emphasising its belief that 'this area has considerable potential for redevelopment if the problems are tackled with vigour and determination'.[13] The Agency were not being sold a hopeless case.

Moreover, the Agency had itself begun to realise the opportunity which its own combination of powers gave it to tackle the problems of areas like Glengarnock, and its capacity, as a body at one remove from the political process, to bring together and co-ordinate the work of the other actors on the urban recovery stage. This realisation made an important contribution to the development of the Task Force. A report in the *Scotsman* written five years after the event gives the romantic view of what happened. A series of meetings, it suggests, held in St Andrew's House in Edinburgh, determined that something should be done. But no one was sure what until, driving back from one fruitless meeting, 'Edward Cunningham, director of planning and local projects, laid back and said: "What we need is some form of . . . task force." After that remark, things began to gel.'[14] In fact, given all the work which had already taken place, the participants in the Glengarnock working party had a pretty clear idea of what needed to be done. The problem was the mechanism for achieving it; and here the SDA's contribution was vital.

The Task Force, a 'small and fast-moving group of people', began work almost immediately and established itself in Kilbirnie in January 1979. As in the GEAR initiative, much attention was paid to involving the local community in its work, and the Task Force office doubled as administrative headquarters and information centre. As in GEAR, moreover, an early action programme was initiated while the details of the Task Force's strategy were fleshed out. This involved construction of advance factories, clearance of some of the more obtrusive dereliction at the lochside, the establishment of a New Business Centre by the District Council, marketing of redundant premises by B S C Industry Ltd., and the co-ordination of promotional work.

The strategy was defined in a detailed document published in June 1979, *Garnock Valley Development: The Strategy for Action 1979–83*.[15] The authors had a clear idea of the importance of their work to the development of an area-based approach to economic development, and note that'the Garnock Valley Project has afforded the Agency an opportunity to develop a new approach to community economic development'.[16] This approach, they suggested, had two main characteristics, organisational and procedural. First, it employed for the first time a style of operation 'which identifies it strongly with the project area and by being resident in the area provides an organisational structure which is close to the ground and essentially practical'. Secondly, it involved a 'threshold' approach under which the Agency's resources were committed only until particular targets of performance had been achieved. This would prevent the Agency becoming permanently locked into an area and 'becoming heavily and permanently involved in a large number of community development projects elsewhere in Scotland'—a problem which was subsequently to concern them in relation to the development of area initiatives.

The 'threshold' approach involved the definition of targets of performance much more sophisticated than the broad—and some might say ill-defined—proposals of the working party. The overall objective defined for the Task Force made explicit what was implicit in the working party report: it was 'to prevent the decline of the local community by implementing both economic and physical development programmes to set in motion a process of regeneration'.[17] Thus the fundamental aim of the five-year development strategy defined for the Task Force was 'to restructure the local economy in order to prevent decline'.[18] The attainment of that aim was to be assessed through a number of objective measures.

First, a target population was proposed for the Garnock Valley for 1983 of at least the same proportion of the population of Cunninghame District Council as a whole as had subsisted in 1979. Secondly, the resident-based unemployment rate should be no higher in 1983 relative to that of Strathclyde Region than it had been in December 1978 immediately prior to the closure of the melt shop (the relative had, in fact, risen from 80 in December 1978 to 137 in January 1979). To achieve this improvement it was calculated, thirdly, that 800 jobs required to be created by December 1983, of which 250 might be in existing firms and 550 in new ones; this, fourthly, would require development of 200,000 square feet of factory space. Training would be necessary to improve the competitiveness of local labour; in particular, steps should be taken in concert with the Manpower Services Commission to increase the availability of apprentice training in the area.

To underpin such action to promote economic recovery it was proposed that there should be a major programme of environmental recovery and infrastructure development. The strategy attached considerable importance to road communications; it was also recognised that it was necessary to ensure 'that supporting infrastructure services are available as required', and in particular that constraints were not imposed by water and sewerage capacities.[19] Finally, there was a nod in the direction of the social development of the area, although it was made clear that 'the problems in the Garnock Valley are fundamentally economic and so far there has been no clear evidence that the local community is particularly demoralised'.[20]

The Garnock Valley Task Force thus entailed close involvement of the Agency and other statutory bodies at the local level, local administration, leadership by a non-political public body, a heavy concentration on public sector solutions, and clearly defined objectives leading to withdrawal of the Agency when certain thresholds in terms of population, unemployment, and the completion of defined environmental improvement programmes had been attained. It is instructive to consider what the Task Force has achieved, to what extent its performance measures remain relevant at a time of increasing unemployment nationally, and whether it is open to the charge of 'organisational redundancy' against which it was necessary to defend the GEAR project.

At first sight the achievements of the Task Force seem impressive. By March 1983 considerable impact had been made in the Garnock Valley in terms of both the regeneration of the physical environment and the provision of infrastructure; physical constraints on economic development had largely been removed; and the large scale dereliction which inhibited the attraction of new jobs had been treated. The Agency had spent £14.2m. out of a total budget of £19m.; it had completed or had under construction 68 factory units providing a total of 371,000 square feet; had completed or had in hand environmental improvement schemes to a value of £3.9m.; and it had attracted 800 business and property enquiries, resulting in 50 new companies and a total of 1,000 jobs created or provided for. The *Scotsman* reported Peter Stott, the Agency's local manager, as making 'the ambitious forecast that some 2000 jobs will be created'.[21]

In short, then, the original job targets of the 1979 strategy for action had been achieved, and the factory building targets had been achieved twice over. At the same time, the area's environment had been transformed and infrastructure constraints had been removed. But the training objectives were forgotten: as elsewhere, the MSC was preoccupied with the attainment of its national objectives in the face of increasing unemployment overall, and significant special treatment for the Garnock Valley did not emerge. The population target was forgotten, too, though it is questionable whether such targets are appropriate as a measure of the success of policies to secure economic recovery. And unemployment in the area remained high. Since the establishment of the Task Force, further redundancies had affected employment levels in the Valley, and the SDA estimated in 1982 that 1,000 more jobs were required in addition to those already in the pipeline merely to reduce unemployment to the level experienced elsewhere in the region.[22] The attainment of a lower level of unemployment than in the region as a whole, as was proposed in the employment target, seems beyond the realms of present possibility.

On the analysis of Booth, Pitt, and Money, the failure to achieve the employment target would be cited as a justification for extending the life of the Task Force. The Scottish Development Agency did not, however, envisage that the organisation should remain in being beyond the end of 1983. The inability of the Task Force to perpetuate itself may be ascribed to a number of factors. The establishment within the Scottish Development Agency of an Area Development Directorate (see below) has given scope for advancement to the Agency's area-based staff unrelated to the continuation of their role in any particular area. The Glengarnock Strategy for Action contained clear goals and thresholds for withdrawal of the Task Force, together with a recognition that targets might require to be adjusted. In the event it became clear that the Task Force's work was primarily a matter of physical recovery; when that was achieved a different organisation might appropriately carry on the work of economic renewal. Hence the Agency decided in early 1983 that the Task Force should be wound up. Peter Stott is quoted as saying 'we have got the patient out of intensive care, and he has to go back to the usual ward now'.[23] In

April 1984 the Task Force was replaced by a local self-help Enterprise Agency, the Garnock Valley Development Executive, established with Agency support to carry on the work. Its co-sponsors are the Regional and District Councils and B S C Industry Ltd., who played an important part in the work of the Task Force, together with two private sector companies, General Accident and the Clydesdale Bank. Besides providing the same kind of business advice services and financial support as other enterprise trusts, the Glengarnock Executive has invested £200,000 in small workshops.

Clydebank

Clydebank, too, required a considerable amount of physical renewal. The town's economy was dominated by manufacturing (in 1976 56 per cent of its employees were in the manufacturing sector by comparison with 30 per cent in Scotland as a whole) and in particular by a small number of externally owned manufacturing enterprises, all of which shed labour throughout the 1970s. Between 1971 and 1976 the town had suffered a fall of 25 per cent in manufacturing employment compared with 9 per cent in Scotland as a whole.[24]

By mid-1979 the town's economy was in crisis. In May Goodyear closed its tyre plant in nearby Drumchapel, following rejection (and subsequent belated acceptance) by the workforce of manning reductions and changes in working patterns: of the 675 employees who lost their jobs, many came from Clydebank. Singer, which in its heyday had employed 16,000 on its 87-acre site, announced in March a rescue programme which would slim its remaining 5,000 workforce to 3,000; in October, the company announced the complete closure of the facility by June 1980.[25] John Brown Engineering Ltd. was also struggling against international trading conditions, and in November announced 600 redundancies. In addition, the Marathon Manufacturing Company of Houston, which had with difficulty been rescued before the 1979 election by the placing of a speculative oil rig order by SEPD and the British National Oil Corporation, had announced its intention to withdraw completely from the former John Brown Shipbuilding Yard, birthplace of the Queens and focus of the Upper Clyde Shipbuilders work-in.

The difficulties at Marathon—and its sensitivity in view of its place in West of Scotland labour mythology—had caused the previous Labour government to give some thought to the possibility of establishing a Glengarnock type of operation in Clydebank, and there was considerable pressure from the Clydebank Campaign on Employment (on which the SDA was represented) for something to be done. In the event, attention was diverted to the rescue of the company, and the departmental officials responsible for what became known as 'task-forcery' were themselves heavily engaged on the rescue. So it was the crisis at Singers which was the immediate prompt for the establishment by the Conservative government of the Working Party on Employment in the Clydebank Area, which first met on 9 October under the chairmanship of the Chief Economic Adviser at the Scottish Office.

The working party, and the subsequent Task Force, followed very much the model established in Glengarnock, and it is unnecessary to pursue their history in detail. As in Glengarnock, the working party included representatives of the central government departments most closely concerned together with the Regional Council, the two District Councils of Clydebank and Glasgow, and the Scottish Development Agency. Like the Glengarnock working party it was asked to report in a short time (by the end of the year), and as in Glengarnock its function was seen as the identification of the 'main problems—physical, economic, social and ad-ministrative—standing in the way of a restoration of balance in the local labour market'; the preparation of 'the main elements of a strategy to begin to reduce these problems'; and the creation of 'appropriate machinery to refine and implement the strategy'.[26]

The working party identified a mix of environmental and economic problems, although infrastructure (apart from the avai-lability of premises for small and medium-sized firms) was not seen as a difficulty, and the area's reputation for poor industrial relations, which the working party thought unwarranted, was singled out for specific action. Hence the working party produced a mix of proposals for remedial action, including improved promotion of the area by the SDA and SEPD, examination of the area's products and markets to identify opportunities for expansion, and development of a range of sites and premises to accommodate small and medium-sized firms. It proposed that steps should be taken to secure the release of land in the ownership of the nationalised industries. The Manpower Services Commission should seek not only to place redundant workers from the Singer plant, but should review its training provision, and perhaps provide special training in vacant premises, 'recruiting redundant skilled workers as instructors'.[27] Consideration should be given to the establishment of an Enterprise Fund to provide risk capital for small firms and, if there was to be an experiment in Enterprise Zones, the claims of Clydebank to be designated as Scotland's zone should be sympathetically considered.

The working party did not propose organisational innovations. As in Glengarnock, a Task Force was to be established by the Scottish Development Agency 'led by an SDA official who would devote himself full time to his work'.[28] Interestingly enough, it was suggested that the SDA should collaborate with SEPD in considering whether any lessons were to be learnt from GEAR to improve the SDA's effectiveness in Clydebank. Little came of that suggestion: the true model of the proposed operation was Glengarnock, and the main lessons of GEAR had already been acted upon through the development of a broad strategy to which all the parties were committed before the establishment of the Task Force. Difficulties could indeed have arisen through the involvement of two district councils: the Task Force area included the former Goodyear factory on the Glasgow side of the District boundary. But Glasgow's involvement at the formative stage (it was represented on the working party by its Chief Executive Designate), together with the recognition that because of the openness of the Clydebank labour market developments there were likely to benefit residents of Western Glasgow, avoided problems of organisational conflict. Arrangements were made to liaise with the Clydebank District Council by means of day to day contacts with officials and three-monthly formal reporting meetings at political level, and a close rapport was established.[29]

The Clydebank Task Force, then, established itself in premises in Clydebank in March 1980 with the task of regenerating the local economy, broadening its economic base, attracting further private sector investment, and improving the environment to attract inward investment. In July 1980, as we have seen, the District Councils were invited to submit an application for the creation of the Clydebank Enterprise Zone, and the zone was designated on 3 August 1981. The Agency regarded the Enterprise Zone as a valuable marketing tool; even before designation the prospect of enterprise zone benefits had a marked impact on the attractiveness of the area. It has been a matter of debate, however, whether designation or the establishment of the Task Force have had the greater impact on Clydebank's economic fortunes. We argued above that, without the very considerable investment in infrastructure overseen and co-ordinated by the Task Force, the Enterprise Zone would have been very much less successful than it has been. The Provost of Clydebank, by contrast, attributes much of the Task Force's success in attracting new firms to the area to the existence of enterprise zone benefits. The fact is that is that both the benefits and the Task Force have worked in the same direction to the advantage of the area.

Wherever the major credit should go, it is clear that the local economy has undergone a remarkable transformation. Environmental improvement, and industrial estate development, including the redevelopment of the Singer site as the Clydebank Business Park, did much to raise morale in the area, as did the attraction of over 140 companies to premises in the area by mid-1983, with the creation of some 600–700 jobs and a potential of some 1,500 jobs by 1985. In the event, 285 new companies had been attracted by March 1985, with some 3,000 jobs created or provided for. The reliance of the economy on outside firms has been somewhat reduced, and the economy has been diversified through the attraction of service and office employment. Private sector investment is being attracted: John Brown Engineering has developed an office block in the area for its own use; Radio Clyde has moved its studios and head office into the Business Park; and Natwest funded a speculative office development in the same location. In 1984–5 three further private sector companies invested in purpose-built accommodation in the area. The Clydebank Enterprise Fund, developed on the recommendation of the working party with funding from the Bank of Scotland and the SDA, had by January 1983 offered loans totalling some £200,000 to 16 ventures,[30] and has continued its work subsequently. The overall effect has been a rebuilding of the town's self-confidence. It is not too much to say that the Task Force has made Clydebank competitive with the New Towns.

Nevertheless considerable difficulties remain. Unemployment continues to be high, and while too much store should not be placed on the local unemployment figures given the considerable amount of commuting to and from the area (the 1981 census showed that only 50 per cent of Clydebank residents in employment worked in the Burgh, and just over half of the jobs in the Burgh were held by non-residents[31]), this does reflect a serious situation. It is simply not possible to isolate Clydebank from the effects of the recession; and the Director of Planning for Clydebank has commented on the high failure rate of new small firms setting up in this area. More requires to be done, moreover, to attract private investment into the area: SDA rental concessions can inhibit private sector factory building, and it was necessary to attract investment from Natwest by offering it a rental guarantee. As elsewhere, it has proved difficult to develop training programmes directed to the needs of local inhabitants and the potential needs of incoming firms, and proposals to second an MSC official to the Task Force foundered because of staffing constraints within the Commission. What can be said, however, is that Clydebank is poised to benefit from an upturn in economic activity in terms of credibility, morale, and attractiveness to potential investors. The Task Force has rebuilt the image of the town, and in that lies the key to the rebuilding of its economy. As Tony Worthington, councillor for North Clydebank on the Regional Council, observes, 'This is a turning point in the town's history. Within five years we'll see the whole town transformed into an entirely different looking animal. Almost every aspect of Clydebank is changing ... it's on its second hundred years in a completely different shape and that takes a lot of faith.'[32] That faith has been generated to a considerable degree by the Clydebank Task Force. But are there any general lessons to learn from the operations of the Scottish Task Forces?

Appraisal

First, one must consider the possibility that the Task Forces have simply confused matters; that they have achieved nothing that would not have been achieved anyway; that they have been unnecessarily imposed on pre-existing organisations: that they are, in short, 'mangos'. This possibility may be readily rejected. A considerable amount of economic activity has been stimulated in Glengarnock and Clydebank. Much of this can be attributed to the activity of the Task Forces, which in effect are means of focusing the powers and resources of the SDA on specific areas and of harnessing those of other relevant bodies; they are not cosmetic. The fact that Clydebank was, in its early stages, the most effective of the first round of Enterprise Zones is telling. The Task Forces have moreover worked harmoniously with the other organisations concerned. In the case of Glengarnock, the two organisations which provided staff for the Task Force—the SDA and BSC(I)—have worked closely together to the attainment of mutually agreed objectives. At Clydebank, close relationships were established at both official and political level between the Task Force and the District Councils. Clear goals were established, if not from the outset, at least early on in the life of the projects, and in the case of Glengarnock were sensibly adjusted. While the staff of the Task Forces have retained their allegiance to their parent organisations, remoteness from headquarters and, in the case of Glengarnock, the spartan accommodation which they shared in the early days of the project soon forged an *esprit de corps* and commitment to the Task Force objectives. The Task Forces are lean and non-hierarchical bodies, working in an entrepreneurial mode and reducing the need for clearances to a minimum. In short, they seem an effective mechanism for securing physical renewal and economic growth.

Nevertheless, the establishment of a Task Force is not a universal solution to economic problems or industrial closures. The bringing together within the SDA of many of the powers relevant to physical and economic renewal is essential to their mode of operation; it could not be duplicated in England without major institutional change. Even within Scotland, the Task Force is costly in terms of resources and, to a lesser extent, of skilled manpower; it is not practicable to manage more than a few at any particular time. Also, a Task Force operation is most appropriate when there is a major job of physical renewal to be done: the Scottish Office resisted calls for the establishment of a Task Force at Linwood precisely because the Chrysler closure did not call for such a response.

The two Scottish Task Forces have, however, been to some extent 'a model for the Agency's work in the rest of Scotland'.[33] This they have been in both a positive and a negative sense. On the positive side, they have confirmed the desirability of securing the commitment of the relevant bodies to an overall recovery strategy and involving the local community in its development and implementation. They have emphasised the benefits of a relatively narrow remit; in this respect the environmental and economic objectives of the Task Forces contrast with the very much broader social goals of GEAR. And they have provided a paradigm for local implementation through the establishment of a small organisation of not more than half a dozen staff, based in the locality but with access to significant powers and resources.

There have also been lessons on the negative side. The Task Forces were, in a sense, imposed on the Agency by political fiat, and the Agency was at risk of becoming victim of its own success. While both Clydebank and Glengarnock had potential as well as problems, there was a possibility that the Agency would be asked to tackle problems where a Task Force approach was inappropriate. Hence it seemed desirable in some way to distance the development and operation of area initiatives from the political process. Secondly, difficulties were experienced in negotiating the withdrawal from Glengarnock, and it became apparent that it would be desirable to set a time-scale on the Agency's operations from the outset despite the initial attractiveness of performance targets and thresholds. Thirdly, liaison with the other bodies concerned was a matter for constant attention: Clydebank District Council complained, for example, that while day to day contacts continued to be close and effective, there was by 1982 too little contact on matters of broad strategy.[34] Fourthly, it became apparent that expectations could be raised too high: at the outset there was, perhaps, too little recognition of the close symbiosis between the performance of the national economy and that of the areas which Task Forces sought to help. Finally, it was recognised that more could be done to harness the resources and skills of the private sector: the extent of the Agency's involvement might indeed inhibit private sector activity in some areas.

At the time of writing, it seems most unlikely that further Task Forces as such will be established in Scotland. The Agency has moved to a more planned and directed approach to local economic development, and by developing arrangements to detect likely crises in advance it has greater scope to plan action to avert them or alleviate their effects. But the lessons of Glengarnock and Clydebank influenced the Agency in its consideration, not simply of measures to assist particular areas, but of its whole corporate approach; and it was this which led to the development of the Integrated Project.

2. Towards an Integrated Approach

Origins of the Integrated Project

At first sight, an Integrated Project is difficult to distinguish from a Task Force, except perhaps in its genesis. Both spring from a crisis in the local economy; both aim to stimulate economic recovery through a combined attack on environmental and economic constraints and through providing assistance to new and expanding firms; both involve the collaboration of a number of public sector bodies. In fact, there are very significant differences, and the new type of project developed not only from the SDA's experience of the benefits of Task Forces, but also from its concerns at the direction in which 'task-forcery' might lead it.

In part these concerns reflected a preference for a planned role, a preference which is readily explicable given the interests and qualifications of the SDA's staff and its relative insulation from the political process. But they reflected also the Agency's worry that a Task Force operation might be wished upon it for an area which in its judgement lacked economic potential, or that it might be asked to establish such operations in greater numbers than its resources could sustain. It was keen, moreover, to develop more precise and definitive mechanisms for locking the local authorities into area projects; in particular, it was anxious to secure appropriate action on social and environmental matters. (Significantly, the local authorities were themselves seeking to lock the SDA into initiatives in their areas: in December 1981, for instance, Strathclyde Regional Council announced, with no prior consultation, twelve area initiatives costing £300m. (of which £200m. was to be provided by the SDA), to tackle environmental, economic, and social disadvantage in hard-hit parts of the Region.[35]) But, most important, experience in GEAR, Glengarnock, and Clydebank had convinced the Agency of the relevance of its unique combination of powers to an integrated approach to local economic problems. This was, in fact, to cause it to reappraise the whole thrust of its corporate strategy.

This reappraisal took place in the course of 1980-1. The Agency's annual report for 1980 gives area initiatives short shrift: the bulk of the report describes industrial investment and factory building policies, and the final chapter, 'A Green and Pleasant Land', is concerned largely with general environmental improvement and puts 'restoring older city areas' second to last and 'special places and cases' (i.e. Glengarnock and Clydebank) last. The report does, however, make a genuflection towards a corporate and collaborative approach to area redevelopment, noting that 'the Agency is involved in several projects in which, by integrating its own wide powers with those of the private sector, it attempts to revive deprived areas'.[36]

The tone of the 1981 report is entirely different. In a passage entitled 'The Agency and the Future' the authors note that the SDA intends to concentrate on

certain local economies identified as clearly performing below their potential. The Agency will adopt a planned and selective approach and will focus resources on identified areas in order to achieve specified objectives within a defined period. Emphasis will be placed on economic and industrial regeneration and the crucial criterion in the selection of areas will be their potential for . . . improved performance . . . The principal mechanism will be the Integrated Project in which the Agency will take an initiative of limited duration under a programme of specified industrial and other activities agreed with the appropriate local authorities and in which the Agency will seek complementary private sector support.[37]

In the meantime, the Agency had entered into agreements for Integrated Projects at Leith (concluded in May 1981) and Dundee, Blackness (concluded in October). In addition, its Corporate Plan for 1981–2 to 1983–4 added to the Agency's defined aims of developing Scottish entrepreneurship, supporting growth sectors, promoting new technology, and improving industrial efficiency and competitiveness a further aim, 'the regeneration of local economies'. Over time, it was suggested, this function should be built up to account for 60 per cent of the Agency's expenditure in the field.[38]

The Integrated Project is, then, a collaborative approach to area development. Its overall aim may be seen as the generation of 'self-sustaining economic development';[39] and its objectives include the creation of jobs to reduce unemployment, improving residents' access to jobs, increasing the level of private investment and of business activity, and upgrading the physical appearance of an area.[40] It involves, in the first place, the negotiation of a Project Agreement with the Regional and District Councils, based on a study of the area's problems and potential and setting out the commitments and responsibilities of each party and the scope for collaboration with other bodies such as BSC(I) or the Scottish Tourist Board. There are 'specific targets over a stated period'[41] (normally envisaging withdrawal by the SDA after three to five years) involving concerted action in a narrowly defined area in terms both of geography and of approach. During the negotiations the SDA typically undertakes an 'early action programme' of environmental recovery and factory building to demonstrate its commitment to the area: this does not, however, form part of the project agreement.

To carry forward the project the Agency generally establishes a team in the area including local authority and sometimes private sector representatives as well (although, as we shall see, others take the lead in the so-called 'self help initiatives'). In the words of its 1982 annual report, 'the Agency operates by placing a small team led by a project manager in an office within the project area for an agreed period, usually three years, where it works for the economic regeneration of that area. Each team identifies strongly with its constituents, hence its physical presence there.'[42]

The team works on a mix of promotion, advice, and support for business, physical renewal, factory building, and letting: in short, the whole range of SDA activities. In addition, the local authority participants are expected to contribute through their responsibilities for infrastructure and for social services generally, in order to achieve 'an overall regeneration of the area which will make it a place where people wish to invest, live and work'.[43]

Organisational Implications

The development of the Integrated Project involved organisational innovations for the SDA at both headquarters and local level. The SDA's new corporate approach was reflected at headquarters in the establishment, from 11 January 1982, of an Area Development Directorate. This involved the merger of the Agency's Urban Renewal Division—formerly responsible for GEAR, Leith, and Motherwell—with the Special Development Unit of the Environment Directorate, which had run the Glengarnock and Clydebank Task Forces. The Directorate's functions are the management and co-ordination of the SDA's programmes in the Project Areas, and involve developing management arrangements for the areas, securing an appropriate input from elsewhere in the Agency and from other bodies, and monitoring progress. The majority of the Directorate's staff are located in offices in the project areas.

It is of note that the new Directorate's role is one of implementation. The initial identification of possible Project Areas,
examination of their potential (if necessary with the help of
consultants), and negotiations with the local authorities are undertaken by the Programmes and Planning Directorate, to which has
been added an Area Programmes Development Division. It is a
moot point whether this split between design and implementation
is beneficial. On the one hand, it limits the potential tension
between the Area Development Directorate and the other functional
Directorates of the Agency: an Area Development Directorate
which was responsible also for planning such initiatives might be
just too powerful, and a separate Planning Directorate can assist
the reconciliation of views on priorities, as well as being in a
position to take a relatively objective view. On the other hand, the
Planning Division may be hampered by lack of direct experience
of implementation, and the Division's experience of negotiating
individual projects might be of use in their execution; policy analysts
stress the importance of binding policy development together with
execution. It is likely that the present distribution of responsibilities
in the Agency owes as much to personalities as it does to any
objective view about the most efficient distribution of responsibilities. But there are close informal contacts between the two
Directorates. The Development Manager of the Dundee Project,
indeed, came from the Programmes and Planning Directorate,
where he was responsible for the pre-planning of the project.

Innovation at local level involved the secondment of local
authority and private sector personnel to work on the Project. The
Glengarnock Task Force, as we have seen, was staffed entirely by
personnel from the SDA and BSC(I), and Clydebank entirely by
the Agency. In Leith, by contrast, the Regional and District
Councils have each funded a part-time officer to join the team,
primarily to work on aspects of the Project which are the
responsibility of their parent authority. The Agency's three members
spring from the Area Development Directorate, the Small Business
Division, and the Factory Policy Division.[44]

In Dundee, to date the most elaborate of the Area Initiatives,
the Project Team consisted in mid-1983 of three SDA staff, one of
them part-time, two part-time staff from the District Council, one

part-time and one full-time secondee from the Region, two private sector personnel, and a secondee from Dundee University. The head of the Project Team had overall responsibility for the Project's execution and for securing appropriate contributions from the participants. He was a member of the SDA's Area Development Directorate who before posting to Dundee was head of the Glengarnock Task Force, where he gained wide experience of both Agency and Local Authority roles in economic regeneration. He was supported by a full-time Development Manager from the Area Development Directorate and by a part-time Development Officer from the SDA's Industrial Services Division, who had specific responsibility for the company development programme. The full-time member from the Regional Council and one of the District's part-timers were responsible for co-ordinating and drawing together the contributions of their authorities. While, for instance, the Regional Council member was not himself a Chief Officer, he nevertheless chaired regular meetings of the Council's Chief Officers in order to concert the inputs of their divisions. The part-time member from the Region, who came from the Tayside Regional Industrial Office (TRIO), assisted in marketing and promotion, while the other District member was primarily responsible for promotion of tourism and conference facilities and the District's industrial support services.

The Project Agreement specified that 'private sector secondees shall be sought to work with and within the Project Team', in particular on 'joint venture and licensing searches, company diversification, funding and advisory programmes'.[45] The two private sector personnel joined the team in early April 1983. One concentrated on the financing of new ventures, including development of an enterprise fund; the other was responsible for high technology projects, licensing deals, and joint ventures (which are becoming increasingly popular with the SDA because they avoid many of the risks associated with branch factories). The university secondee had the dual role of seeking commercial applications for the products of university research and encouraging Dundee colleges to meet the training needs of companies already established in Dundee and of potential newcomers. The Project's Training and Education Development Group, for which he was responsible, was working on two initiatives in particular: a technological awareness programme, and a skill-training service for US companies.[46]

Deliberate steps were thus taken to meld together the various aspects of the project within the Project Team. But that was not all. Superimposed on the Project Team is a steering committee to oversee strategy, review progress, and agree programmes. The Project Agreement requires this committee to meet at least quarterly. Its chairman is the Agency's Deputy Chairman (a distinguished Dundee businessman); the other members are the SDA's Director of Estates and Environment and its Deputy Director of Area Development, and one elected member and one official from both Region and District. In addition, the Agreement specified that four other representatives were to be appointed by the Agency with the approval of the Region and the District to cover private sector and trade union interests;[47] in the event the managing directors of two large firms and one small firm in the area and the district organiser of one of the larger unions were appointed. Thus the local authorities and other interested parties are closely involved not only in the execution of the Project, but also in the development of strategy.

In the organisational arrangements established for the Integrated Projects we have, then, to use Keating's term, a 'framework' in which the problems of conflicting priorities both within and between organisations can be resolved.[48] At the intra-organisational level, the SDA has developed a corporate approach to its activities and is encouraging local authorities to work on similar lines. Between organisations, there is joint involvement in policy-making, both at the negotiating stage and thereafter, and there is joint involvement in implementation. We shall consider below the effectiveness of this framework in resolving conflict. Perhaps the body least affected has been the Scottish Office. Even here, however, there is, as we have seen, much closer collaboration between SEPD and SDD on such matters than there is between DI, DOE, and DE. The responsibility for area initiatives and regional policy was brought together in one division of SEPD (now IDS) in January 1982. And the arm's-length relationship of the Scottish Office to the area initiatives, noted by Keating, does reduce the possibility of conflicts on priorities within and outside the office. Distance does breed content.

The Project Agreement
The Project Agreement is at the heart of the Integrated Project, and it is worthwhile examining their negotiation and subject-matter in some detail. As we have seen, negotiation is generally preceded

by a consultancy study, commissioned by the SDA, to identify the area's problems and potential. Local authorities have complained that, too often, such studies are over-general or simply regurgitate facts and opinions only too well known to the people on the ground,[49] but an independent view is necessary background to the negotiations: the local authorities are, after all, in one sense supplicants for a Project. With the help of the study, the Plans and Programmes Division of the Agency seeks to define constraints and opportunities, delineate the project area, and estimate the resources needed for remedial action. The negotiations with the local authorities are designed to secure agreement on a package of measures to be undertaken by the participants in order to generate sustainable economic growth in the area. The Project Agreement details such measures and the action to be taken by each of the parties, and specifies 'financial commitments, support activities, organisational arrangements, performance targets and a definition of roles, including private sector participation'.[50] It also defines who is to take the lead in the Project, and, in cases where the lead is taken by the SDA, the arrangements for it to phase out its leadership role, on a defined time-scale, and hand over responsibility to the local authorities. In other words, the Project Agreements are a paradigm of the policy cycle, and pay appropriate attention to each element in it. They involve (*a*) a decision to decide on the establishment of a project; (*b*) a decision how to decide; (*c*) a definition of the problems to be tackled; (*d*) the setting of objectives and targets; (*e*) arrangements for implementation and control; (*f*) means of evaluation and review; and (*g*) arrangements for termination.[51] In this respect, the Integrated Projects represent a considerable advance on the Task Forces, which were truncated in the first two stages, well developed in the definition of the problem and the arrangements for implementation and control, and less than fully satisfactory in the setting of targets, means of evaluation, and, in particular, termination.

The Integrated Projects themselves have, nevertheless, developed over time, particularly in relation to the breadth of the project and the nature of the local authority involvement. A comparison of the Agreements for the Leith Project (signed in May 1981) and the Dundee Project (signed in November 1982) makes the point clear. The focus of the Leith Project is 'business development'. The target is to 'create and safeguard' 800 jobs, primarily in manufacturing.

The objectives of the programme, which has a budget of £7m., include, in addition, assisting Leith residents to gain access to jobs and improving the environment; but both of these appear to have very much a subsidiary role: as paragraph 6 of the Agreement puts it, 'to support the main economic thrust, the project will also include some physical development works as well as housing, social and community programmes'.[52]

The £24m. Dundee Project is far more ambitious. Starting life as an exercise to revitalise the waterfront area of the city on lines akin to the Blackness Project (a small-scale project designed to regenerate a mixed tenemental and industrial area near the city centre), it grew into nothing less than a major attempt to revitalise the economic life of the city. The project was designed to 'integrate and co-ordinate the existing activities of the Agency in Dundee and will initiate a new development momentum in the city based upon technology industries, and aligned to the training, infrastructure, skills and locational attributes of Dundee'. The target was the creation of 1,200 jobs over three years, together with the es-tablishment of sufficient momentum to lead to a further 3,500 jobs in the following five years.[53]

This ambitious target was to be achieved through the development of a high technology park, training initiatives, the preparation of city centre sites for hotel, recreational, and commercial users, and intensive promotional efforts aimed at encouraging tourism and conferences, attracting overseas business, and stimulating oil-related developments (which hitherto had largely passed Dundee by, for reasons both of industrial history and of geography).

The Dundee Project was, then, of far greater scope than that at Leith in terms of area, finance, and objectives. But it shared the basic economic orientation of the Leith Project; there was none of the all-embracing universality of GEAR. Even the training initiative was presented, not in terms of improving residents' access to jobs, but in terms of 'the precise training requirements of individual companies', which would be met in the main through the use of local authority and European Community resources; the MSC was not envisaged as playing a significant role.

The Project Agreements for Leith and Dundee differ also in the extent to which they define the local authorities' commitment to the project. Perhaps inevitably, given the emphasis on business development, the Leith Project imposed the greater burden on the

SDA, which, apart from administrative costs, was committed to spend up to £7m. over three years on provision of sites and premises (£5m.), financial assistance to firms (£1m.), and environmental treatment (£1m.). No price tag was put on the contributions of the Region and the District, and much of the support required of them consisted in consultation on their statutory activities. Partly because of dissatisfaction at the one-sided nature of this agreement—the local authorities could criticise the SDA's contribution, but were insulated from such criticism themselves—later agreements were far more specific about the contribution of the local authorities. Thus the Agency's £18m. expenditure on the Dundee Project was matched by a commitment by the Region to spend £5.5m. over the four years 1982–3 to 1985–6, covering road developments and access (£3.6m.), support for site developments and improvements to the railway station (£0.7m.), external servicing of the Technology Park (£1m.), and provision of a sewer (£0.2m.). While no additional finance was provided by central government to help the Region meet this commitment, the Region adjusted its programmes to accord with the Project's priorities. The District, by contrast, came off fairly lightly, partly perhaps because of its ambiguous attitude to the Project during the negotiations: while it was anxious to secure additional resources from the SDA, it wished to retain the lead itself in economic and industrial development in Dundee. Thus its commitment was a mere £0.5m. on unspecified land acquisition, servicing, and support work, a commitment against which much of its normal expenditure would score.

By mid-1985 the integrated projects in Leith and Dundee had made substantial progress. In Leith, during the initial three years of the Project some £6m. of public funding for environmental improvement, industrial promotion, and business development stimulated over £25m. worth of private investment, and the project was extended for a further two years to 1986. Of particular note has been the willingness of private sector developers to take on the role of providing factory premises, the refurbishment of older buildings for private housing, the development of small workshops, and the attraction of high technology and media-related companies to the area. By March 1985, 124 new companies had established themselves in the Project Area, and 1,450 jobs had been created or provided for.[54]

The Dundee Project faced a broader challenge; hardly surprisingly, set against the overall problems of the city, progress has been slower than in Leith. The Project Team is seeking to promote strategic change in the city's economy, and is placing a special emphasis on high technology developments and tourism. Thus the Project's Technology Initiative is designed to assist existing companies to capitalise on technological change through education, training, and technological awareness. The Dundee Technology Park aims to provide an attractive environment for high technology companies, and has already had some significant successes in attracting investment from such companies. The Project has, in addition, identified the potential for Dundee to provide significant tourist activity, and, as elsewhere, the Project Team, together with the Dundee Industrial Association (the local Enterprise Trust), is providing support for the development of small businesses. By March 1985 some 150 new companies had been attracted to the Project area, and 2,300 jobs had been created or provided for; but the success of the project can only be assessed in the longer term against its primary aim of securing a fundamental shift in the balance of the local economy.[55]

Self-help Initiatives

In Leith and Dundee the SDA took the lead in planning and implementation, and this is true of most of the other area initiatives in which the Agency is involved. But the Agency has also supported local initiatives led by others. In north-west Ayrshire, for example, it provides, alongside the Region and District Councils, ICI, and Shell, one-fifth of the operating costs of the Ardrossan, Saltcoats and Stevenston Enterprise Trust, which was established under an independent chairman and director in 1981, following the closure of ICI's nylon works, with the aim of reducing unemployment to the Scottish average, diversifying the area's economic base, and providing a 'one door approach' to industrial promotion. By March 1985, ASSET had assisted over 260 companies and helped to generate over 1,000 new jobs and training places. In Kilmarnock, an autonomous Business Development Unit has been established to provide intensive support and advice for small and medium-sized firms. Responsibility for implementing the project rests with the District Council, but the Agency is represented on the Project's Steering Group, which includes also the Chief Executive of the

District Council, a senior official from the Regional Council, and two representatives from the private sector. The aim is to create some 1,000 new jobs by encouraging local entrepreneurship and expansions of existing firms and providing guidance and advice. Funding comes from the Agency, the Regional and District Councils, and the private sector: the Clydesdale Bank, for example, has funded the expenses of the Business Development Unit.[56] In Bathgate, the Agency is collaborating with Lothian Region, West Lothian District, and British Leyland in Bathgate Area Support for Enterprise (BASE), which aims to regenerate industry and commerce in the area.[57]

These self-help initiatives are akin to the Enterprise Trusts pioneered in the South in particular through their stress on stimulating the private sector and encouraging large firms to help small. The director of the Kilmarnock Business Development Unit, a secondee from United Biscuits, is quoted as saying that 'We are trying to pull the people together to make them work for themselves. It is in the private sector that we see the biggest opportunity for growth.'[58] The involvement of public sector bodies in their sponsorship, does, however, provide a somewhat greater possibility of public sector support for their aims. In north-west Ayrshire, for instance, the SDA is committed to a programme of land renewal and factory building amounting to £3m. over three years. As the Agency notes in its evidence to the Environment Committee, 'A key characteristic of these initiatives is a co-operative approach by several parties co-ordinated by a small team located in the area, able to market to firms there, and to call on the assistance available from the sponsoring bodies.'[59]

Appraisal: the Resolution of Conflict

How effective have the Integrated Projects been in securing the regeneration of local economies? It is too early yet to produce a conclusive balance sheet, but early indications are that they are developing into an effective means of tackling supply-side constraints on economic recovery and that they are having a favourable impact on the areas where they are located. The Leith Project, for example, has removed some of the fundamental constraints on new development in the area: a shortage of sites and premises suitable for modern industry and an environment which, if not scarred by the kind of industrial dereliction afflicting parts of the west of Scotland, certainly lacked the amenities and the quality of environment which attract firms to the New Towns. The Agency's 'pump priming' has, as we have seen, attracted considerable private sector interest.

The Integrated Project is, then, a means of releasing an area's economic potential through harnessing the resources of the relevant public and private sector bodies in a collaborative venture. But clearly, and despite the efforts to avoid conflict described above, it can create the possibility of conflict between policies and organisations. How significant are such conflicts, and how have they been resolved?

There was a risk, first, that area initiatives might run counter to regional policy. The SDA was adamant that areas of potential should be chosen, and this, on the face of it, could mean preferential treatment for areas with lesser problems than those which were rejected. Some of the new areas might, indeed, be outwith the assisted areas altogether, as indeed was Leith, although it seems somewhat naïve to suggest that the Agency's involvement here originated in the area's loss of assisted area status.[60] In fact, the risk was more apparent than real. Regional policy, even when substantially curtailed after the reforms of 1979, remained a relatively broad and essentially reactive mechanism for influencing the location of economic activity; more closely focused and pro-active area initiatives were unlikely to conflict to any major extent with traditional policy, and most of the areas singled out for treatment were in any case within the assisted areas. Integrated Projects soon became regarded as an adjunct to regional policy, not as a competitor; and, as we have seen, responsibility for the two subjects has been brought together within the Scottish Office organisation.

A related area of potential policy conflict concerned the extent to which the SDA should focus it activities on particular places rather than spreading its resources over the whole of lowland Scotland (the Highlands and Islands are largely catered for by the HIDB). There was a possibility of criticism from those who considered that the Agency should give all parts of lowland Scotland an equal opportunity to benefit from its activities. No such criticisms have, in fact, emerged. Neither problems nor opportunities are equally spread, and effective deployment of the Agency's not unlimited budget requires concentration. While such concentration does encourage the local authorities who are not benefiting from area initiatives to bid for similar preferential treatment, this can in fact increase the SDA's capacity to secure an appropriate local authority input.

There is, secondly, the possibility of conflict within organisations. The focusing of effort on specific areas through an Area Directorate was not intended to diminish the autonomy of individual Directorates within the Agency or the thrust of its sectoral programmes. Not all Directorates, however, will necessarily share the priorities of the individual project team, and their co-operation is essential to the success of the project teams' work. In the event, the 'strategy of harnessing resources towards specific areas of need and potential'[61] was seen as supportive of the Agency's other objectives. The Agency's sectoral work has been used as the foundation for particular business initiatives in project areas: part of the Clydebank Business Park is being given over to electronic and medical research industries, and Dundee Technology Park is being promoted for electronics, health care, and energy-related industries.[62] The potential for inter-divisional conflict was handled through transferring members of the other divisions into the project teams and developing a matrix organisational structure, under which the head of the Project Teams has day to day control of the members of his team, who nevertheless continue to report to the head of their original division. Whether this will develop into an appropriate means of resolving dissonance it is perhaps too early to say: it does seem likely that, as they work in the field, team members will develop a primary loyalty towards their team rather than their parent division.

Similar intra-organisational conflicts are possible within the local authorities and central government. For the local authorities, the benefits of securing a major SDA presence in their area are likely to be sufficient to secure collaboration, although, as we have seen, there have been difficulties in some areas. For the central government there is little conflict at the level of the Scottish Office: Keating noted 'a coherence to central policy which is often lacking in England'.[63]

Finally, there is the possibility of inter-organisational conflicts of the kind which dogged the early stages of GEAR and the Merseyside Task Force. Such conflict could arise both from concern that the SDA was seeking to influence democratically determined local authority priorities, and from the wish of the local authorities to take the lead in local economic development. The Agency has taken deliberate steps to minimise such conflict through involving the local authorities in the formulation, steering, and implementation of the projects. Local authority involvement at the planning stage can help to ensure that the authorities' priorities are reflected in the project; if the local authorities are not content, they need not participate (although that does carry the penalty of loss of the intensive SDA support provided by the project). The considerable financial resources available to the Agency provide it with the 'leverage' to negotiate appropriate inputs from the local authorities, and to encourage them to bend their programmes to accord with project priorities. The representation of local authority interests on the SDA board may, moreover, help to make the Agency's close involvement in matters which the local authorities might consider as their own more acceptable than the analogous involvement of the DOE in the South; the existence of a quango has helped to defuse potential local–central conflict. Thus both the structure of government and the arrangements adopted by the SDA are such as to minimise conflict.

Nevertheless, conflict can never be eliminated in areas of overlapping function, possibly conflicting priorities, and a high degree of political salience. The arrangements provide a framework for the resolution of conflict; they do not remove conflict. That can only be done through careful negotiations in the case of each individual project. Conflict is perhaps more likely in cases where the Regional and District authorities are of different political persuasions: we have seen, for instance, how opinions on the merits of the Dundee Project differed, leading to a markedly smaller contribution by the District than the Region, and to the controversy over the Dundee Centre for Trade and Industry.

Conclusions

Integrated projects have become a popular means of tackling local economic decline in Scotland. In 1985 the SDA was involved as leader of such projects in Leith, Motherwell, Dundee, and Coatbridge, and was providing close support for a private sector led area project, the Inverclyde Initiative. Such projects have advantages for all the major participants, and this is one explanation for their popularity.

For the central government, Integrated Projects have the advantage of making possible a finer-grained approach to local problems than traditional regional policy does (although, *pace* Boyle and Wannop,[64] it is misleading to regard them simply as a substitute for the declining influence of regional policy). In addition, they provide a means of focusing assistance on particular areas other than directly through the local authorities or through central government action of the kind we have seen on Merseyside. The provision of assistance through the local authorities is constrained through the relatively crude mechanisms of the Rate Support Grant and capital expenditure controls: there is no sure means of ensuring that additional resources are applied for the purpose they were granted, or go to the authorities intended. Such assistance could, moreover, run counter to central government attempts to reduce the totality of expenditure by certain authorities: Dundee District has, in the past, been in conflict with the Secretary of State about its expenditure programmes. And it could reopen questions about local government support for industry. Direct action by the central government would create problems of acceptability and discrimination, although it is perhaps stating matters too strongly to suggest, as does the *Scotsman*, that the projects allow Scottish Ministers to do things which would be 'classed as heretical a little nearer Downing Street'.[65] The DOE is doing similar things in the South; and integrated projects are not so much 'classic examples of pump-priming by the public purse, a concept which is too close to the Keynesian consensus to have much attraction to those who adhere to the monetarist orthodoxy', as a means of reducing supply-side constraints, something far closer to the heart of the new orthodoxy than increasing demand through public expenditure.

For the Agency, Integrated Projects have the advantage of insulating it to some extent from political pressures from the central government, of supporting its other objectives, of harnessing the powers of the local authorities, and of facilitating a planned approach to local economic regeneration. Finally, for the local authorities such initiatives have the benefit of offering evidence that they are taking positive action to deal with local economic problems, either through participation in an existing project or through seeking the establishment of a project in their own locality, and they offer the possibility of harnessing SDA resources to action in their area.

But Integrated Projects would not be so popular if they did not deliver results in terms of improved economic performance in the communities where they are based. In part this can be measured by their impact on employment in the areas—although many of their benefits will only come to fruition in the longer term. But it can also be measured by the impact on business confidence in these communities—and willingness to invest is a measure of such confidence. Stuart Gulliver has shown that, for the year ending March 1983, 'Agency investment of £7.1m. in businesses and share capital etc. brought in some £25m. of private investment—a leverage rate of 3.5'.[66] This is some measure of the impact of the projects.

If the GEAR project 'raises a question about the general utility of the "area approach" ',[67] the Integrated Projects have done much to resolve it. Their innate flexibility reflects the diversity of the problems which they are intended to tackle, from a single major industrial closure to deep-seated and long-standing economic decline. They have done much to raise the morale of communities in decline. They are becoming increasingly credible with the private sector, both because of private sector involvement and because of the increasing evidence of success on the ground. They can do much to improve the supply side of the local economy. But supply-side improvements will not create their own demand,[68] and for this reason too much weight should not be placed on job targets which, at a time of increasing unemployment nationally, can only be a crude measure of a project's progress. Area initiatives can place local economies in a better position to benefit from increased demand than hitherto; but they cannot—except to a limited degree—create that demand. That is the province of national economic policy.

Notes

1. Boyle, R. M. and Wannop, U. A., 'Area Initiatives and the SDA: the Rise of the Urban Project'; op. cit., pp. 46-8.
2. Keating, M. and Midwinter, A., *The Government of Scotland*, Mainstream, Edinburgh 1983, p. 34.
3. Keating, M., Midwinter, A., and Taylor, P., *Enterprise Zones and Area Projects: Small Area Initiatives in Urban Economic Renewal in Scotland*, Department of Administration, University of Strathclyde, Glasgow 1983, p. 13.

4. Great Britain, *Steel: British Steel Corporation: Ten Year Development Strategy*, Cmnd. 5226, HMSO, London 1973.
5. See Checkland, S. G., *The Upas Tree: Glasgow 1875 to 1975*, University of Glasgow Press, 1975.
6. SEPD, *Glengarnock Working Party: Report*, Edinburgh 1978.
7. Ibid., para. 2.
8. Ibid., *passim*.
9. Ibid., para. 30.
10. Scottish Office Press Notice 1110/78, 31 October 1978.
11. Op. cit., para. 30.
12. Ibid., para. 50.
13. Ibid., para. 50.
14. *Scotsman*, 15 June 1983, p. 13.
15. SDA, *Garnock Valley Development: The Strategy for Action 1979-83*, June 1979.
16. Ibid., para. IV, 2.
17. Ibid., summary, para. 4.
18. Ibid., para. II, 1.
19. Ibid., para. II, 4.
20. Ibid., para. II, 5.
21. *Scotsman*, 15 June 1983, p. 13.
22. SDA, *Annual Review of Special Projects* (*excluding GEAR*), 28 April 1982.
23. *Scotsman*, 15 June 1983, p. 13.
24. SEPD, *Working Party on Employment in the Clydebank Area: Report*, Edinburgh 1979.
25. See Hood, N., and Young, S., *Multinationals in Retreat*, Edinburgh 1982, pp. 134–52, for a full treatment of the Goodyear case, and pp. 42–60 for Singer.
26. Report, op. cit., para. 1.3.
27. Ibid., para. 5.11.
28. Ibid., para. 3.2.
29. Interview with Clydebank Task Force, November 1982.
30. *Scotsman*, 28 January 1983, supplement on Clydebank, p. i.
31. Cited in Report, op. cit., para. 2.8.
32. *Scotsman*, 28 January 1983, supplement, p. iii.
33. S. Gulliver, Deputy Director, SDA Area Development Directorate, quoted in *Scotsman*, 28 January 1983, supplement, p.i.
34. Interview with Clydebank District Council, November 1982.
35. Cited in Keating, M., Midwinter, A., and Taylor, P., op. cit., p. 30.
36. SDA, *Annual Report 1980*, Glasgow 1980, p. 50.
37. SDA, *Annual Report 1981*, Glasgow 1981, p. 62.
38. See SDA, *Annual Review of Special Area Projects* (*excluding GEAR*), April 1982, pp. 4–6.

39. Ibid., p. 8.
40. Ibid., pp. 8–9.
41. Ibid., p. 4.
42. SDA, *Annual Report 1982*, p. 55.
43. SDA, *Review*, op. cit., p. 4.
44. See SDA, *Leith Project Agreement*, May 1981.
45. SDA, *Dundee Project Agreement*, October 1981, para. 18.
46. Interview with head of Project Team, March 1983.
47. SDA, *Dundee Project Agreement*, paras. 14–19.
48. Keating, M., Midwinter, A., and Taylor, P., op. cit., p. 38.
49. Ibid., p. 20.
50. SDA, *Review*, op. cit., p. 6.
51. Adapted from Hogwood, B. W. and Gunn, L. A., *Policy Analysis for the Real World*, Oxford 1984, p. 4. See also Hogwood, B. W. and Peters, B. G., *Policy Dynamics*, Wheatsheaf, Brighton 1983.
52. SDA, *Leith Project Agreement*, May 1981, para. 6.
53. SDA, *Dundee Project Agreement*, November 1982, paras. 2, 5, and 6.
54. SDA, *Annual Report 1985*, p. 65.
55. Ibid.
56. *Scotsman*, 25 May 1983, p. 14.
57. *Scotsman*, 20 November 1982.
58. *Scotsman*, 25 May 1983, p. 14.
59. Evidence, op. cit., p. 289, memorandum submitted by Scottish Development Agency, para. 24.
60. Boyle, R. M. and Wannop, U. A., op. cit., p. 52.
61. SDA, *Annual Report 1982*, p. 17.
62. See SDA, 'Sectoral and Area Initiatives: the Experience of the Scottish Development Agency', paper delivered to the Regional Studies Association, November 1982, and *Scotsman*, 25 October 1982, p. 5.
63. Keating, M., Midwinter, A., and Taylor, P., op. cit., p. 41.
64. Op. cit., p. 52.
65. *Scotsman*, leader, 11 February 1983.
66. Gulliver, S., 'The Area Projects of the Scottish Development Agency', *Town Planning Review*, vol. 55, no. 3, 1984.
67. Booth *et al.*, op. cit., p. 70.
68. See Gilmour, Sir Ian, *Britain Can Work*, Martin Robertson, Oxford 1983, for an entertaining critique of Say's law.

8
Conclusions

The task of securing the regeneration of local economies raises important economic, organisational, and political issues. Regeneration involves fundamental questions about the nature of local economic decline and the efficacy of measures to reverse it. It poses problems about the allocation of portfolios and functions between and within government departments and agencies, the relationship between central and local government, and the co-ordination and implementation of policy. And it raises issues about the role of government which come close to the heart of current debate about the frontiers of the state.

We have seen that since the war there have been a number of more or less adequate attempts to define the nature of the problem, involving, for instance, views on congestion, the need for dispersal, the cycle of decline, and social disadvantage. Recent analysis has, however, suggested that local and regional economic problems are closely related, and that they are likely to respond to a variety of measures designed to improve the supply side of the local economy. Improving the access of entrepreneurs to finance, facilitating technological change, providing small factories and workshops, and land assembly, reclamation, and improvement are all of importance. So too are measures to help local residents compete in the labour market and the diversification of housing tenure in the inner cities. Much of this prescription involves a fine-grained and pro-active approach, designed and implemented at local level; and this is the keynote of many of the initiatives which we have considered. But local design and delivery raise acute questions of local–central and inter-agency relationships, a matter to which we shall return.

Alongside this approach there remains a need for the more broadly based and reactive approach of traditional regional policy, designed not so much to remove particular constraints on development as to assist the adaptation of a region's economic structure to modern needs. There is little doubt, however, that regional policy, as it operated throughout much of the 1970s, was in need of reform. Large automatic subsidies for immobile capital-intensive projects are not cost-effective, and the use of regional aids to shore up companies on the point of collapse is likely to hinder rather than assist the process of regional adaptation. More might be done instead to assist growth sectors in the regions.

But calls to confine regional assistance to employment creation in sunrise industries located within closely defined areas need to be examined critically. In the first place, the encouragement of large capital-intensive manufacturing projects within the regions can have important spin-offs in the local economy (although experience of the Scottish motor industry suggests that linkages with the rest of the economy must be fostered). It is, moreover, to the long-term advantage of a region for its manufacturing firms to become more capital-intensive: if they do not, they may simply disappear. Secondly, new firms, whether or not in sunrise industries, cannot over the short term replace the jobs lost through a major closure or deep-seated decline. The health of local economies depends not only on the generation of new firms, but also on the competitiveness of those which already exist. More attention might, therefore, be given to existing companies. The development of 'early warning systems' (such as the SDA is introducing in its Area Initiatives) could have significant benefits, not in saving lame ducks (which is not an appropriate aim of policy), but in preventing them becoming lame in the first place. Finally, it is neither feasible nor desirable to define the same boundaries for all forms of spatially discriminated assistance. It is not an appropriate use of regional aids to support dependent service sector activity in the regions; but it may be a very appropriate use of local aids to encourage its development in one rather than another place within a region. It is, however, clear that the map which was in use between 1979 and 1984, despite the simplifications introduced in 1979, was too complicated, particularly in the conurbations, and that benefits would flow from its rationalisation. Such a rationalisation did indeed result from the 1984 review of regional policy.

In the longer term the health of local and regional economies depends not simply, or even primarily, on government aid, but on the initiative and resourcefulness of the areas' inhabitants. The centralisation of decision-making in the United Kingdom has both compounded the problems of its regions and localities and made their solution more difficult. The Berlin school of regional economists, as Hallett notes, argues that the level and spatial distribution of technology and skill 'depend to a large extent on organisational structure, in both public administration and industry'.[1] This view is persuasive, and has important implications for mergers policy—as well as for the structure of government.

The improvement of the supply side of the local economy is, we have argued, the key to local economic regeneration. Improvements in the supply side can go some way towards creating demand, for example, for goods which would otherwise require to be imported. But they cannot create sufficient demand to mop up the underutilised resources with which the regions are endowed: this can be achieved only through general economic policy. It is, of course, often argued by critics of the Government's overall economic policy that attempts to regenerate local economies are, for this reason, purely cosmetic. But unless the right conditions are created in the problem regions and districts they will not share in the success of general policy. The initiatives which we have considered are designed to enable them not only to share in, but also to contribute to, national economic recovery by creating the conditions for self-sustaining economic growth. Despite the presentational advantages which they can offer, they are thus very much more than cosmetic exercises.

Such initiatives have not always been assisted by the institutional structure through which they must be implemented. Indeed, the development and delivery of appropriate measures to tackle local economic problems raise many of the problems discussed in Hood's *The Limits of Administration*.[2] The 'policy space' is crowded, and the 'policy map' is complex both geographically and institutionally. We have seen cases where implementation has been hampered by unclear or conflicting objectives, inter-organisational rivalries within and between hierarchical layers, intra-organisational tensions, and the sheer weight of bureaucracy. 'Multiple or ambiguous political objectives' (to use Hood's phrase) hinder administrative success. The structure of central government raises its own difficulties: Mawson and Miller note that 'there is little point in central government arguing for greater co-ordination of regional and local agencies if it doesn't have a clear idea of its own position'.[3] Relationships between central and local government are not always easy, and there are tensions between the two tiers of local government, and between local government and other local and regional organisations involved in the same task.

It would be nice to be able to wish such problems away by the establishment of an all-embracing organisation or by a clear and agreed division of labour. But it is naïve to suppose that, in a complex and advanced state like the UK, they could be removed by administrative or political fiat. Problems of conflicting objectives, overlapping functions, multi-organisations, and a complex map are an inevitable consequence both of the subject and of the political process. The problem for the politician and the administrator is not to define an unambiguous best solution to such problems (they will not find one) but to find a solution or solutions which satisfy most of the constraints.[4]

We have considered four solutions in particular—reorganisation, charisma, negotiation, and what for want of a better word we might term privateering. All of them have a place, and each of them raises its own difficuties. Reorganisation has produced powerful and effective regional development agencies in Scotland and Wales. But it cannot provide an instant solution to local and regional economic difficulties, and it does, as we have seen, have costs and raise problems of its own, shifting the boundaries of conflict rather than resolving it, and in some cases causing considerable short-term disruption. Comprehensive public sector agencies, moreover, can discourage involvement by the private sector, a problem with which the Urban Development Corporations, to their credit, are grappling.

Charismatic leadership, such as was given by Mr Heseltine on Merseyside, can overcome bottle-necks and produce useful activity on the ground. But it is inevitably limited in scope—one man can only do so much for so long—and it also creates problems. It is essentially non-strategic and *ad hoc*; the led do not always wish to follow; and once the leader departs there is a need to normalise such leadership into 'bureaucratic' modes of action. The transfer of some of the Department of the Environment's regional functions (for example, responsibility for the Urban Programme) from Manchester to Liverpool could be seen as an example of such normalisation; but there remains a major problem of securing effective joint action among the different agencies involved.

Negotiation—the development of a joint and agreed approach to local economic regeneration among the parties with relevant powers—can secure effective action where the institutional framework permits it and where there is sufficient agreement on strategy from the outset. But it cannot solve problems of joint action where such agreement is lacking.

Privateering—the encouragement of a major private sector role in local economic regeneration—can and does bring useful dividends. But it cannot provide the only answer, particularly where there is a major task of land assembly and renewal to be done, or where the private sector is traditionally weak. We have seen how attempts to secure private sector involvement through removing burdens on industry and commerce are of doubtful success on their own (although they remain an important part of industry policy generally); a more fruitful approach is the continued encouragement of Enterprise Trusts and Agencies and of partnership between the public and private sectors. This, indeed, is a major emphasis of current policy.[5]

In the end, whether or not the private sector is involved, charismatic leadership is supplied, or new institutions are created, organisations require to work together. As the Environment Committee concluded, 'The effective management of urban renewal rests ... on the successful orchestration of joint action and the successful "packaging" of multi-agency involvement in schemes.'[6] Co-ordination is the prerequisite for such orchestration and packaging. It does not remove the cause of conflict, and it can indeed cloud the issues. But some mechanism is necessary to bring the parties together, and this can be provided through co-ordinative machinery. Effective co-ordination does, indeed, appear to be essential to any attempt at regeneration, and even the private sector Enterprise Trusts have found it essential to develop machinery to ensure the collaboration of public sector bodies in their area. But the fewer the organisations, the fewer the boundaries across which measures require to be co-ordinated and the easier implementation is likely to be. (While, as we have seen, there remain problems of co-ordination within organisations, experience suggests that it is easier to secure concerted action in a single organisation than among separate organisations.) One cannot avoid the conclusion that, in terms of structures and institutions, Scotland is better placed to design, implement, and secure the regeneration of local economies than her neighhbour to the south. But there is a penalty to pay in terms of a lesser commitment by the private sector. And, unless one were to contemplate institutional reform, involving for instance 'more substantial changes in the structure of metropolitan government and Ministerial responsibilities, and the integration of urban and regional policies',[7] one cannot generalise from Scottish experience.

Is it possible at this stage to assess the effectiveness of the various initiatives which we have considered? It is too early in the life of many of the projects to estimate their cost-effectiveness; when the time comes for such an assessment it must, however, take account not merely of jobs created, but also of the wider economic impact of the measures—for example on growth, output, productivity, and migration—and of social costs and benefits. In the meantime, however, it is possible to reach some impressionistic and tentative conclusions.

First, all of the initiatives which we have considered tackle some of the causes of local economic decline, although some are more comprehensive than others and one—the Enterprise Zone—has stumbled upon its most effective role in local economic regeneration almost by accident. It is not, however, the case that the broadest initiatives are necessarily the most effective: both the Glasgow Eastern Area Renewal project and the Merseyside Task Force appear to have been hampered by the broadness of their remit, and the private sector initiatives appear, at least in terms of the jobs which their sponsors claim they have created and their small cost to the public purse, to be an effective means of securing local regeneration. But it is not possible to make a direct comparison of initiatives, for each must be designed to meet local circumstances. The reclamation of land requires a different approach from the encouragement of entrepreneurship.

Secondly, it appears that, in the short term at least, initiatives which are designed with regard to the institutional framework are likely to raise fewer difficulties of implementation than those which run across the grain of existing organisations. New organisations, such as Urban Development Corporations, which by their very nature are direct competitors with the local authorities, are likely to raise particular difficulties.

Thirdly, there is a major role for local organisations—and particularly the local authorities and local enterprise agencies—in the design and implementation of local initiatives. Because of the need to take account of local circumstances in design, attempts by the central government to control such initiatives are unlikely to improve their effectiveness, even if they worked. Much of the activity of the local authorities need cause no concern to the central government: the encouragement of local entrepreneurship and indigenous growth, even at the expense of the ratepayer, seems unlikely to distort national fiscal or industrial policies to a noticeable extent and can indeed make an important contribution to national economic recovery. But certain matters, and particularly the attraction of inward investment and the provision of financial assistance to incoming companies, are best left to be handled, or at the least co-ordinated, by central government and its agencies.

Fourthly, there are particular problems in relation to the provision of finance for the entrepreneur in the English regions. The institutions are becoming interested in the provision of venture capital for the new firm; more might be done to encourage the development of regional venture capital funds.

Fifthly, while through its special programmes for the unemployed the Manpower Services Commission has made a valuable contribution to physical regeneration in local areas of decline, the Commission might do more to assist disadvantaged inner city residents to enter the labour market. It is to be hoped that the New Training Initiative will develop along these lines.

Ultimately local initiatives will stand or fall with the national economy. They are dependent on the success of broad economic policy, and this provides a basic limit to their effectiveness. But the most important limit is provided not by the macro-economic environment but by the bounds of political acceptability, and the boundaries of acceptability have shifted with the breakdown of the regional policy consensus. Hood comments that 'schemes which benefit many territorial areas are typically preferred to schemes benefiting more concentrated areas', so that, despite economic arguments to the contrary, aid is generally offered over a relatively broad area.[8] We have noted that, at one point, regional policy in Britain covered 40 per cent of the working population. On this analysis, tensions are likely because of the close focus required in measures to improve the supply side of local economies. But the underlying question is not how closely such measures should be focused, but whether it is appropriate to have any kind of spatially biased policy at all. This study has proceeded on the assumption that it is. There are, as we have seen, social and economic arguments for this view, but the question is essentially political. It concerns the role of government and the limits not of administration, but of the state.

Notes

1. Hallet, G., *Second Thoughts on Regional Policy*, p. 51.
2. Hood, C. C., *The Limits of Administration*, John Wiley, London 1976.
3. Mawson, J. and Miller, D., 'Agencies in Regional and Local Development', paper presented at the conference of the Regional Studies Association on 'Local Enterprise Agencies: their Role in Regional Development', Manchester, 12 November 1982.
4. Hood, C. C., op. cit., p. 56.
5. Moore, C. and Richardson, J., 'Shifting Parameters: Public–Private Partnership in Local Economic Regeneration', paper delivered to Public Administration Committee's Fifteenth Annual Conference, York, September 1985.
6. House of Commons, Environment Committee, Report, op. cit., p. xxxix.
7. Ibid., p. xl. See also the Labour party, 'Alternative Regional Strategy', op. cit. It is a pity that the Environment Committee did not return to this issue following the 1983 General Election.
8. Hood, C. C., op. cit., p. 9.

Bibliography

Adam Smith Institute, *Freeports in the United Kingdom*, London 1982.

Archbishop of Canterbury, *Faith in the City*, report of Archbishop's Commission on Urban Priority Areas, Lambeth 1985.

Association of British Chambers of Commerce, *The Widening Role of Chambers*, report of the ABCC Annual Conference, 1982.

Booth, S. A. S., Pitt, D. C., and Money, W. J., 'Organisational Redundancy? A Critical Appraisal of the GEAR Project', *Public Administration*, vol. 60, no. 1, spring 1982.

Boyle, R. M. and Wannop, U. A., 'Area Initiatives and the SDA: the Rise of the Urban Project', *Fraser of Allander Institute Quarterly Economic Commentary*, vol. 8, no. 1, Glasgow 1982.

Brown, G. (ed.), *The Red Paper on Scotland*, EUSPB, Edinburgh 1975.

Building Design Partnership, Roger Tym and Partners, *Enterprise Zone Workshop 1983: Report of Proceedings*, London 1983.

Bush, H., 'Local Intellectual and Policy Responses to Localised Unemployment in the Inter-war Period: the Genesis of Regional Policy', unpublished D. Phil thesis, Nuffield College, Oxford 1980.

Butler, S. M., *Enterprise Zones: Greenlining the Inner Cities*, Heinemann Educational Books, London 1982.

Carrington, J. C. and Edwards, George, *Financing Industrial Investment*, Macmillan, London 1975.

——, *Reversing Economic Decline*, Macmillan, London 1981.

Checkland, S. G., *The Upas Tree: Glasgow 1875 to 1975*, University of Glasgow Press, Glasgow 1975.

Damesick, P., 'Issues and Options in UK Regional Policy: the Need for a New Assessment', *Regional Studies*, vol. 16, no. 5, October 1982.

Dawson, M. W., 'The Scottish Development Agency', *Public Enterprise*, 19, autumn 1980.

Deloittes, Haskins, and Sells, R. Tym and Partners, *GEAR Review, Business Development and Employment Strategy*, SDA, Glasgow, October 1982.

Dennison, S. R., *Location of Industry and the Distressed Areas*, Oxford University Press, London 1939.

Department of the Environment, *Enterprise Zones*, DOE, COI, London 1982.

———, *Enterprise Zone Information 1983–4*, DOE, London 1985.

———, *Urban Programme Management Guidance Note No. 1*, DOE, London May 1985.

———, Urban Programme, *Ministerial Guidelines for Partnership and Programme Authority Areas*, DOE, London May 1985.

———, Department of Trade and Industry, Manpower Services Commission, Department of Employment, *City Action Team: Your City and Your Government*, DOE et al., London 1985.

———, Scottish Office, and Welsh Office, *Local Authority Powers to Assist Industry and Commerce*, DOE et al., London 1982.

Environment Committee, *Problems of Management of Urban Renewal*, Evidence, session 1982–3, HMSO, London 1982–3.

———, *The Problems of Management of Urban Renewal (Appraisal of the Recent Initiatives on Merseyside)*, HMSO, London 1983.

Fairley, J., 'Training Policy: the Local Perspective', *Regional Studies*, vol. 17, no. 2, April 1983.

Falkirk District Council Planning Department, *Application for the New Scottish Enterprise Zone*, Falkirk, September 1982.

Firn, J., 'External Control and Regional Policy', in Brown, G. (ed.), *The Red Paper on Scotland*, EUSPB, Edinburgh 1975.

Fothergill, S. and Gudgin, G., *Unequal Growth: Urban and Regional Employment Change in the UK*, Heinemann Educational Books, London 1982.

Friedman, M. and Friedman, R., *Free to Choose*, Martin Secker and Warburg, London 1980.

Gilmour, Sir Ian, *Britain Can Work*, Martin Robertson, Oxford 1983.

Goddard, J. B., 'The Changing Environment for Regional Policy in the UK', *Regional Studies*, vol. 16, no. 5, October 1982.

Grant, W., *The Political Economy of Industrial Policy*, Butterworths, London 1982.

Great Britain, *Policy for the Inner Cities*, Cmnd. 6845, HMSO, London 1977.

———, *Regional Industrial Development*, Cmnd. 9111, HMSO, London 1983.

——, *Royal Commission on the Distribution of the Industrial Population* (Barlow Report), Cmnd. 6153, HMSO, London 1940.

——, *Steel: British Steel Corporation Ten Year Development Strategy*, Cmnd. 5226, HMSO, London 1973.

——, *The Brixton Disorders April 1981, Report of an Enquiry by the Rt. Hon. Lord Scarman OBE*, Cmnd. 8427, HMSO, London 1981.

Greater London Council, Popular Planning Unit, *Jobs for a Change*, GLC, London 1983.

Green, W. and Clough, D., *Regional Problems and Policies*, Holt, Rinehart and Winston, London 1982.

Gudgin, G., Moore, B., and Rhodes, J., 'Employment Problems in the Cities and Regions of the UK: Prospects for the 1980s', *Cambridge Economic Policy Review*, vol. 8, no. 2, December 1982.

Gulliver, S., 'The Area Projects of the Scottish Development Agency', *Town Planning Review*, vol. 55, no. 3, 1984.

Hall, P. (ed.), *The Inner City in Context*, Heinemann, London 1981.

——, Harrison, B., and Massey, D., 'Urban Enterprise Zones, a Debate', *International Journal of Urban and Regional Research*, vol. 6, no. 3, 1982.

Hallett, G., *Second Thoughts on Regional Policy*, Centre for Policy Studies, London 1981.

——, Randall, P., and West, E. G., *Regional Policy for Ever?*, Institute of Economic Affairs, London 1973.

Harvie, C., *Against Metropolis*, Fabian Tract 484, London 1982.

Higgins, J., Deakin, N., Edwards, J., and Wicks, M., *Government and Urban Poverty*, Basil Blackwell, Oxford 1983.

HM Treasury, *Freeports in the United Kingdom*, report of a working party under the chairmanship of the Economic Secretary to the Treasury, HM Treasury, London 1983.

Hogwood, B. and Gunn, L. A., *Policy Analysis for the Real World*, Oxford University Press, Oxford 1984.

Hogwood, B. and Peters, B. G., *Policy Dynamics*, Wheatsheaf Books, Brighton 1983.

Holland, S., *Capital versus the Regions*, Macmillan, London 1976.

Home, R. K., *Inner City Regeneration*, E. and F. N. Spon, London 1982.

Hood, C. C., *The Limits of Administration*, John Wiley, London 1976.

—— and Dunsire, A., *Bureaumetrics*, Gower, Farnborough 1981.

Hood, N. and Young, S., *Multinationals in Retreat: the Scottish Experience*, Edinburgh University Press, Edinburgh 1982.

Johnson, N. and Cochrane, A., *Economic Policy-Making by Local Authorities in Britain and Western Germany*, George Allen and Unwin, London 1981.

Keating, M., 'Enterprise Zones: from Rhetoric to Reality', *Municipal Journal*, 21 August 1981.

—— and Midwinter, A., *The Government of Scotland*, Mainstream, Edinburgh 1983.

——, Midwinter A., and Taylor, P., *Enterprise Zones and Area Projects: Small Area Initiatives in Urban Renewal in Scotland*, Department of Administration, University of Strathclyde, Glasgow 1983.

Kirwan, F. X., 'Scottish Development Agency: Structures and Functions', *Studies in Public Policy* 81, University of Strathclyde, Glasgow 1981.

Labour Party, *Alternative Regional Strategy: a Framework for Action*, Parliamentary Spokesman's Working Group, London 1982.

Lawless, P., *Britain's Inner Cities; Problems and Policies*, Harper and Row, London 1981.

——, *Urban Deprivation and Government Initiative*, Faber and Faber, London 1979.

Lever, W. F. and Moore, C., *City in Transition: Policies and Agencies for Economic Regeneration in Clydeside*, Oxford University Press, Oxford 1986.

London Docklands Development Corporation, *Annual Report and Accounts 1984–5*, London 1985.

Lythe, C. and Majmudar, M., *The Renaissance of the Scottish Economy?*, George Allen and Unwin, London 1982.

Maclellan, D. and Parr, J. B. (eds.), *Regional Policy: Past Experience and New Directions*, Martin Robertson, Oxford 1979.

Madgwick, P. and Rose, R. (eds.), *The Territorial Dimension in United Kingdom Politics*, Macmillan, London 1982.

Marquand, J., *Measuring the Effects and Costs of Regional Incentives*, Government Economic Service Working Paper 32, London 1980.

Mawson, J. and Miller, D., 'Agencies in Regional and Local Development', paper presented to Regional Studies Association conference, Manchester, 12 November 1982.

McCrone, R. G. L., *Regional Policy in Britain*, Allen and Unwin, London 1969.

McGregor, A., *Urban Unemployment: a Study of Differential Unemployment Rates in Glasgow*, Central Research Unit, Scottish Office, Edinburgh 1980.

Merseyside County Council, *Targets for Merseyside for the 1980s*, MCC, Liverpool 1977.

——, *The Merseyside Economy: Performance and Prospects to 1986*, MCC, Liverpool 1981.

Monopolies and Mergers Commission, *The Hong Kong and Shanghai Banking Corporation, Standard Chartered Bank Ltd. and the Royal Bank of Scotland Group Ltd.: a Report on the Proposed Mergers*, HMSO, London 1982.

——, *Charter Consolidated PLC and Anderson Strathclyde PLC: a Report on the Proposed Merger*, HMSO, London 1982.

Moore, B. and Rhodes, J., 'A Second Great Depression in the UK Regions: Can Anything Be Done?', *Regional Studies*, vol. 16, no. 5, October 1982.

Moore, C. and Richardson, J., 'Shifting Parameters: Public–Private Partnership in Local Economic Regeneration', paper delivered to Public Administration Committee conference, York, September 1985.

Mukherjee, S., *Strathclyde Employment and Development Agency: a Proposal for Discussion*, Scottish International Educational Trust, Edinburgh 1973.

Myrdal, G., *Economic Theory and Underdeveloped Regions*, Methuen, London 1956.

Nove, A., *Planning: What, How and Why*, The Fraser of Allander Institute Speculative Paper No. 1, Scottish Academic Press, Edinburgh 1975.

OECD, *Decision of the Council Concerning a Co-operative Action Programme on Local Initiatives for Employment Creation*, c (82) 99 Final, Paris 26 July 1982.

Owen, D. W. and Coombs, M. G., *An Index of Peripherality for Local Areas in the United Kingdom*, Scottish Economic Planning Department, Edinburgh 1983.

Parry, R., 'The Scottish Office', in Rose, Richard (ed.), *Territorial Ministries in British Government*, Oxford University Press, Oxford (forthcoming).

Pearce, J., *Can We Make Jobs?*, Local Government Research Unit, Paisley College of Technology, Heatherbank Press, Glasgow 1978.

Pressman, J. L. and Wildavsky, A. B., *Implementation*, University of California Press, London 1973.

Roger Tym and Partners, *Monitoring Enterprise Zones: Year One Report*, London 1982.

——, *Monitoring Enterprise Zones: Year Two Report*, London 1983.

——, *Monitoring Enterprise Zones: Year Three Report*, London 1984.

——, *Monitoring the Freeport Experiment: Progress Report 1985*, London 1985.

Rothwell, R., 'The Role of Technology in Industrial Change: Implications for Regional Policy', *Regional Studies*, vol. 16, no. 5, October 1982.

Scottish Affairs Committee, *Prestwick Airport*, first report of the Committee on Scottish Affairs, session 1982–3, HMSO, London 1982.

Scottish Council (Development and Industry), *The Influence of Centralisation on the Future*, SC (D and I), Aviemore 1970.

——, *Report of the Committee on Local Development in Scotland*, SC (D and I), Edinburgh 1952.

——, *Inquiry into the Scottish Economy 1960–61*, SC (D and I), Edinburgh 1961.

Scottish Council of the Labour Party, *Scotland and the NEB*, SCLP, Glasgow 1973.

Scottish Development Agency, Annual Reports, SDA, Glasgow 1977 to 1985.

——, *Annual Review of GEAR*, SDA, Glasgow 1982.

——, *Annual Review of Special Area Projects (excluding GEAR)*, SDA, Glasgow 1982.

——, *Dundee Project Agreement*, SDA, Glasgow 1981.

——, *Garnock Valley Development: the Strategy for Action 1979–83*, SDA, Glasgow 1979.

——, *Leith Project Agreement*, SDA, Glasgow 1981.

——, 'Sectoral and Area Initiatives: the Experience of the Scottish Development Agency', paper delivered to Regional Studies Association, Manchester, November 1982.

Scottish Economic Planning Department, *Glengarnock Working Party: Report*, SEPD, Edinburgh 1978.

——, *Working Party on Employment in the Clydebank Area: Report*, SEPD, Edinburgh 1979.

Slowe, P., *The Advance Factory in Regional Development*, Gower Press, Aldershot 1981.

Stephen, F., 'The Scottish Development Agency', in *The Red Book on Scotland*, EUSPB, Edinburgh 1975.

Storey, D. J., *Entrepreneurship and the New Firm*, Croom Helm, London 1982.

Strathclyde Regional Council, *Strathclyde Regional Report*, SRC, Glasgow 1976.

——, *Urban Deprivation*, SRC, Glasgow 1976.

Taylor, S., 'The Politics of Enterprise Zones', *Public Administration*, 59, winter 1981.

Index